T0294845

Positioning Your Museum as a Critical Community Asset

AMERICAN ASSOCIATION FOR STATE AND LOCAL HISTORY

BOOK SERIES

SERIES EDITOR

Russell Lewis, Chicago History Museum

EDITORIAL ADVISORY BOARD

Anne W. Ackerson, Leading by Design
William Bomar, University of Alabama Museums
Jessica Dorman, The Historic New Orleans Collection
W. Eric Emerson, South Carolina Department of Archives and History
Tim Grove, National Air and Space Museum
Laura Koloski, Pew Center for Arts & Heritage
Jane Lindsey, Juneau-Douglas City Museum
Ann E. McCleary, University of West Georgia
Laurie Ossman, Preservation Society of Newport County
Sarah Pharaon, International Coalition of Sites of Conscience
Laura Roberts, Roberts Consulting
Sandra Smith, Heinz History Center
Kimberly Springle, Charles Sumner School Museum and Archives
Will Ticknor, New Mexico Department of Cultural Affairs
William S. Walker, Cooperstown Graduate Program, SUNY Oneonta

STAFF

Bob Beatty, AASLH
Charles Harmon, Rowman & Littlefield Publishers

About the Series

The American Association for State and Local History Book Series addresses issues critical to the field of state and local history through interpretive, intellectual, scholarly, and educational texts. To submit a proposal or manuscript to the series, please request proposal guidelines from AASLH headquarters: AASLH Editorial Board, 1717 Church St., Nashville, Tennessee 37203. Telephone: (615) 320-3203. Website: www.aaslh.org.

About the Organization

The American Association for State and Local History (AASLH) is a national history membership association headquartered in Nashville, Tennessee. AASLH provides leadership and support for its members who preserve and interpret state and local history in order to make the past more meaningful to all Americans. AASLH members are leaders in preserving, researching, and interpreting traces of the American past to connect the people, thoughts, and events of yesterday with the creative memories and abiding concerns of people, communities, and our nation today. In addition to sponsorship of this book series, AASLH publishes *History News* magazine, a newsletter, technical leaflets and reports, and other materials; confers prizes and awards in recognition of outstanding achievement in the field; supports a broad education program and other activities designed to help members work more effectively; and advocates on behalf of the discipline of history. To join AASLH, go to www.aaslh.org or contact Membership Services, AASLH, 1717 Church St., Nashville, TN 37203.

Positioning Your Museum as a Critical Community Asset

A Practical Guide

Edited by
Robert P. Connolly
and Elizabeth A. Bollwerk

ROWMAN & LITTLEFIELD
Lanham • Boulder • New York • London

Published by Rowman & Littlefield
A wholly owned subsidary of The Rowman & Littlefield Publishing Group, Inc.
4501 Forbes Boulevard, Suite 200, Lanham, Maryland 20706
www.rowman.com

Unit A, Whitacre Mews, 26-34 Stannary Street, London SE11 4AB

Copyright © 2017 by Rowman & Littlefield

All rights reserved. No part of this book may be reproduced in any form or by any electronic or mechanical means, including information storage and retrieval systems, without written permission from the publisher, except by a reviewer who may quote passages in a review.

British Library Cataloguing in Publication Information Available

Library of Congress Cataloging-in-Publication Data
Names: Connolly, Robert Patrick, 1952- editor. | Bollwerk, Elizabeth A., editor.
Title: Positioning your museum as a critical community asset : a practical guide / edited by Robert P. Connolly and Elizabeth Bollwerk.
Description: Lanham, Maryland : Rowman & Littlefield, 2016. | Series: American Association for State and Local History book series | Includes index.
Identifiers: LCCN 2016040537 (print) | LCCN 2016041832 (ebook) | ISBN 9781442275690 | ISBN 9781442275706 | ISBN 9781442275713 (ebook)
Subjects: LCSH: Museums—Public relations. | Museums—Educational aspects. | Museums—Social aspects.
Classification: LCC AM124 .P67 2016 (print) | LCC AM124 (ebook) | DDC 069—dc23
LC record available at https://lccn.loc.gov/2016040537

∞™ The paper used in this publication meets the minimum requirements of American National Standard for Information Sciences—Permanence of Paper for Printed Library Materials, ANSI/NISO Z39.48-1992.

Printed in the United States of America

Contents

Figures

Tables

Acknowledgments

This book is one that we have wanted to see put together for several years. As is so often the case, if you talk about how much a book on a particular subject is needed, ultimately, it will be suggested that you take on the project. Such was the case when we raised this idea with Bob Beatty, chief of engagement for the American Association of State and Local History. Bob's enthusiasm for this project provided the assurance that the book got off the ground. The support and guidance of Charles Harmon and Kathleen O'Brien at Rowman & Littlefield has been exemplary. On multiple occasions we have commented to each other that we could not have envisioned a more efficient and professional publishing experience.

This volume marks our third joint editing project. We have aimed for these projects to increasingly move beyond theory to a very practical and hands-on application of community engagement. We believe this volume is our most successful effort in achieving that end. We thank all of the individuals we have met along the way, many of whom are contributors to this volume, who have inspired us with their projects. And most importantly, we thank the thirty contributors to this volume for their commitment and professionalism in delivering a quality product, in some instances on very short notice.

Introduction

"Learn what aid the community needs: fit the museum to those needs."

—JOHN COTTON DANA (1917:38)

This book is explicitly a "how-to guide" for museums to integrate themselves into the communities they serve. This book is not meant to convince the reader of the need for that integration. We consider the need a settled matter. We stand with John Cotton Dana's 1917 mandate for museums to act on their community's expressed needs, whether those needs are directly or indirectly stated.

We envision this book within the framework of museums co-creating with their communities. Ellen Hirzy (2002:16) writing in the American Alliance of Museums' seminal publication *Mastering Civic Engagement* noted, "What is needed are reciprocal, co-created relationships that connect the assets and purposes of organizations." Anthropologist Erve Chambers's (2004:194) understanding of engaging "with others who are trying to make decisions related to particular heritage resources" also is a key component of this co-creation perspective. We do not envision this co-creation as museums simply being more attuned to community needs. Co-creation means making a commitment to working *with* a community to address those needs. Co-creation does not mean working *for* the community based on what a museum *perceives* are a community's needs. Instead co-creation means working *with* the community to address the needs as *expressed* by the community itself.

We consider this volume as the instruction manual for our previously edited volumes that discussed the concept of co-creation for cultural heritage professionals and museums. In 2012 we published *Open(ing) Authority through Community Engagement*, which provided a theoretical overview and ten case studies on co-creation with museums and their communities. In 2015, we published *Co-creation in the Archaeological Record*, which brought the discussion squarely to the fieldwork, curation, and interpretation in the discipline of archaeology.

In our application of co-creation we prioritize acting on the public's *expressed* needs and interests. In the field of museum studies, a considerable amount of ink is spilled over theoretical and methodological approaches to best determine those expressed community needs. To simplify that process, we rely on Dana's mandate written one century ago: "Learn what aid the community needs: fit the museum to those needs."

We intend for this volume to fill methodological and logistical gaps in attempting to implement Dana's mandate. For example, our experience over the past several years demonstrates that for many museums, particularly smaller ones, the ability to carry out a community oral history project that can be curated online with universal access or create a new low-cost exhibit based on important community curated collections are often not considered feasible because of economic, staffing, and other constraints. At the same time, over the past ten years, we have encountered dozens of individual projects that overcame these problems and implemented such community-driven engagement work.

Drawing on that experience, this volume is not a discussion of the relevance or need for museums to engage with their community. We assume that the reader does not need to be convinced of the importance of such actions. Instead, our contributors introduce specific themes of engagement, supported by applied case studies.

The volume's themes and case studies will be particularly relevant to small- and medium-sized cultural heritage venues with a limited or even no full-time staff. Our contributors to this book needed to be certain their "how-to" projects could be completed for $1,500 or less to ensure that cost was not a prohibitive factor. We are pleased that all of our contributors came through on that challenge. Excluding labor costs, all of the projects discussed in this volume can be completed for $1,500 or less, along with standard operating equipment such as a computer and basic office supplies. Within the individual case studies, the contributors make recommendations and list those material costs.

Some museums might find that even a $1,500 expense to implement a project is prohibitive. For that reason, we challenged our authors to provide their "go-to" resources to raise a quick $2,000 to fund a project. Our authors also were tasked with providing a thorough list of digital and cost-effective resources to assist the reader in carrying out projects based on the case studies. All of these results are included in the Resource Guide of this volume.

Positioning Your Museum as a Critical Community Asset: A Practical Guide is organized into six parts. Each part begins with a thematic discussion relevant to a museum's engagement with the community they serve. The discussion considers a community from both geographic and interest perspectives. Each thematic discussion is followed by three to six case study applications. The final part of this book links to an extensive Resource Guide that will be regularly updated and include digital links to forms, workbooks, and guides used in the case studies presented. The Resource Guide also contains an extensive bibliography on museums and community engagement. The guide is introduced in Part VI of this volume with the full resource guide available digitally on the Internet (www.museumcommunities.com).

In Part I, Jody Stokes-Casey uses the concept of meaning-making to consider educational opportunities that museums provide for their communities. Drawing on her experience in education and programming at the National Civil Rights Museum in Memphis, she notes that a museum-making approach extends beyond the learning of facts and figures and moves to contextualize that process within the prior experience and knowledge of community members. Meaning-making takes the museum visit and integrates that experience into the daily lives of the visitor. The five case studies that follow Stokes-Casey's essay draw on a similar meaning-making approach and range from international rural settings (Gustavo Valencia Tello and Elizabeth Cruzado Carranza, to the urban U.S. Midwest (Shana Crosson). The case study presented by Nur Abdalla and Lyndsey Pender reports how a high school used museum collections as a curriculum resource. Mary Anna Evans's contribution shows how book studies and writing exercises can link schools with their museums to tell stories about their community contextualized within the mindset of the makers. Brian Failing's case study is an example of how a student's course work in higher education can be used to further museum programming that addresses a community need. Techniques for determining community needs in museum educational programming are taken up by Shana Crosson's work at the Minnesota Historical Society.

Elizabeth Bollwerk's discussion of Open Authority in Part II places the concept of co-creation in museum and community contexts. The concept of open authority is a logical extension of this volume's co-creative framework and provides museums and their communities considerable latitude in the product created in and for museums. The four case studies in this part are diverse examples on how Open Authority can be applied. The case study by Elizabeth Cruzado Carranza and Leodan Alejo Valerio illustrates how a museum altered its planned activity based on the input from educators in a rural Andean community. The resulting change created a program that met an expressed community need for a written record of their history. Porchia Moore describes how the commitment to incorporate a community's voice in Columbia, South Carolina, empowered community members to provide guidance for a renovation project at a historic house with traditional ties to the African American community. The case study by Lisa Young and Susan Sekaquaptewa details a project that featured the voice of a Native American community in the interpretation of cultural materials curated at a museum nearly 2,000 miles away. All three of the case studies demonstrate how a co-creative and Open Authority approach prioritize the voice of typically underserved peoples in a cultural heritage venue. In a different vein Rebecca Price's case study shows the value of building trust with private collectors. Her museum's project, which focused on building a shared understanding of the importance of opening collections, enabled the historic house venue to acquire critical materials on a poorly documented national movement that were then shared with the public.

Advocacy is often perceived as an area of work that requires extensive training, political connections, and insights best left to the experts and beyond the reach of the typical small- to medium-sized museum professional. Sarah Miller draws on her long-term work in cultural heritage advocacy to challenge that notion. She provides an overview of the many avenues for museum advocacy that build strong and sustainable community relationships. Ember Farber's case study is geared toward small museum advocacy based on resources available through the American Alliance of Museums. Robert Connolly reports on simple educational and economic impact statements and their important role in ensuring continued support from the governing authority of the small museum where he is a director. Melissa Prycer presents a compelling case study for advocacy from her work at the Dallas Heritage Village. Prycer's consistent focus on community advocacy at her small museum, with a staff of four, led to increased visibility, visitation, and funding for this once forgotten venue that now plays a key role in the urban redevelopment of South Dallas. Miller's advocacy overview and the three case studies are all based on an approach that is doable by the small museums with limited staff and financial resources.

In Part IV, Robert Connolly focuses on opportunities for museums to become partners and social assets for the people and communities in which they serve. Based on his nearly ten years as the director at the C.H. Nash Museum at Chucalissa, he reports how that museum moved from being viewed as a venue of academic privilege and passive engagement to one that is now considered an integral community asset. The shift is marked by increased volunteer participation, hosting of community events, family programming, and educational opportunities with the local community. Colleen McCartney's case study is also based at the C.H. Nash Museum where she organized a project to make the institution inclusive of users with special needs. Ashley Rogers's case study reports on the New Orleans area Whitney Plantation's efforts to incorporate the voice of the surrounding community residents who are descendants of those enslaved in the pre–Civil War era. Mary Wildermuth's case study of Iowa's Muscatine History and Industry Center is an excellent example of how a small museum and the city's manufacturing interests partnered to create a unique cultural heritage venue. Contextualized within the recent civil unrest, Melanie Adams's case study reports on how long-term community outreach allowed the Missouri History Museum to play a mediating role in response to the 2013 events in Ferguson, Missouri. The case study by Allison Hennie draws on community outreach in the preliminary stages of a museum project. Additionally, Suzanne Francis-Brown's study focuses on low-tech ways of engaging aging and geographically disparate university alumnae to preserve important stories that are in danger of being lost.

In Part V, the essays includes numerous how-to guides for navigating the important yet often daunting opportunities available through digital technology. Brigitte Billeaudeaux and Jennifer Schnabel focus particularly on digital preservation and presentation technologies. Their essay considers both the preservation needs of the museum and the community served. The case studies here detail and expand on the thematic essay and include creating a digital library of ephemera from the historic A. Schwab Drug Store on Beale St. in Memphis (Brigitte Billeaudeaux), the social media outreach program at the National Underground Railroad Museum (Jamie Glavic and Assia Johnson), a reusable podcast series (Rebecca Price), multimedia documentation of an often ignored labor force in the sport of horse racing (Holly Solis), and a step-by-step case study of how to create a website for a historic house museum (Kelsey Ransick). The content is enhanced by a rich set of resources. For example, Rebecca Price's study concludes with "Technical Guide: How to Podcast for Free." When discussing digitization standards, Brigitte Billeaudeaux and Jennifer Schnabel provide links to national best practices for all of their projects.

The final part of the book is the Resource Guide. We consider this to be a crucial part of our how-to volume. As we noted above, we challenged all contributors to recommend resources for financing small projects. A summary of their recommendations is provided in the Resource Guide. In the case of the advocacy work covered in Part IV, our contributors provided nearly twenty major online resources that range from the American Library Association Advocacy Action Plan Workbook to the American Association of Museums Speak Up for Museums website. Although we include references to hard-copy resources when possible we focus on materials that can be digitally accessed. Our contributors have also included copies of their surveys, presentations, and other products specifically related to case studies presented in this volume. Only an introduction to the resources is contained in this book. The extensive lists and their updates are available online (www.museumcommunities.com).

Positioning Your Museum as a Critical Community Asset: A Practical Guide is a book that demonstrates any museum, regardless of size, staffing, or financial resources, can engage with their communities in a vibrant and co-creative way. We truly believe that such an approach where museums and communities co-create with each other will result in cultural heritage venues that are viewed as social assets with value that must be preserved and maintained.

Part I

COMMUNITIES MAKING MEANING IN MUSEUM EDUCATION

Jody Stokes-Casey

RECALL YOUR MOST powerful museum experience. Was it an opportunity to use new materials to replicate the historic or artistic process of making an object? Was it a moment when you made a connection between what you already knew and exciting new information presented in an exhibition? Perhaps it was seeing an expression of understanding dawn across a visitor's face or hearing an excited exclamation from a guest making his or her own connections. The primary goal of museum educators is to create opportunities for guests to experience similar and significant *meaning-making* moments. Going beyond information gathering through labels or lectures, meaning-making experiences are those in which the visitor is actively engaged in the learning process, making choices, and building on prior knowledge to create new connections both personally and within communities.

Take a moment to consider the following questions. What are the educational goals of my institution? How will we know if we accomplished our goals? Are the programs and educational materials of my institution fulfilling the museum's mission? How does the museum currently collaborate with the community? Scribble your answers in the margins and return to them after reading this chapter.

Educators in cultural institutions tackle a plethora of challenges. They work to create engaging, meaningful programming and educational experiences for guests of all demographics while fulfilling the mission of the institution. With an ever-expanding to-do list and limited staff, how can small museums enhance their educational resources? Throughout this chapter and the following case studies, the authors offer an array of tools and techniques for museum educators. Brian Failing reminds educators of the ephemeral artifacts in museum collections and demonstrates their potential as powerful primary sources for student learning. Shana Crosson offers insight on teachers' use of digital collections in the classroom. Nur Abdalla and Lyndsey Pender detail steps taken to establish an institutional partnership between their small museum and a local charter school while engaging students through internships. Gustavo Valencia Tello and Elizabeth Cruzado Carranza show the impact of a Perúvian museum in preserving and renewing community interest in a rich cultural heritage. These case studies stem from research, interviews, online forums, and on-the-job practice. This chapter is organized around these recurring themes of mission-driven materials and programming, collaboration, and evaluation that contribute to meaning-making in the museum.

Mission-Driven Materials and Programming

How do museum educators sustain, influence, and inspire lifelong learners to continuously seek opportunities for growth in cultural institutions? Museums are places for informal, or free-choice, learning. Odds are you picked up this book, flipped through to the table of contents, and honed in on a particular essay. Before diving in completely, you likely slid your thumb along the crisp pages flipping through until an interesting phrase popped out and piqued your curiosity. You made a choice on the ideal way to explore this compilation. Museums offer guests similar opportunities to choose the best way to approach exhibitions, objects, and ideas through a process of informal learning. Ben Garcia writes, "Formal and informal educational environments—schools and museums—should serve as the yin and yang of learning in a healthy community: equally necessary for education of the whole person."[1] As Garcia notes, informal learning is vital to the holistic education of a person *and* a community.

The theory and practice of education in museums comes from a long lineage of philosophy establishing the importance of informal learning. Museum educators recognize the influential power of these free-choice learning opportunities for visitors of all ages. In *Learning from Museums: Visitor Experiences and the Making of Meaning*, John Howard Falk and Lynn Diane Dierking provide museum educators with extensive research on the learning that occurs within museums. They argue the power of visitor choice as crucial to the cumulative, long-term process of meaning-making. Educators are often actively involved in the planning of exhibitions. They may write copy, design learning materials, and even select objects for display. In support of free-choice learning, museums must provide enough material for visitors to interpret the exhibitions as well as offer supplemental resources for those who want more.

Educational Materials

The primary goal of museum educators is to create opportunities for meaningful museum experiences. To inspire lifelong learning, museum educators need to offer a variety of activities to meet the needs of teachers bringing their classes to the museum as well as community members bringing their friends and families. With such a tall order, getting started can be overwhelming. Here are some simple steps to consider. First, examine the mission of your institution. What goals are stated? How will your materials accomplish the goals?

Second, peruse the exhibitions and collections with those goals in mind. What themes emerge? What stories are waiting to be told? What objects from the collection will tell the story best? Finally, begin constructing materials. It is natural to craft materials full of rote information about artifacts at this stage. However, to ensure materials are more meaningful, consider the enduring ideas embedded in exhibitions and collections.

To illustrate this, I will refer to my work at the National Civil Rights Museum (NCRM) in Memphis, Tennessee. The educational materials in place at the NCRM primarily highlighted historic individuals and their specific stories, trials, and triumphs. After a massive renovation at the museum, we updated the educational materials to reflect the new exhibitions. The mission of the museum was not only to provide information about significant episodes of the Civil Rights Movement but also to inspire participation in civil and human rights. Focusing only on the accomplishments of historic individuals created a barrier to empathy. Those using the materials were disconnected from the struggles of heroic figures of the past and unable to see the relevance to their own lives. With guidance and support from educators, scholars, and colleagues, I retooled the education materials to focus on the enduring idea of courage. The new materials were designed to help users connect with historic individuals while finding courage within themselves. Aligning with the museum's mission, the materials not only chronicle key episodes of the movement but also create contemporary connections showing guests *how* to participate in civil and human rights issues of today. The Courage Educator Resource is available on the National Civil Rights Museum website.[2]

Enduring Ideas

Enduring ideas or themes are central to the human experience. They transcend time and place, relating to people throughout history. They are interdisciplinary, intergenerational, and multicultural. Within an enduring idea, artifacts from a collection provide material culture and primary sources allowing school groups as well as community members to explore a museum as it directly relates to their lives.

In the example above, courage is the enduring idea connecting the past with the present. In the following case study by Tello and Cruzado, the Maria Parado de Bellido School Museum of Archaeology established a mission to maintain the cultural heritage of local people. Through multiple enduring ideas including equity, the relationship between humans and nature, and citizenship, the museum incorporated archaeology and artifacts to educate students and community members about the rich culture and history of their town, Nivín, in Ancash, Perú. The museum not only encouraged a greater understanding and appreciation of the past, but uncovered it by locating archaeological sites of historic significance. Enduring ideas allow for a stronger connection to history through visitor choice ensuring mission-driven meaning-making.

Constructing Materials

After selecting an enduring idea to align with the collection and museum's mission, begin constructing materials. While developing the Courage Educator Resource at the NCRM, we worked with newly renovated exhibits drawing on a motif within them called "Acts of

Courage." The resulting materials incorporated audio/video oral histories of courageous acts. Our materials were intended primarily for teachers of seventh through twelfth grades, but adaptable to any learner.

To determine the audience for educational materials, ask if they are for teachers, families, children, teens, or the broader community. Multiple online resources, such as the University of Massachusetts at Dartmouth link in the Resources Guide of this volume, explain different styles of learning (visual, auditory, and kinesthetic) and offer suggested activities to accommodate each. "Helpful Hints" boxes are examples from the Courage Educator Resource that articulate strategies to meet diverse learning styles when visiting the museum. Be certain to research appropriate methodologies to align learning objectives and activities. For example, in their case study Abdalla and Pender highlight *design thinking* and *mind mapping* as specific methods to meet the needs of their program.

Information should be presented in the language and style appropriate for the intended audience. Consider incorporating components of a traditional lesson plan, especially if materials are for teachers. Table 1.1 can be used as a guide for creating plans. Constructed materials for families, children, and teens can follow a similar plan. Research similar insti-

Table 1.1.   Components of a Lesson Plan, General Definitions, and Examples, 2015.

COMPONENT	DEFINITION	EXAMPLE
Title of Lesson	Include titles and subheadings	How to Write a Lesson Plan
Grade Level/Age Group		All ages
Objectives	The measurable goal(s) of a lesson	Using Table 1, museum educators will construct a lesson plan which includes all components.
Materials	Tools and resources needed in order to teach the lesson	Computer, pen, paper, copy of Table 1, etc.
Vocabulary	Vocabulary appearing in the lesson or necessary to understanding the lesson unfamiliar to the targeted age group	Some states have academic vocabulary lists by subject and grade level available on their Department of Education websites.
Standards	Local, state, and national curricular learning objectives	Find them on state Department of Education websites.
Body	The body of the lesson plan will include a hook or introduction, any informational notes for the teacher, and step-by-step instructions on the activity.	Use a riddle, statistic, exciting, fact, etc. as a hook. Include everything the educator needs to successfully teach the lesson in step-by-step instructions.
Closure	The wrap-up to solidify the lesson	Review key points; draw conclusions

tutions and explore a variety of museum, gallery, and exhibition guides to gather inspiration for your museum's educational materials.

Graphic Design

Aesthetics and design are just as important for conveying messages as words on the page. Good design is a form of trust. We often iterate the trope "don't judge a book by its cover," but tend to trust a well-designed cover to contain a quality story. Educational materials must not only be full of excellent content, but also aesthetically pleasing.

Unfortunately, many museum staff are off-put by the idea of designing educational materials themselves, but there are countless resources for design advice and tutorials readily available online and in books. PrintPlace.com and CreativeLive are free YouTube channels offering a series of art and design videos. *The Non-Designer's Design Book: Design and Typographic Principles for the Visual Novice* by Robin Williams is a good print resource. Consider taking an introductory course in design through a university or Lynda.com. If your museum does not have access to the Adobe Creative Suite, Microsoft Publisher offers features beyond typical text-editing software. Lucidpress.com is an online app available for a small monthly fee and promotes an intuitive interface and professional document layouts without needing a design team. At the NCRM, our Courage Educator Resource was created using Microsoft Word, though it is not the most design-friendly software. No matter your tools, ensure consistency of font, colors, and graphics with all other museum materials for a clean, branded, and trustworthy design.

Have multiple readers edit for content and grammar and consult the opinion of designer(s) to ensure educational materials are of high quality. Outside of the museum, designers may be found in the community as freelance, enrolled in a local university, teaching art at a nearby K–12 school, working at a newspaper, or even on the museum volunteer team. Skills for Change (http://skillsforchange.com) is a microvolunteering website where nonprofits receive free consults on a wide variety of design and marketing tasks.

Educational Programming

Creating educational materials is only one component of the responsibilities of a museum educator. In small museums, educators are usually the primary producers of programming. From school tours to special programs, both the mission of the museum and how the participants make meaning must remain at the forefront in all decisions.

School Tours

School tours need clear objectives. But why identify objectives and standards in the museum when informal learning is the primary goal? Teachers often must justify to administrators why the museum is integral to the lesson(s) taught in the classroom and how the visit connects to state, local, and national education standards. Stating clear objectives does not close the door on informal learning; it adds structure. Be creative in working with docents, tour guides, educators, and volunteers in designing tour experiences that maximize informal learning opportunities.

Use open-ended questions and enduring ideas as tools to help achieve this goal. For example, the NCRM Courage Educator Resource was used to train tour guides, but also became a document for pre- and post-visit activities for teachers, and provided a theme to form personal connections with history for students in school groups.

Step-by-step procedures for tours help achieve a uniform and effective experience for all visitors. Museum educators must know how people learn best, including addressing Maslow's Hierarchy of Needs[3] by ensuring museum guests first know where to find the restrooms! Establish procedures for housekeeping, time for meaning-making, and space for reflection to give tour groups the best experience.

Special Programs

The types of educational programs a museum can offer are as numerous as the stars, but they (should) all share the common goal of mission-driven meaning-making. Museum educators often must acquiesce to the demands of funders in program development. If your museum is fortunate to have many funders, congratulations! This fortune can also come with the need to create a different program for each funder's ideas and requests to the detriment of staff time and energy. Juggling multiple projects with different goals and needs is extremely challenging. It is always critical that the programs align with the mission of the institution. How will programs meet the mission and create meaningful experiences for the participants? How do the requests for programming align with what the museum already offers? Try to find overlap in programs and projects; that is, work smarter, not harder.

Consider how you are communicating about your institution's educational programs and events. Is there a difference between a community program and a family program or a teen program and a young adult program? Be consistent and concise to increase potency. Use your graphic design skills to create a recognizable aesthetic for the different types of programming.

Ultimately, when planning programs consider (1) the audience, (2) the primary takeaway/objective, (3) how the program will meet the objective and museum mission, and (4) how success will be measured.

Collaboration

Collaboration is a route to meaning-making. Communication with museum users is key to meeting their needs on programming, educational materials, exhibitions, and nearly every museum operation. Find opportunities to invite new or underrepresented voices into the museum to express their needs. Be prepared to listen and collaborate to meet those needs. There are varying levels of collaboration including advisory groups, school partnerships, and sharing authority with the community.

Advisory Group

The last thing a busy museum educator needs is another meeting. However, developing an education advisory committee or teacher advisory group is invaluable as Shana Crosson's case study demonstrates. The purpose of the group will depend on the museum and encompass a variety of tasks such as reviewing materials, offering suggestions for programs or special projects, advocating, networking, weighing in on assessment tools, and especially ensuring the museum is meeting the community's needs. Brainstorm ways the advisory group can help the museum. Be certain to articulate the expectations when recruiting advisory group members.

When recruiting for your advisory group, offer incentives such as free admission, museum store discounts, or a complimentary meal. Include educators at varying levels of their profession (new, seasoned/veteran, and retired), teachers or professors in fields directly aligned with your mission and those in other subjects to incorporate science, technology, engineering, the arts, and math (STEAM). Consider museum educators in your region and Internet video conferencing if travel and schedules are problematic. It is also beneficial to invite one or two museum board members to serve on advisory groups or committees.

Start with a smaller committee of around ten individuals. Schedule meetings for three to four times per year or as frequently as the museum educator needs. To find out more about forming an education advisory committee, post a query on a listserv such as museum-ed.org. Also, *The Museum Educator's Manual: Educators Share Successful Techniques*, published by the American Association for State and Local History, contains information on advisory groups.

School Collaboration

Museums, libraries, and schools are the primary institutions of learning within communities. While museum educators should understand the classroom teacher's approach to presenting information, it is also vital for museum professionals to educate teachers and school administrators on the types of learning that can only occur in museum settings. Communication is key to sorting through logistical challenges that arise when collaborating with schools. Shana Crosson's case study in this chapter provides a framework for working closely with classroom teachers to determine their needs, while Nur Abdalla and Lyndsey Pender's case study highlights the importance of institutional communication.

Often, partnerships and collaborations occur on a personal level in which the museum educator builds a relationship with an administrator or teacher at a school. While personal relationship building is crucial to successful collaboration, sustaining a partnership relies on institutional relationship building and communication. Establish clear objectives for the collaboration. Compare the objectives to the mission statements of the museum and the school. Timelines and checkpoints are useful tools to ensure success. Consider pre- and post-evaluations before the collaboration begins.

Collaborations between cultural institutions and universities are as important as working with primary and secondary schools. Institutions of higher learning provide museums with potential resources and knowledge. Collaborations with them can prove to be mutually beneficial. Nearly all of the case studies included in this section incorporate projects to benefit both museums and universities. With trial, error, and excellent communication skills collaborations between museums and educational institutions create optimal learning opportunities for all involved.

Community Collaboration

Cultural institutions are designed to serve their communities. According to a post on April 22, 2015, on her blog Museum 2.0, Nina Simon defines communities with three factors: geography, identity, and affinity.[4] Spend time identifying the geographical, identity-, and affinity-based communities served by your institution and ways the museum can meet its needs within the parameters of the mission.

Tello and Cruzado's case study illustrates ways a Perúvian museum met community needs through co-creation. When the community began losing sight of its historical legacy, the museum responded by collaborating with a local school to generate socially relevant and meaningful learning for all community members.

Communities trust their cultural institutions and appreciate collaborative efforts to build and sustain culture. Explore ways your educational programming and materials incorporate community needs. What ways can community collaboration fulfill your museum's mission statement?

Evaluation

If communication with museum users is key to meeting needs, evaluation provides data to determine if visitors' and the community's needs are met. Evaluate programming and educational materials through surveys, focus groups, or interviews. Keep a record of attendance at special programs and events. These forms of assessment will lead to data. Data leads to advocacy.

When a visitor participates in a program or uses educational materials in the process of informal learning, the personal, qualitative results of their meaningful experience are often not evident or articulated at the end of the event or the conclusion of a tour. The museum experience is part of the identity of the individual as a lifelong learner and manifests itself in different ways. One individual's experience may lead him or her to be a museum visitor for life where before he or she had never had an interest in museums. Another's museum experience may be an influential decision in his or her career path. Someone else may be inspired to become more socially engaged due to the museum visit. These factors make it very difficult for museums to assess the immediate and long-term impact of educational materials and programming. Educators must constantly advocate for their work both within the institution and the community.

Assessment

The best times to collect data are at the beginning and end of a program, tour, or lesson. Pre-experience information will provide data to determine change or growth. Formative assessments can be done quickly during a tour or at a midpoint in a program by gathering simple data. For example, a tour guide could ask for a thumbs-up or thumbs-down if a crucial point was made clear on the tour or a programming host could ask for a show of hands or applause to determine the participants' level of engagement. Post-experience data is a summative assessment to determine if objectives were met and may be in the form of verbal questions or written surveys.

Align assessments with the goals of the program, event, or materials being evaluated. The key to obtaining great feedback is clear articulation of objectives when planning materials, programs, and assessments. Choose the appropriate methodology to determine if goals were met. There are many evaluation methods available online. For example, the Institute of Museum and Library Services has a webpage dedicated to evaluation resources including templates, toolkits, and terminology to help you build the appropriate assessments for your programs.[5] The AASLH small museum blog also contains links to evaluation resources.[6]

At the beginning of this essay, I posed a few questions with the prompt to scribble answers in the margins. The objectives for the section on museum education were also presented. Use those notes as preassessment tools to evaluate your learning after reading this essay. When finished, return to the questions and determine how your answers may have changed.

Advocacy

While Part III in this volume provides excellent advice on advocating for the museum, a unique challenge in museum education is internal advocacy. To maintain (or gain) a seat at the museum's decision-making table, museum educators must continuously advocate for their work. Internal advocacy is supported by assessments to demonstrate data-driven success, educating staff on the work of educators, and creating mission-driven programming and materials.

Museum educators must become keenly aware of the costs and revenue of educational programs. The *Journal of Museum Education* published "Mission, Money, and Authority" in two parts (Volume 35, Numbers 2 and 3) in summer and fall of 2010. Several of the essays, particularly John W. Durel's "No Mission, No Money: No Money, No Mission," emphasize the museum educator's role in strategic thinking for financial viability. To advocate for our work, we must know how it affects both the mission and the budget.

While considering costs and revenue, keep the museum mission at the forefront. If a funder wants to contribute but has strict stipulations on developing a new program, carefully consider how the program is serving the mission. Educators can quickly become overwhelmed when the demands of too many customized programs deviate their work from the mission. Keep an open mind for new ideas and advocate for the programs your museum does best.

Advice and Networking with Fellow Museum Educators

Peers and mentors understand the challenges of being a museum educator. Listservs are excellent resources to learn from the collective wisdom, compare lessons learned, or solve challenging issues. Listserv subscriptions are free. An informal query soliciting advice on museum education from the listserv, Talk@MuseumEd generated the excellent advice from museum educators summarized below.

Be Flexible

As museum educators, many curveballs are thrown our way. Tour groups arrive late. Three surprise meetings are scheduled on a day with big deadlines. A hard rain floods the classroom space. Be flexible in your plans; it is guaranteed they will change. Always be overprepared and organized, allowing for maximum flexibility. On a personal note, be flexible with scheduling to create a healthy work/life balance.

Listen

Educators work hard to perfect materials and create stellar programming. During these processes don't forget to listen to the needs of those who will use the materials and attend the programs. However, be cautious of categorizing audiences; instead listen and respond directly to their expressed needs. Emerging professionals, your voice will be heard, but don't forget to listen to your colleagues.

Reflect

Evaluate your performance as a museum educator. For example, write what strategies worked well after a tour and note ideas for improvement. Ask yourself if you are taking on projects that are both meeting the museum's mission and also challenging you personally and professionally. Reflective practice will make us all better professionals.

Peers are your greatest resource. Build relationships with other museum educators and professionals to learn about and contribute to the field together.

Conclusion

Educators in cultural institutions play a vital role in upholding the mission. Museum educators generate well-designed materials to meet the needs of diverse learners. We work in collaboration with every branch of the museum as well as schools and communities. Educators plant seeds of experience in museum visitors and are often not around when they grow. Therefore, we must collect evaluative assessments and advocate for our mission-driven work. Our role is to inspire personal connections between museum visitors and our institutions and collections. By sticking to the mission, we create opportunities for all guests to make meaning.

Notes

1. Garcia, Ben, "What We Do Best: Making the Case for the Museum Learning in Its Own Right," *Journal of Museum Education*, 37(2012):52.
2. http://civilrightsmuseum.org/wp-content/uploads/2014/01/COURAGE.pdf.
3. http://www.learning-theories.com/maslows-hierarchy-of-needs.html.
4. http://museumtwo.blogspot.com/2015/04/how-do-you-define-community.html.
5. https://www.imls.gov/research-evaluation/evaluation-resources.
6. http://blogs.aaslh.org/together-we-can-listen-incorporating-evaluation-pt-3/.

Developing High School Curriculum

The C.H. Nash Museum and Freedom Prep Charter School Project

Nur Abdalla and Lyndsey Pender

FOR DECADES, the relationship between museums and schools has been rather modest, most often serving as a field trip destination that passively supplements a classroom curriculum. However, in evolving to meet twenty-first-century needs, museums are presented with opportunities to explore more active avenues of engagement and outreach. Of interest to our work are the opportunities to develop proactive and engaged relationships between schools and museums. In our case study, we discuss how one small museum, the C.H. Nash Museum at Chucalissa (CHNM), is taking advantage of engagement and outreach opportunities to form an institutional relationship with a neighboring charter school, Freedom Preparatory Academy (FPA). We report our experience developing and directing summer internship camps with FPA students. We then present these camps as a model for use by other small museums.

An Organic Relationship: The C.H. Nash Museum and Freedom Preparatory Academy

The CHNM, a unit of the University of Memphis, is located in Southwest Memphis on a prehistoric Native American site in a neighborhood that is predominately African American. The museum was founded in 1956 and throughout its early history focused solely on the interpretation of Native American culture, overlooking the significant African American cultural heritage of the area. In 2010, the interpretive focus of the CHNM shifted with the inclusion of an exhibit titled the *African American Cultural Heritage of Southwest Memphis* (AACHSWM), the creation of the southwestmemphis.com website, along with the museum hosting Black History Month and Veteran's Day activities.

In 2013, to fulfill their community service hour requirements, FPA students began to participate in monthly volunteer opportunities at the CHNM. The museum saw the service hours as an opportunity to strengthen its partnership with the school, aligning with the CHNM's mission "to provide the University Community and the Public with exceptional educational, participatory, and research opportunities on the landscape's past and present Native American and traditional cultures."[1]

The mission allows the CHNM to serve as an asset for local schools beyond field trip visits and volunteering. Museum staff met with the FPA dean of students to discuss creating a formal institutional relationship between the two organizations. The relationship would strengthen the ties between the CHNM and FPA at an institutional rather than on an individual level, which could develop into a long-term partnership. As a next step toward this relationship, in 2015 the CHNM proposed hosting a series of summer internship camps for FPA high school students. The camps would fulfill internship requirements for FPA students and generate new content for the museum's AACHSWM exhibit and website.

Learning by Doing: The Camps

By focusing on the AACHSWM exhibit and website, students explored different themes of their community's cultural heritage. The themes included military veterans, the role of women, African American cemeteries, urban gardening, a state park founded in the Jim Crow era, and a nearby folk temple known as Voodoo Village. Each of the five camps explored the themes using a variety of research methods including (1) an oral history camp where participants interviewed veterans, (2) a video/audio camp where students edited the collected oral history footage, (3) an archaeology camp that examined curated cultural materials at the CHNM for potential use in the AACHSWM exhibit, (4) a web design camp where campers updated the existing website, and (5) an event-planning camp to organize a special public event to highlight students' work over the summer. In each camp, there were three or four FPA students and two museum staff. Each camp met for four eight-hour days over a two-week period.

FPA and the CHNM wrote a grant proposal to fund the camps, which was not awarded. However, the CHNM was able to provide funds from its operating budget to meet the minimal economic requirements for the camp including staff salaries, digital recorders, and office materials. The more expensive supplies such as laptops, digital cameras, and projectors were already available at the CHNM. Another important, yet intangible resource the museum provided was flexibility. Each camp flowed from the earlier one in a continuum, so it was imperative that each camp's students create a product. However, we were flexible in how these products were created. Flexibility allowed the students constant input and thus maintained the co-creative experience of the camps. We use the term "co-creation" here in line with that popularized by Nina Simon, meaning to represent a partnership between a museum and community members that includes presenting a community's narrative, representation, and needs through their voice in a museum setting.[2]

We also created an overall operating framework for the camps. Each camp began with a half-day orientation that included watching the museum's introductory video and brief lectures about the relationship between the CHNM and FPA and the concept of co-creation/community partnerships. Also included in the orientation was a scavenger hunt to introduce the AACHSWM exhibit, viewing the southwestmemphis.com website, and viewing the twenty-minute documentary video on the AACHSWM project. Next, students performed a word association exercise writing down all the words and phrases they could think of that related to the term "Southwest Memphis" and the five camp themes.

Students received a detailed introduction to their camp theme and the work completed by the previous camps. On the first day, each camp created a research question/problem based on what they learned during orientation. For example, the oral history camp created their research question: "How can we get more people to share their stories of Southwest Memphis in a more accessible and creative way?"

The process led to an abbreviated version of a brainstorming/problem-solving methodology known as Design Thinking. For the purposes of this camp, we relied on the five-stage Stanford University's Design School Design Thinking model.[3] The first stage, *empathy*

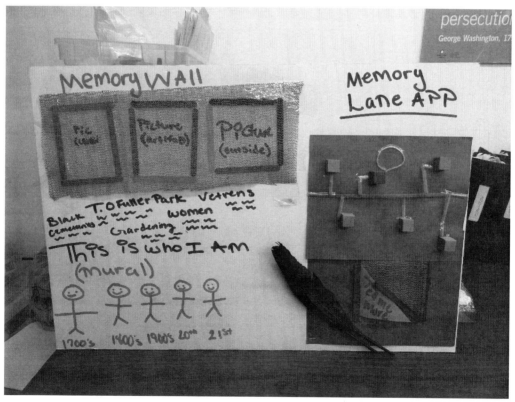

Design thinking prototype created by students. Photograph by Nur Abdalla.

(knowing your audience), and the second stage, *define* (creating a research question/problem), were completed during orientation. On the second day, students used sticky notes to complete the third stage, *ideation*. They proposed written solutions to the problem, realistic or unrealistic, for ten minutes. Working together, they separated the different ideas into themes to complete the fourth stage—creating a *prototype*. Using various office supplies, students created prototypes first individually and then collectively as a team. Afterward, the students presented their group prototype. Due to time constraints, the students were not able to *test and refine the prototype*, the final stage of Design Thinking.

To accommodate our time frame, we introduced each camp's focus utilizing multiple crash courses on the topic. For instance, before beginning the web-editing camp, we trained students on the conventions of web design. Students used "Writing for the Web," an online resource, and together we discussed best practices of online design.[4] If the interns violated any of the conventions of editing, we used the resource information provided to redirect their efforts. We supplemented the verbal discussion of web design conventions with a slideshow of poorly designed websites assembled by Jo Throup titled "Top Ten Worst Websites You'll Wish You Hadn't Seen."[5] While viewing each website students identified the gaffes.

The other main components of the camps were the hands-on learning workshops. For instance, all camps had a writing component. Each student wrote their own content, using a mind-mapping activity to help develop their subject matter and organize their text. Mind

African American Cultural Heritage Exhibit

The African American Cultural Heritage in Southwest Memphis Exhibit, at the C.H. Nash Museum at Chucalissa.

In the summer of 2010 nine high school students, from the Southwest Memphis area, took part in the African American Cultural Heritage project at Chucalissa. The students spent the summer researching neighborhood history and recording interviews with

Southwestmemphis.com website prior to student upgrade. Source: http://www.southwestmemphis.com

Southwestmemphis.com website after student upgrade. Source: http://www.southwestmem phis.com

mapping, as developed by Tony Buzan, uses lines to illustrate connections between phrases, words, ideas, and images (2012 MindMapping.com).[6] Using a simplified version of mind mapping, students started with a word in the center of a large sheet of paper and then jointly wrote down subtopics around the centered word and drew connections. Taking turns, students constructively analyzed their own writing, identifying at least one positive aspect and one aspect to be improved. Next, other students and instructors offered constructive criticism of each other's writing. Students collectively edited and selected pieces of their writing to combine into one cohesive document. The collective process was particularly important since not all students were on the same writing level. Field trips focused on the relevant camp theme were also included.

Conducting the camps for the first time resulted in unexpected obstacles. For example, in the video/editing camp, after experiencing technical and logistical difficulties, instructors moved to a Plan B. Creating a call-to-action video about abandoned African American cemeteries became the new focus for the camp. By evenly distributing production, students completed an original, four-minute video on the topic of abandoned cemeteries. For the web design camp, instead of focusing on updates to the existing southwestmemphis. com site, the second half of the camp focused on generating original content, including articles about a small, predominately Caucasian neighborhood in Southwest Memphis, the CHNM community garden, and abandoned African American cemeteries in the neighborhood.

The Results: Steps and Missteps

The internship camps were insightful, and we learned many general and specific lessons through their operation. For example, during the web design camp, we realized that Wix, the website platform used to perform the edits, only allowed one user to make edits at a time. Therefore, we will use a different platform for future projects. Additionally, although we reviewed conventions for online writing and design, students still made some of the mistakes covered in the lessons. We will need to spend more time on this process in future camps.

A series of evaluation questions distributed at the end of each session assessed camp length, content, favorite/least favorite activities, and a word association of the themes to measure student evaluation of the experience. The student response was overwhelmingly positive. Most students stated they left the project more informed about their camp theme but disappointed that the internships were so short. Students particularly enjoyed the field trip and lecture on historic African American cemeteries by a local resident.

Other lessons learned include:

- The camps needed more time to address the assigned themes. Longer camps also will allow the opportunity to move beyond the orientation phase to engage experts who complement the instructors' areas of expertise. Engaging other experts introduces the CHNM and FPA to additional institutional and individual resources in the community.
- Rather than five separate groups of students, we concluded that a single group of students over a longer period will result in a more effective experience.
- A major concern was the lack of communication between FPA and the CHNM on organizational logistics for the camps.
- We found that talking to teachers to incorporate aspects of the current curriculum into the camps will connect the camps to classroom learning, enhancing the overall educational impact.

The Bigger Picture: Key Lessons

The tangible results of the camps were the student-generated products. However, more importantly, the camps confirmed that, with some refinement, a small museum such as the CHNM could sustain similar types of activities with local schools. We operated the camps with a semi-structured format with considerable flexibility on the outcome expectations. During the early stages of planning for the camps, communication was inconsistent and buy-in with FPA was dependent on a few staff at the school. After the internship camps, both CHNM and FPA staff realized that such projects are not only doable but fill a specific niche of cultural heritage education and outreach that are a part of each institution's mission. The camps demonstrate that a museum is a viable resource for student needs beyond field trip and volunteer opportunities. This result proved to be a major incentive toward further planning and collaboration between the two institutions. Through a co-creative process rooted in the Southwest Memphis community, students can continue to generate content at the CHMN, providing a hands-on supplement to curriculum at FPA.

The Future: Focusing on the Bigger Picture

The camps were a further step in the process of institutionalizing a relationship between the CHNM and FPA. We found that our next and perhaps biggest step is deepening the lines of communication between the two organizations and understanding the broader potential of the camps. Thus, involvement from both institutions must include CHNM staff, FPA students, teachers, parents, and other community stakeholders. We suggest that a broadly based partnership is the only way to create a sustainable and viable relationship. Forming such networks can also help address limited project resources, including the financial means to support the camps and accessing other expert knowledge that proved important to the program. In a follow-up meeting with FPA and CHMN staff, some of these next steps are already completed or planned for implementation, including a presentation to FPA teachers about curriculum support the CHNM can offer, the publication of an oral history book, co-hosting the museum's community garden, and co-hosting our sixth annual Black History Month event in 2016. As well, our two institutions will collaborate in seeking grant support to fund future projects.

In conclusion, there are many avenues to advance the link between museums and schools. Museums must proactively connect to their neighboring schools and/or reexamine their existing relationship. As in our case, many schools are not aware of the opportunities to collaborate with museums beyond the traditional field trip. These institutional relationships can take many shapes but should consider the needs and mission of both institutions when planning. Through partnership and collaboration, our two institutions of service and learning not only strengthened each other but also enhanced their commitment and place in the southwest Memphis community.

Table 1.2.   Project Material Expenses

3 voice recorders: Olympus WS-802 voice recorder	$355
Bulk pack of headphones & 2 lapel microphones	$70
Notepads, Exacto knives, sticky notes, mounting spray, whiteboard markers, flip chart markers	$80
Design Thinking crafting supplies (foam pieces, straws, pipe cleaners, cardboard, feathers, poster board, glue, etc.)	$30
Total	$535

Acknowledgments

We thank the staff of the C.H. Nash Museum at Chucalissa and Freedom Preparatory High School and the residents of Southwest Memphis for their assistance in the project.

Notes

1. The mission statement of the C.H. Nash Museum at Chucalissa was retrieved from their website at http://www.memphis.edu/chucalissa/.
2. http://www.participatorymuseum.org/chapter8/.
3. For more information on the Stanford Design Thinking model, see the Resource Guide.
4. http://www.usability.gov/how-to-and-tools/methods/writing-for-the-web.html.
5. https://www.branded3.com/blog/top-10-worst-websites/.
6. For more information about mind mapping and Tony Buzan, see http://www.mindmapping.com/theory-behind-mind-maps.php and http://www.tonybuzan.com/about/mind-mapping/.

Creating a Museum in a School

Cultural Heritage in Nivín, Perú

Gustavo Valencia Tello and Elizabeth K. Cruzado Carranza[1]

HOW CAN A MUSEUM be integrated into and become essential to a classroom curriculum? Over the past few years, this question has been addressed in a small rural school in the village of Nivín on the north coast of Perú. The Nivín school functions not just in the traditional role as an educational institution for scientific and social knowledge, but also serves to strengthen the cultural identity of the students and teachers.

Addressing the issue of cultural identity allows the local residents to evaluate and embrace their past. Through this process students learn from their history and have that history reflected in the contemporary cultural identity of their community. In turn that identity is directly informed by an understanding of the local culture, including the cultural heritage, historical events, and iconic characters. For these reasons, knowledge of the local cultural heritage should be taught to all students and residents of each community, so they can truly appreciate their homeland, and its history.

Not just in Perú, but throughout the world, the social dynamics of the last fifty years have favored a more regional or even national set of contemporary values and have dismissed the value of the local culture and communal identity. Though an international concern, specifically in Perú, these processes have generated a disconnect of contemporary generations from the Perúvian pre-Hispanic past.

In 2011, to begin building a link between the present and the past, the teachers in the local school in Nivín, Ancash, Perú, led by Professor Gustavo Valencia Tello, created a small museum with archaeological artifacts donated by the local community. The village of

Nivín is situated adjacent to a large unprotected archaeological site from which residents have collected artifacts for many years. The purpose of the donations is to use the materials in the classroom as tools for developing a cultural identity and teaching about the cultural heritage of Nivín.

Maria Parado de Bellido of Nivín: Where the Change Began

The educational Institution No. 88104 Maria Parado de Bellido is a rural school located in the town center Nivín, 23 km from the city of Casma, on the bank of the Rio Grande River valley. This portion of the valley is characterized by a dry environment, with sparse rainfall and very warm temperatures most of the year.

The school is in the process of an administrative and academic reorganization by transitioning from a traditional curriculum to one based on applied learning projects. The Nivín School projects are developed in collaboration with the students, teachers, and community members as a demonstration of mutual interest in the school's educational focus. The school is the main actor in the community and seeks to propose and provide solutions to local social problems and opportunities, through an applied approach to education.

Nivín Archaeology: Seeking Identity

When analyzing the current state of Nivín, teachers noted a lack of concern by government authorities to assess and conserve the regional cultural heritage. This attitude leads to the destruction of archaeological sites and the loss of movable and immovable cultural heritage. Students at the Nivín School are no strangers to the current situation that results in alienation, lack of cultural identity, an indifference to preservation and economic development, and lack of respect for traditional local heritage. All these factors reflect a lack of information, accompanied by official regional and national policies that do not support the assessment, preservation, and integration of the tangible cultural heritage left by the ancient inhabitants in small communities.

In response, one objective of the school is based on the urgent need to identify, recognize, study, and assess the historic and monumental pre-Hispanic legacy of the area. The teachers recognized not just the duty of Nivín residents to care for the archaeological resources, but the fundamental right of every person to know of and celebrate their own identity. In 2011, the campaign of *Nivín Archaeology: Seeking Our Identity*, was created with an aim to promote educational opportunities for the development of local cultural identity with students from the local school and the village residents.

The Seeking Identity project values a respect for life, democratic participation, sense of belonging and cultural identity, and seeks the acquisition of social, historical, and ecological knowledge. The study of cultural heritage also allows students and the community to identify, register, document, design, and implement preventive measures for the conservation of heritage properties. This project educates on the local cultural identity and results in new knowledge and a deepening of moral values.

Exhibit in Nivín Archaeology Museum. Photograph by Elizabeth Cruzado Carranza.

The Nivín Museum and Mission

As the material cultural heritage of Nivín is threatened with destruction its protection requires preservation actions by several entities, but above all, by the local community. To promote this work, the school principal of Nivín takes part in community activities that aim to protect the past. The school jointly assumes the responsibility for the preservation and enhancement of the community's cultural heritage. Therefore, the Seeking Identity campaign created a school museum. The museum promotes the mutual participation of the school and the community in valuing and promoting the preservation of Nivín's cultural memory and heritage resources. The Maria Parado de Bellido Museum of Archaeology is a major effort of the school and community in this work.

Teachers, students, and the community use the museum to curate materials recovered from the archaeological sites near the school. The museum promotes the preservation of archaeological sites with the support of cultural heritage professionals in the region. Currently ceramics, lithics, human remains, and textiles are curated in the museum. Most of the artifacts were obtained through the patient advocacy work with local townspeople and farmers who acquired the materials from their agricultural fields.

The mission of the museum as a community cultural center is to serve society and its development. The school museum plays a decisive role in the creation of spaces for reflection and production of knowledge about heritage and culture. Besides working to achieve significant changes in the preservation of culturally important material remains, this work has enhanced the cultural identity of Nivín's people.

Educating with Archaeology in Nivín

In Perúvian education, prehistoric national heritage traditionally is presented as a distant concept from the day-to-day life of the contemporary student. The national curriculum focuses on ancient complex societies, such as the Inca, Moche, and Chimú. Within this academic vision, the teaching of local history, archaeology, paleontological heritage, living or intangible culture, and local cultural landscapes is typically not included. The exclusion leads to the lack of appreciation of cultural heritage by the local people.

Therefore, at the Nivín school cultural heritage is incorporated into the curriculum through a range of educational projects. A concept developed by Nivín teachers is that children and adolescents learn to see with historical eyes, and critically assess the local cultural heritage. Therefore, the Nivín School aims to teach through an approach that demonstrates the importance and preservation of cultural heritage.

Nivín educational curriculum stipulates that the content must be developed comprehensively across all disciplines. This approach allows for cultural studies to cross through multiple subject areas. In this context, the role of the museum as part of the school has increased in the last few years. The teachers consider the school museum as a place that provides education in and for the community. This perspective benefits the school, the teachers, and the community members, because the museum provides creative and active educational learning experiences, based on the goal of promoting respect for democratic participation, cultural

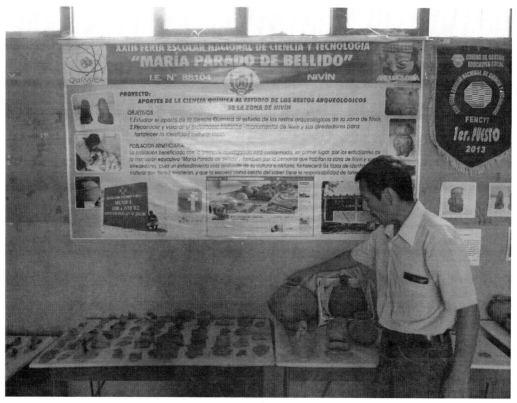

Gustavo Valencia Tello with exhibit in Nivín Archaeology Museum. Photograph by Elizabeth Cruzado Carranza.

patrimony, and local individuals. With this interaction, the school has created networks with local residents for educational programs that meet their needs.

Similarly, in the social sciences classes, the lessons are created based on the key issues of the local community that affect cultural heritage, especially the preservation of archaeological objects at the school museum. The students identify, register, document, design, and implement actions for the preservation of their cultural patrimony.

Each educational class type has the potential to explore different aspects of the importance of cultural heritage in Nivín's local education. For example, during science lessons, students conduct research using the scientific method, which allows them to create arguments, hypotheses, and record test results. These lessons also allow students to develop critical thinking skills that enable them to consider historical and cultural events from local and regional perspectives.

In the museum, educational activities also focus on the subject area of chemistry as related to the development of archaeological research. For example, the study of soil phosphates of an archaeological site provides information about the presence of human activity. This chemical analysis can determine if the site was used as a kitchen area, pasture, garden, animal pens, midden, or an agricultural area. This information is crucial to the reconstruction of the pre-Hispanic use of the area and can inform students about present-day activities as well.

Another activity is linked to the science of human anatomy. Human skeletal material curated at the museum is used in biology courses. The materials include actual human remains along with ceramic and plastic casts from museum displays. In this way the students study human anatomy in their biology class through the use of pre-Hispanic residents of the region and develop a recognition and respect for the men and women who lived in ancient Nivín.

Results and Conclusions

The teaching of cultural heritage in the Nivín School museum is characterized by using material culture for many subject areas. In Nivín, education is based on building links with the local cultural identity and direct engagement with community members who participate in events that support this learning method.

Inserting the issue of cultural heritage into the school and community agendas has been a challenge that teachers face. But with perseverance the campaign around cultural identity has led to changes in the attitude of Nivín community members and students.

The work has led to recognizing six major archaeological sites near the school. There is no official record of these archaeological sites except for a brief mention in the Perúvian scholar Julio C. Tello's volume on the archaeology of the region some eighty years ago.[2] To date most of the archaeological sites in the region remain unknown to local cultural heritage professionals, and result in the neglect and ignorance of the local past. Therefore, the work of the Maria Parado de Bellido School in Nivín is an important first step to inform not just the local community but the regional and national archaeological community of the existence of these sites so that they are incorporated into the story of pre-Hispanic Perú.

The archaeological work in Nivín, centered at the school museum, is an essential educational project for achieving meaningful learning. The importance of the project has been noted by Perú's Ministry of Education, which recognized the campaign's potential to be replicated across the country.

This approach of including the teaching of local cultural heritage has also been included in two recent editions of the Perúvian National Science and Technology Fair and through inclusion of Nivín student archaeological heritage projects in provincial-level competitions. In addition, in 2014, the project *Nivín Archaeology: Seeking Identity* was the winner of the National Award for Best Teaching Practices by the Ministry of Education of Perú.

Notes

1. A Spanish language version of this article is available at www.museumcommunities.com.
2. Julio C. Tello, *Arqueología del Valle de Casma* (Editorial San Marcos, Lima, 1956).

Meeting Teacher Needs

Digital Collections in the Classroom

Shana Crosson

Introduction

IN 2008, the Minnesota Historical Society (MNHS) received support from the Minnesota Arts and Cultural Heritage Legacy Fund that empowered staff to focus on how to meet the changing needs of the twenty-first-century learner. Based on our information-gathering techniques, which ranged from observations of student behavior on field trips to conversations with teachers and classroom observations, we knew that the educational needs of today's students were changing as outside forces impacted the educational landscape. Building on the work from the Institute of Museum and Library Services 21st Century Skills Project,[1] we wanted to know how technology in classrooms was impacting the ways teachers taught and changing how students learned. How did technology open up new doors to learning? How could MNHS help address these twenty-first-century skills? This special funding gave MNHS an opportunity to build new programs and products specifically to address these new skills.

This case study will focus primarily on the impact of using digital collections in classrooms. Museums have lots of "stuff": objects, maps, photos, documents, and more. Teachers love to show this "stuff" to students as primary sources to make history real and help students understand their place in history. But getting the "stuff" to the students and actually using it can be tricky. Websites and online collection repositories have made it much easier to bring these primary sources into the classroom, especially now that many students have ready access to the Internet, whether through their own device (phone/tablet), classroom computers or iPads, or a 1:1 program with a school-provided device for each student. However, many teachers still do not access primary sources or don't know how to use them.

Given that the shift to digital technology in the educational landscape is new, we needed to get into classrooms and connect directly with teachers in their world. We needed to go to schools, observe classes, meet with district staff and teachers, and listen to their concerns and needs. As part of the move to understand twenty-first-century learners, we asked why teachers weren't using digital collections and started collaborations with teachers to learn more about how teachers are—and are not—using digital primary sources. As it turns out, teachers welcomed and greatly appreciated being asked for their input. Needless to say, these experiences significantly impacted the programs we created at MNHS.

Planning

Before developing new resources, MNHS staff wanted to know about how teachers used primary sources. Our research questions included:

- What age of students can use primary sources?
- What types of primary sources do teachers use in the classroom?
- How do students respond to primary sources?
- What activities do teachers do with students using primary sources? Do teachers incorporate sources into daily class work?
- Where do teachers find primary sources? What do teachers like and not like about online repositories?
- How do teachers instruct students to find primary sources?
- How do teachers validate the sources?
- How do teachers instruct students to validate the sources?

This research led to the development of curriculum products, training, and online tools that will hopefully meet the needs of teachers and students into the future. The research also allowed MNHS staff to better understand the needs of teachers in this changing educational landscape and to develop close ties to a number of teachers that have evolved into ongoing partnerships. The teachers continue to provide input, feedback, and motivation to develop more tools and resources that meet the educational needs for using primary sources. These partnerships are mutually beneficial. As one of the partner teachers said: "What is valuable about working with museums? For a classroom teacher, access to resources is a huge challenge. Students learn history best using authentic artifacts. Putting artifacts in students' hands—physically, and more importantly, digitally—gives students an experience that is 'hands-on' in a classroom. Since museums are curators of that type of resource, teachers and students have the opportunity to learn and ask questions that can be answered through the partnership with a museum."

Implementation

The first step in our research entailed reviewing literature about twenty-first-century learning and skills. There are a variety of online sources and books about these topics (see Resource Guide of this volume at museumcommunities.com). However, the most valuable research came from delving into the online conversations with teachers, which meant going out of our comfort zone and using Twitter! There is a robust online community of teachers actively involved in discussions regarding twenty-first-century skills that connect using social media tools such as Twitter and blogs. They are eager to engage in conversation. As part of this work, the MNHS staff members on this project were active on Twitter and maintained their own blog to document the findings.[2]

The next step of research involved a series of focus groups exploring the role of technology in the classroom. The five focus groups of between seven and ten participants lasted approximately two hours. Teachers were given a small compensation and snacks. Some focus groups consisted of teachers from the same school, while other groups included teachers from multiple schools. Almost all grade levels were represented and teachers came from a variety of content areas, including a self-contained elementary classroom, high school history (including world and American history), middle school science, and media specialists. The same set of questions was asked of each group. The questions explored how teachers used digital tools, their perception of the role of technology in the classroom, how they were teaching twenty-first-century skills, and what resources they wanted for their classrooms.

Additional focus groups concentrated on field trips and twenty-first-century skills. These focus group participants included teachers, and in separate groups, chaperones (usually parents) and students. As with the technology focus groups, participants were paid for their time and provided with snacks. The participants in these groups were drawn from lists of teachers who had brought students to a historic site or museum for a field trip in the last year.

The third step of research was a "Teacher Camp" where ten teachers spent a week in conversation about using primary sources and preparing materials that MNHS staff could use in project development. Camp participants taught grades 1–8 and mostly elementary self-contained or middle school social studies. The Teacher Camp was funded by a grant. Teachers were paid for their time and provided with lunch, snacks, parking, and, very importantly, a behind-the-scenes tour of collections storage. Activities for the week included:

- presentation of a classroom activity using primary sources,
- discussions about criteria used when selecting primary sources,
- identification of information teachers wanted about the primary sources, and
- team development of a "wrapper" of content about a primary source that would be part of any online collection designed for classrooms.

During the time period of the camps and focus groups, MNHS staff attended conferences for educators, including sessions about technology in education. Attending and eventually presenting at these conferences shifted our perspective and informed our approach to program development.

Classroom observations were crucial to the project. Partner teachers welcomed us into the classroom. Sometimes we just observed; other times we interacted with students. These partnerships continue to provide MNHS staff with a place to test new products and ideas. Teachers benefit by getting curriculum and classroom resources that best suit their needs.

Results

Our research on twenty-first-century skills has markedly influenced how MNHS staff develop programs for the K–12 audience, including curriculum products, online tools, professional development, and field trips. For example, we have developed a set of packets of primary sources that include twelve to eighteen items (images, maps, photos of objects, letters, etc.), context about the objects, and the topic and suggested activities. Many field trip options have been changed to include twenty-first-century skills such as more critical thinking, collaboration, and creativity.

The relationships between MNHS staff and teachers that developed from this research continue to be mutually beneficial for all involved. MNHS staff members have access to continuous feedback from teachers about products and programs; teachers have significant input in how products and programs are created. Teachers have commented that they appreciate having better access to the resources of the organization. Some of the teachers have developed their own partnerships with local historical organizations in their town. They then have access to local primary sources such as photos, maps, and objects that make history even more relevant and accessible to students. One teacher commented on the significant impact of local primary sources on his students in seeing then/now images of their town and the original plat maps with names that are still familiar today. According to one of our partner teachers, "What makes it attractive for a teacher to partner with a small museum? Since all history is local, a small museum might be the perfect fit for a classroom teacher. Often the local history is missing from district curriculum and state standards so a small museum provides a classroom teacher with a hook that is more accessible to students."

Ongoing partnerships have led to our increased participation in conference presentations (both museum and education conferences), curriculum development in classrooms, and a new level of understanding between teachers and museum educators.

The findings about the teachers' use of primary sources, and digital primary sources in particular, have been consistent through all of our research efforts:

- Teachers find most digital repositories overwhelming. Teachers welcome the option where fewer, specifically selected sources are presented.
- Teachers want additional context about an object. Stories about a specific object and background context make an object/primary source much more useful. This "wrapper" includes additional content about the source, such as information about the owner, how the object was used, contextual information about the time period, and the place or event in which the source originated. The wrapper as designed by the teachers also included links to additional sources, Common Core standards, and suggested questions/activities.

Anti-Vietnam demonstration in Dinkyton, Minneapolis, April 11, 1967. Photograph by St. Paul Pioneer Press. Courtesy Minnesota Historical Society.

Anti-Vietnam demonstration in Dinkyton, Minneapolis, April 11, 1967. Photograph by St. Paul Pioneer Press. Courtesy Minnesota Historical Society.

- Teachers use specific criteria to select primary sources. They want to use primary sources to engage students to ask questions and think critically about content. For example, when presented with two images of the same event, teachers selected Image 1 because it provided more context and more room for questions. Regarding Image 1 one teacher said. "There are so many more questions that could be asked, and some of them will be answered and some of them won't necessarily be answered." Teachers thought Image 2 was "too easy, it's too simple."

Lessons Learned

This case study project successfully changed the mindset of MNHS education staff and resulted in developing ongoing partnerships with teachers. It became very clear through this research that input from teachers is the most important part of project development. There is nothing better than having teachers evaluate products and programs while in development. The process results in a better final product. Teachers have distinct needs that may be quite different than a researcher's or a museum-goer's.

The teacher input impacted the selection of projects. After we knew more, initial ideas were changed or scrapped because we could identify what would work better. MNHS staff continue to utilize the lessons learned in all program development. The underlying change in how MNHS staff approach education projects has been significant. This process challenged long-held practices and approaches to working with students and teachers. Most staff have embraced the changes, but change can be difficult. These changes have been no different. However, the ongoing partnerships continue to provide positive impact.

Some of our research methods have become an integral part of project/program development and evaluation. For example, many projects now include focus groups either in early developmental phases or in program evaluation. Attendance at education conferences, as opposed to only museum conferences, has proven essential for keeping an eye on educational trends and for building and maintaining relationships.

Similar research can be undertaken by institutions even with a very small budget:

- Focus groups can be done at a very low cost. Compensation for participants can be made within a small budget, or perhaps through tickets to an event, a book, or small gift certificate donated by a business. Food, however, is critical! It isn't necessary to do a series of focus groups. One focus group is often enough to learn a great deal.
- Similar results could be achieved by simply meeting with a small group of teachers. For example, one possibility is to contact a local middle school and ask for a twenty-minute meeting with the social studies teachers. Meet at their convenience—maybe attend a staff meeting—and bring treats! Then, just listen to their needs and be open to change.
- Develop relationships with local teachers. Reach out to teachers who bring field trips and teachers you may know in your community. Invite them to test your programs. Ask to observe in their classrooms. Send them evaluations after field trips asking

for their input on the experience. If you write grants to develop programs, include funding to pay teachers to participate.

- Organizers of educational conferences often welcome presentations by museum staff. These presentations should not be an advertisement for a museum, but rather an opportunity to present skills and pedagogical approaches. Consider proposing a session with a teacher. Topic ideas could be about how teachers use primary sources (digital or physical) in the classroom, how to help students do historical research online or in person, or how to evaluate a historic image/object.
- Being present in online spaces where teacher communities are active is free and easy to do. Follow known thought leaders on Twitter and read their blogs.

Next Steps

MNHS continues to focus program and product development using the lens of the twenty-first-century learner. The biggest threat to continuing to build on what we've learned is the number of competing projects and finding ways to make new products and programs financially sustainable. It is also important to continue this research by following educational trends and making sure the conversation and partnerships don't fade away.

Museums can easily implement approaches to deliver primary sources. For example, a curator or educator could put together small sets of (twelve to fifteen) primary sources that deal with the local city/town, a local event, or famous person. Take photographs (objects) or make copies (printed material, images) and gather them into a packet. Copies for print packets can be as simple as a 5 × 7 photo or even a photocopy. Write the stories about the primary sources: who owned it, where did the museum get it, what was it used for, and when was it used (see Mary Anna Evans's case study, this volume). These packets could be distributed in print or online using free blogging tools, such as Blogger.com or WordPress.com.

Museums are natural partners of schools and teachers. It just takes a conversation to start a partnership that benefits everyone: the museum, teachers, students, and the entire community.

Table 1.3. Essential Expenses for Two Focus Groups (ten participants per group)

Payment can vary depending on your relationship with the participants. Recommend minimum payment of 25.00.	$500
Refreshments	$200
Transcriptions	$400
Recording of focus groups can be done with an inexpensive smartphone, tablet, video camera, or digital recorder.	$200
Miscellaneous office materials	$100
Total	$1,400

Notes

1. https://www.imls.gov/assets/1/AssetManager/21stCenturySkills.pdf.
2. Unfortunately this blog is no longer available.

Using Postcard Collections as a Primary Resource in the Classroom

Brian Failing

HAVE YOU EVER THOUGHT about the educational possibilities a collection of postcards can bring to your local museum? Do you fear that your museum does not have the time or skill to complete a digitization project? Within every museum is a collection of ephemera, much of which goes unused and underappreciated, that if digitized would provide far greater public access to the curated material. This project began as a classroom assignment in my Research Methods in American Local History class while I was a student in the master's program in historical administration at Eastern Illinois University (EIU).

Planning

I initially found several postcards at a local antique store and decided to form a project around the items. To my surprise, I learned that the DuPage County Historical Museum (DCHM) in Wheaton, Illinois, curated a collection of nearly 600 postcards depicting Du-Page County. I ultimately decided to add these postcards to my project. At the time my class was reading Fay Metcalf and Matthew Downey's *Using Local History in the Classroom*, which examines the ways local sources could be used to teach history.[1] The authors' model divides local sources into four thematic areas: family history, economic history, social history, and political history. Through each section the authors discuss a variety of sources; however, they do not include the analysis of postcards. After reading Metcalf and Downey, I applied their thematic model to postcards at the DCHM. I explored why postcards were important and how they could be used as historical evidence.

I titled my project *Using Postcards as Historical Evidence*.[2] The significance of the collection of postcards at the DCHM included much more than just pictures and inscriptions. The postcards illustrate an important part of twentieth-century history and cover a variety of subject areas. The postcards depict businesses, churches, community events, parks, residential homes, and street scenes of the community. In essence, the postcards capture a visual and written memory of the past. The collection of postcards lent itself perfectly to Metcalf and Downey's model. Eastern Illinois University featured my paper on the postcard project on their Localities website—a digital repository that provides local history pages pertaining to the history of the university and region and features the work of EIU history students.[3]

To further develop the usefulness of my paper and the Localities website, I created an accessible digital collection of the DCHM postcards.[4] This project, entitled *Postcards of DuPage County: A Digital Collection of the Past*, allowed me to work with the DCHM while meeting the requirements of the Historical Administration Program at EIU. The project also aligned with DCHM's mission to provide avenues for public access to curated historic records and enabled me to develop an applied educational experience. Ultimately, the project expanded well beyond my original intentions.

Creating the Digital Collection

The basis of public history is to take traditional historical work and make it accessible to all. The first application of public history in this project began in one of my graduate courses by creating the online resource *Using Postcards as Historical Evidence*.[5] The intent of this digital component was to make an academic paper accessible to the public through the Localities webpages. The Localities webpages are an integral part of the EIU total website, allowing my project to be placed alongside other local and regional projects that focus on Illinois history. Moreover, the presence of *Using Postcards as Historical Evidence* on the Localities website gives the user access to information about the history of postcards and allows them to examine related resources and repositories and explore the use of postcards as evidence in local history research.

Using Postcards as Historical Evidence was designed to be readily accessible by teachers, students, and researchers. I wanted the webpages to be useful as both a stand-alone asset and as a teaching tool. The site includes a variety of discussion- and inquiry-based questions linked to specific postcards. For example, a postcard of the then Adams Memorial Library (now the DuPage County Historical Museum) is featured on the webpage.

Linked questions urge the user to compare the image on the postcard shown at the bottom of page 39 to other postcard images of the same building through time. The user is then encouraged to consider how the multiple views of the same structure reflect social, economic, and architectural changes over the period reflected in the postcard images. The site includes many examples of postcards for each thematic area.

Using Postcards as Historical Evidence page on Eastern Illinois University's Localities website. Source: http://www.eiu.edu/localite/postcardshisth ome.php. Accessed November 30, 2015.

Postcard of the Adams Memorial Library. Source: Memorial Library, Wheaton, Illinois, 1907–1908. DuPage County Historical Museum, Wheaton, Illinois.

While having access to the Localities website was useful, there are many digital platforms appropriate to make similar research projects available to the public. Website "creators" or platforms such as Squarespace, WordPress, Weebly, and Wix allow users to drag and drop components such as headlines, text blocks, and images onto the website pages. All of these platforms offer free website hosting and little web design experience is required beyond basic computer skills.

As a small museum, DCHM did not have the resources to complete the project without additional support. The project used PastPerfect, a collections management software, to develop a catalog of the museum's postcard collection that included relevant metadata such as the publisher, publication date, and the scene depicted. PastPerfect also features components to add images to each catalog entry, create virtual exhibits, and make the catalog accessible online to the public. DCHM already owned PastPerfect, including the multimedia component, which allowed the scanned postcards to be attached to their respective catalog records. Making the digitalized postcards accessible on the web required purchasing the software expansion, PastPerfect Online. PastPerfect Online is $285 to set up and $440 per year. All these prices can be reduced by 20 percent with an AASLH membership. The museum is a member so the cost was $228 and $352, respectively. I scanned each postcard, front and back; created a file name; edited or cleaned up the file; and then uploaded the file into PastPerfect.

Besides PastPerfect, uploads of scanned images can be made through no-cost alternatives such as a wiki-based site or open source database management. Omeka.net is a data management software package that is based online and can host up to 500 megabytes of files for free. Omeka is a low-cost alternative for museums who do not already have PastPerfect.

In addition to the noted software the project required a digital scanner and editing software to prepare the images for upload. Suitable scanners range from as little as $200 (Epson V550) to a more elaborate system for several thousand dollars (Epson 11000XL model). The photo-editing software typically included with the scanner can be used or software packages such as Corel PaintShop Pro, Adobe Photoshop, or Adobe Lightroom allow for greater image manipulation and metadata storage.

Lessons Learned

This project developed entirely from my graduate course work and demonstrates the value of such projects to museums. As a student, I sought an opportunity to create a project from a topic of interest to me—postcards. Through a class assignment, I was able to achieve that goal and provide a public resource for the DCHM. The postcard project expanded throughout my graduate curriculum for paper and project assignments in two classes and provided me with grant application experience and an internship required for my degree program.

Graduate students working on real-time applications can take ownership and become invested in the project and the museum. Graduate students have access to resources from their home institutions not necessarily accessible to the small museum. For example, in this project I received mentoring and guidance from EIU faculty and received a Research/Creative Activity Grant from the Graduate College to purchase PastPerfect Online for the DCHM. Such awards are often readily available from universities but require student involvement and initiation.

Next Steps

The *Using Postcards as Historical Evidence* project has a potential to expand the work of the DCHM and provide a framework for other practitioners or users to follow. Such projects can also further engage graduate students and university programs in the work of a small museum. Both the museum curator and museum manager and educator are excited by the possibilities the postcard projects hold for the DCHM. At small museums, where resources are often stretched thin, collections often are underutilized because researchers do not know the materials exist or are unable to access them. However, postcards of DuPage County are one of the most requested collections at the DCHM, making them a clear priority for patrons. Michelle Podkowa, museum manager and educator, notes that "by providing some of our primary sources, such as the postcards, on our website we hope that we can get part of our rich collection, much of which has not been seen in decades, out there for the public to use."

The *Using Postcards as Historical Evidence* project relied extensively on the work I completed through several of my graduate classes, an internship, and volunteer hours. Ashley Downing, museum curator, recommends that museums "build relationships with graduate students and programs at local universities to see what resources and skills they can bring to the table." Placing the postcard collection online is an example of building a stronger connection between a university, community, and museum. The postcards depict settings of a majority of the towns in DuPage County, thus illustrating the far-reaching geographic extent of the museum's collection.

Online collections can address logistical considerations in archive access. An online collection is accessible no matter where the user is located or when they require access. A typical on-site collection access in the museum necessitates making an appointment to view a more narrow range of curated materials. More than one person can use an online collection simultaneously—valuable for group and class projects in schools. Digital collections help to preserve the original postcards through reduced physical handling of the objects by users and museum staff. Additionally, an online collection does not require staff to facilitate access.

Using Postcards as Historical Evidence can be developed further. A museum-sponsored educational workshop could provide instruction on how to read primary sources and stress the importance of postcards as a resource. The DCHM experienced firsthand how working with internal and external groups made this project a reality. The postcard project can serve as a model for other museums to utilize their underutilized collections to further their public history and educational work.

The items digitized in this project do not represent the entire collection of postcards and other ephemera curated at the DCHM. The remaining postcards of the region can be digitized and added to the digital archive that has proven quite popular with both the general public and the educational community of DuPage County. *Using Postcards as Historical*

Evidence is an example of a project that is low cost and can be completed by small museums with a limited staff.

Acknowledgments

I thank Dr. Terry A. Barnhart, professor of history at Eastern Illinois University, for his guidance. This project received support from DuPage County Historical Museum and a Research/Creative Activity Grant from the Graduate College at Eastern Illinois University.

Notes

1. Fay D. Metcalf and Matthew T. Downey, *Using Local History in the Classroom* (Nashville, TN: The American Association for State and Local History, 1982).
2. *Using Postcards as Historical Evidence* began as a paper, which was translated into a digital resource by the same name on the Localities platform.
3. "Localities," Eastern Illinois University, accessed November 30, 2015, http://www.eiu.edu/localite/.
4. "DuPage County Historical Museum," Wheaton Park District, accessed November 30, 2015, http://www.dupagemuseum.org/. The completed archive of digitized postcards available on PastPerfect Online will be available through the museum's website.
5. Brian Failing, "Using Postcards as Historical Evidence," Eastern Illinois University, Fall 2014, accessed November 30, 2015, http://www.eiu.edu/localite/postcardshisthome.php.

Words, Stone, Earth, and Paint

Using Creative Writing to Engage a Community with Its Museum

Mary Anna Evans

I'M A NOVELIST, which is only one of many ways to be a storyteller. The goals of a storyteller are not materially different from the goals of a museum and the people who bring it into being. We are all interested in reaching people where they are most human.

When creating a story, a writer seeks to create empathy, putting the reader into the shoes of another person living in another place and, perhaps, in another time. Isn't this the aim of a museum? To put visitors into the place of Galileo, crafting his own instruments in hopes of bringing invisible stars close enough to see? Or to let them stand in front of re-articulated mastodon bones, letting them feel the way the earth trembled when that beast was whole and alive?

I am often asked to present educational programs at venues like museums, schools, and libraries. As I prepare, I think, "What is our goal for this program?" and I try to go beyond the easy answer: "I'm supposed to teach these people how to write a story." Time and again, I come back to the idea of empathy. When designing a museum program, this leads me to a straightforward question with many not-straightforward answers: "How can I use the museum's collection to help its community engage with the people who populate their cultural heritage? How can I help them use that empathy to write stories that resonate with their heritage?"

My favorite museum-based program is supremely simple. It can be accomplished in an hour by anyone of any age. It can also fill a weeklong summer camp. I can think of no museum where some version of the program wouldn't work. It requires no equipment beyond paper and pencil.

I gather the participants and I talk to them about the making of cultural things or objects by saying something like this:

> Every item in every museum is chosen for its relationship with the human experience. This is true of historical museums that put the day-to-day lives of long-ago humans into contexts that museum-goers can understand. It's true in art museums, where the paintings and sculptures were made by human beings who were saying, "This is what the world looks like to me."
>
> Sometimes art and history collide, allowing artists whose fame has made them almost mythological to be human beings again. I have read that when the ceiling of the Sistine Chapel was restored the restorers found bristles from Michelangelo's brush in the plaster. They also found the prints of his fingertips where he tested the plaster to see if it was dry enough to paint. Thinking of this very physical connection with Michelangelo after all these centuries gives me chills, but then I remember that his paintings give us that same connection. So does every historical artifact in this museum, every sculpture, every document, every stone tool. These things were made by human hands, which is the definition of the word "artifact." Even those things in this museum that weren't made by human hands—dinosaur bones, meteorites, petrified wood—were found by humans, chosen for display by humans, and preserved for us by humans.
>
> Your assignment is to take a slow walk through this museum until you encounter an object that speaks to you. Read any interpretive material, then settle yourself in front of the object and take out your pen and paper. Spend the next forty-five minutes living with this object and writing. You may divide your time between those activities as you see fit. I don't want you to write about the object, however. Write about the making of it. Imagine yourself in the shoes of the maker and then tell me about that maker's life. The first word of your piece should be "I."
>
> Beyond that, the story is your own. You can let your narrator tell me the story of making this piece. You can let your narrator describe a completely unrelated event. If you choose an object without a human maker, you can tell about the person who found it or the person who prepared it for display or the person who drove the truck that brought it here. Surprise me.
>
> If you have questions or if you finish early and want to talk about the assignment, come talk to me, but try to take the whole time for your writing. Sometimes stories come slow. Wait for yours and see what comes.

These instructions can be tailored for the museum's collection. Since I write mysteries about a North American archaeologist, I have a small box of artifacts given to me by an archaeologist. I open the box and hand them around, letting students have a tactile experience of the past. They can test the edge on a spear point. They can fit their thumb into the depression on the side of a scraper, where someone else rested a thumb while scraping hides long ago. They can hold a clay ball made at Poverty Point World Heritage Site in Northeast Louisiana 3,500 years ago, thrown into a fire, heated and used like a charcoal briquette to cook food by the heat it retained. This clay ball is my favorite way to put a human face on the past. Impressed in its surface are the shapes of its maker's fingers. When people put their own fingers in those impressions, the past and its people come alive. This is the power of empathy.

Putting the Process into Practice

I teach creative writing at the University of Oklahoma, where I recently used this exercise with two of my classes. I took one class to the Fred Jones, Jr. Museum of Art, and I took the other to the Bizzell Memorial Library, which has standing exhibits of paintings, sculptures, and historical artifacts. While some of the students may not have visited the art museum, they almost certainly had been in the library. I wanted to explore whether they'd ever interacted with the library exhibits or whether they'd even noticed them in their hurry to get to the books.

They uniformly responded with enthusiasm, spending time walking among the exhibits, trying to choose just the right object to write about. Some stood to write and observe. Some found a bench with a handy vantage point. And some just sprawled on the floor, pen in hand.

I'd seen trepidation flit across their faces when I said "forty-five minutes." Three-quarters of an hour is a long time to be still and quiet in a public place, but I already knew that. I consciously chose the time frame to push the boundaries of what they were willing to do. I just as consciously kept the writing time under an hour. The phrase "an hour" has a psychological heft; it sounds like a really long time. Forty-five minutes falls short of that psychological barrier, but it requires some effort for adults to sustain their focus for even that long while doing an exercise of this sort. (I would assign a shorter period to younger students, perhaps a half hour for teenagers and fifteen minutes for younger children.)

Despite being daunted by the assigned time, the students quickly fanned out into the galleries and got to work.

After the full time period was over, we gathered to share their work and discuss the experience. One student made the comment that forty-five minutes had sounded like too long, until she sat down to write and got immersed in her task. When she checked her watch, the time was gone. Judging by the length and thoughtfulness of the other pieces, this may have been a common or nearly universal response.

Their pieces were genuinely insightful and they varied widely in tone, touching on topics that included isolation, grief, and the passage of time. Some took me up on the invitation to surprise me. For example, after I pointed out that the library itself, an impressive Gothic-style structure dating to 1929, was made by human hands, two students independently wrote about the people who made it. One chose to speak as its proud architect and the other chose to speak as an uneducated carpenter angry that the architect got the credit for this beautiful thing that he had made. Hearing the essays in juxtaposition put the students' imagined versions of long-dead people into dialogue. The serendipity of hearing the unplanned counterpoint between their voices was a gift. These two essays, like all the others, delved deeply into the assigned task of feeling empathy for someone the writer had never met.

The simplicity of this observing-and-writing exercise makes it endlessly flexible. If given a half day with the students, I would follow it with something like this:

> Use your phones (or, if available, computers in the facility's classroom) to research your chosen piece. Can you find out more about the maker, the piece itself, or the history of the piece? Can you research what life was like in the area where the maker lived at the time the piece was made? Can you find out what life is like for paleontologists who dig up fossils like the one you chose? Spend some time putting yourself in the shoes of the human beings that brought this experience to you; then use that insight to rewrite or add to your story.

If given a full day and access to art supplies, I would ask students to make an artwork that was inspired by the original piece. Then I would ask them to write about the sensory experience of art making. How did the paint smell? How did the clay feel in their hands? Did those sensations make them feel closer to Michelangelo painting the ceiling of the Sistine Chapel or to a prehistoric resident of Poverty Point squeezing a ball of clay?

Because of my interest in North American archaeology, I enjoy visiting museums that feature ancient earthworks on-site. Those earthworks can inspire a whole-body activity that gets participants moving, with no more materials than some laundry baskets and a pile of children's blocks. After some time spent looking together at photographs of mounds in cross section, with the outlines of individual basketfuls of earth clearly visible to show us how the mounds were built, teams of students can be given baskets of blocks and asked to carry them several yards, dump them out, then give the basket to someone else to load and carry. This exercise is best done outdoors, in the shadow of the earthworks themselves, and it is best done until the participants begin to sweat. After hauling a few baskets and absorbing the reality of the volume of earth contained in even a moderate-sized Mississippian mound, students writing an essay from the viewpoint of a mound builder will be able to give a tactile, even visceral, description of the effort it took to build such massive structures.

If you have even more time with your group, collaborative possibilities open up. Small groups can be assigned to write dialogues or short plays in which their characters interact. With access to art supplies, students can craft props and costumes. The final meeting can be devoted to performances. Where appropriate—for example, at earthwork museums or living history museums—the museum itself can provide a backdrop for these plays.

Unless time is at an absolute minimum, however, I urge you to save class time for a strategy to teach writing that is frequently overlooked—reading aloud together. Too often relegated to primary classrooms, the act of reading together is a communal experience of yet another art—the art of storytelling. There are many texts appropriate for museum groups of different ages and interests. Memoirs and biographies of historical figures highlighted in the museum can be very effective. Poetry that is inspired by art can engage learners who are more attracted to sounds than to visual stimuli; Keats's *Ode on a Grecian Urn* comes immediately to mind. Fiction about artists or scientists or historical figures appropriate to the museum brings collections to life.

I write about an archaeologist who occasionally stops in wonder to consider the sweep of history encompassed by the work she does. I'll close with a brief excerpt from one of my books that you are welcome to use in your own programs.

Excerpt from *Effigies*, by Mary Anna Evans[1]

Faye Longchamp had work to do, but it could wait. A tremendous backlog of unfinished tasks seemed to be her lot in life. Taking a weekday afternoon to immerse herself in history and religion simultaneously seemed like an efficient way to use her time. Granted, it was someone else's religion, but Faye had never been too finicky about that kind of thing.

Joe, on the other hand, had a direct connection to the silent mound of dirt beneath their feet. His Creek ancestors believed that their history began here at Nanih Waiya, the Mother Mound. Or maybe in a cave under a natural hill somewhere across the creek. The issue was murky, as spiritual issues tend to be.

Faye considered Nanih Waiya, constructed at about the time Christ walked the earth, to be a most impressive perch. She and Joe sat atop it, forty feet above the natural ground level, surveying Nanih Waiya Creek and a lush forest and a very ordinary pasture full of cattle grazing just outside the fence surrounding the great mound. She had noticed a sour, familiar smell as she climbed the stairs sunk into the old mound, but couldn't quite put her finger on its source. The creek's banks were brimming, so she thought perhaps she was sniffing the musty, peaty smell of a swamp at high water. Either that, or somebody needed to empty the garbage bins at the state park across the road.

Only when her head cleared the top of the mound and she could see the grassy open area beyond did she put a name to the odor. Cow manure.

Did it bother Joe to see this sacred place shorn of its trees and planted in pasture grass? He didn't look perturbed. Faye thought about cows for awhile. They fed their calves out of their own bodies, then fed the land with their manure. Eventually, they fed the land with themselves. Maybe the Mother Mound liked having cows around.

Not being nearly as spiritual as Joe, she figured her revelation about the holiness of cows was the deepest thought she was likely to have that afternoon.

My best wishes go out to you as you work to use empathy as a magnet that draws people to their museum and the heritage it preserves.

Note

1. Evans, Mary A. *Effigies*. Scottsdale, Arizona: Poisoned Pen Press, 2007.

Part II

THE VALUE OF OPEN(ING) AUTHORITY AND PARTICIPATORY FRAMEWORKS FOR MUSEUMS

Elizabeth A. Bollwerk

Introduction

A great deal has been written about how museums can increase their relevancy. But how do organizations that were built on a model of raising up individuals with education—that is, being the experts that educated the masses—deal with populations that are increasingly challenging the notion of the "expert"? This is no doubt a difficult transition and one that has ebbed and flowed for decades. This thematic chapter focuses on a concept called Open Authority, which was coined by Lori Byrd Phillips (2013, 2014) and grew out of the ideas of the Open Source movement in the digital realm. The primary goal is to break down the traditional hierarchy that defines museum professionals as "experts" and visitors as "learners" in the museum environment. Although museum experts have training and specialized knowledge that is vital for ensuring museums operate smoothly, collections are cared for, and research is conducted, arguably there is also a great deal to be gained from engaging individuals outside of the museum profession—community members, K–12 educators, descendant communities—as active contributors and partners.

This part begins with a brief discussion of the history and development of Open Authority and related participatory frameworks. It also provides a few examples of its implementation that are contained in this volume as well as other projects. It concludes by exploring what museums and cultural institutions have learned from these efforts to date and considers what the future holds for this movement.

Open(ing) Authority—A Definition

It is important to note that the issue of sharing authority is not a new one. The movement for museums to be more inclusive has taken many forms over the last century. As early as 1917, John Cotton Dana's *The New Museum* pushed for museums to shift their focus from solely accumulating and caring for collections to responding to expressed public needs. In 1971, Duncan F. Cameron posited that a museum should be both a temple and a forum—an authoritative space and a place for dialogue that coexist within a museum but remain separate (Cameron 1971 in Phillips 2013:221). Starting in the late 1980s the postmodern movement in museum anthropology pushed museums to be more inclusive and think carefully and critically about their relationship to and depiction of descendant and non-Western communities (Ames 1995; Butler 2000; Karp and Lavine 1991; Karp et al. 1992; Karp et al. 2006; Krouse 2006; Sleeper-Smith 2009; Stocking 1988).

Other scholars and practitioners have taken up this call, noting that museums should not only seek to disseminate information/knowledge but must also encourage knowledge sharing and creation that is reciprocal. In this context, successful engagement necessitates an exchange rather than a one-way dissemination of information with the general public and descendant communities. In recent decades museum scholars and practitioners have also focused on inclusivity for the general public (Connolly et al. 2013; Crooke 2007; Harden et al. 2015; Kuo Wei Tchen 1992; Satwicz and Morrissey 2011; Schultz 2011; Simon 2010; Stein et al. 2008; Weil 2002). In particular, the rise of the World Wide Web and digital realm has spurred new conversations about the role of museum engagement as Wikipedia, social media, and mobile computing create opportunities for sharing and connecting on an unprecedented level (Adair el al. 2011; Cairns 2013; Phillips 2013, 2014; Proctor 2010, 2013; Ridge 2013, 2014; Rodley 2015; Rodley et al. 2015; Shirky 2012). These considerations have spurred critical reflection about the complex dynamics of communities and remind us that one-size-fits-all methods generally will not work (Golding and Modest 2013; Karp et al. 1992) because even tight-knit communities are comprised of diverse individuals with a variety of needs (Wong 2015, 310–11).

The Engagement Spectrum

This part's definition of engagement draws from the Public Participation Model portrayed by Simon (2010) and the Open Authority Spectrum created by Phillips (2013, 2014). Both of these models were originally based on the model of "Public Participation in Scientific Research" (Bonney et al. 2009, 11). Simon's Public Participation Model envisions museums and cultural heritage institutions serving as platforms "that connect different users who act as content creators, distributors, consumers, critics, and collaborators." In a related vein Byrd Phillips's Open Authority model primarily focuses on museums and digital engagement by bringing "together the museum's established expertise with the contributions of broad audiences through collaborative virtual platforms" (Phillips 2013, 220). Simon's model has four major levels: contributory, collaborative, co-creative, and hosted. Although Byrd Phillips envisions Open Authority Spectrum as a spectrum or continuum the divisions of the spectrum (participatory, collaborative, and co-creative) have similar focal points as Simon's model.

The first level consists of contributory/participatory projects. Participatory projects try to create engagement by providing users or audiences with the opportunity to actively participate in an exhibit or project using digital or physical platforms. The next type of engagement consists of collaborative projects that make outside communities active partners in the design and implementation of the project. Projects that include outside community members from the start and make them *equal partners* in the design and implementation of a project are co-creative. Co-creative projects have diverse user groups that help shape the exhibition, program, application, or platform with their perspectives and knowledge. In many cases the platform is created as a resource for a community rather than being a platform for the general public. In the growing literature on community engagement different terms have been used that mean roughly the same process, including co-production or co-management. Finally, Simon's model also includes hosted projects, where an institution "turns over a portion of its facilities and/or resources to present programs developed and implemented by public groups or casual visitors" (Simon 2010). In other words, these programs are entirely developed by community members and happen in the museum's space with input from the museum.

These models have been applied in a variety of ways by a host of different museums. Nina Simon's blog, The Participatory Museum (www.participatorymuseum.org) chronicles a variety of projects. Lori Byrd-McDevitt has led and advocated for Wikipedia/Digital projects (2013, 2014) as well as community blogging and community-centered content creation. The next few sections are brief discussions of different examples of such projects organized under a few overarching themes that roughly align with the levels of the Participatory/Open Authority Spectrum: open access, crowdsourcing and community sourcing, and getting outside the museum walls.

Open Access

One way museums and cultural heritage institutions have sought to operationalize Open Authority is by opening their collections and making them accessible to descendant communities and the general public. The goal of these programs is to invite visitors into spaces they aren't normally allowed in. Museums have instituted open access by putting collections online (Boast and Biehl 2011; Gorgels 2013; Johnson 2015) and creating visible or open storage collections spaces (Kedmey 2016; Kehl 2015; Schultz 2011).

While the movement to get collections into the hands of the public is widespread and has notable benefits, there are a number of challenges that make this difficult for large and small museums alike. At a practical level, putting collections online can be expensive.

However, a number of the case studies in this volume demonstrate tools that have been developed to help smaller museums and institutions keep up with this trend (see Billeaudeaux and Schnabel, Failing, Solis, and Young and Sekaquaptewa). Omeka is one example of a digital platform that has been created to help communities, museums, and cultural heritage institutions digitize collections or create digital archives and make them accessible to the public. Omeka (omeka.org) is a "free, flexible, and open source web-publishing platform for the display of library, museum, archives, and scholarly collections and exhibitions." Created by the Center for History and New Media (CHNM) at George Mason University, this system can be scaled to address the needs of a variety of institutions including small and large museums, libraries, and cultural heritage sites. CHNM has also secured funding to create Omeka.net, which is a free hosting platform. By offering easy to use software, Omeka enables institutions to easily digitize and share their collections using online galleries and exhibit software.

While putting more of collections, or collections metadata, out in the galleries or online is an important step forward, a number of museum professionals have argued open access should not be considered an end in itself. Museums must be "promiscuous but discriminating" (Rodley 2015, 228). It is vital that museums make information and collections available but they cannot "open up" without well-developed plans for doing so and careful reflection on what they are releasing. Empowering community members to interact with collections necessitates creating safe spaces for engagement. Ideally this means that museums should spend "more time on creating and spreading and less on trying to control access" (Rodley 2015, 232). Furthermore, engagement spaces and projects should be created and iteratively evaluated with input from user communities.

One example of a longstanding program with an open access focus is the "Revisiting Collections" project in the United Kingdom, which created "toolkits and guidance documents to show museums and archives how to run sessions where individuals and groups of external participants were prompted and supported to explore what they know, feel, and think about individual objects and records and to critique the language and information contained in current catalogues and interpretation" (Reed 2013, 4). Such toolkits are valuable resources for museums although Reed (2013) notes that evaluation of these programs has proved challenging. In a related vein Rebecca Price's case study in this volume is an interesting case study of an innovative project that provides a helpful model for opening access to what are traditionally closed-off collections—those in the hands of private collectors. Price demonstrates that a great deal of trust must exist for these types of projects to be successful and a lot of time goes into determining how to share and how to communicate both with the collection owner and the public.

While spending time on sharing collections is vital, careful attention must also be given to what is appropriate to spread. A number of scholars have argued that the authority to make those decisions should not lie solely with the museum. Deference should be given to descendant communities and their cultural and intellectual property concerns. Museums should make it a priority to have conversations with communities about collections and related knowledge and connect communities with assets and context whether digital (Beale and Boast 2012; Christen 2011; Rowley 2013; Young and Zange 2015) or physical (Karp and Lavine 1991; Karp et al. 1992; Karp et al. 2006; Krouse 2006; Sleeper-Smith 2009).

An interesting example that addresses these concerns is the Murkurtu Content Management System (CMS). The Murkurtu CMS "is a grassroots project aiming to empower communities to manage, share, preserve, and exchange their digital heritage in culturally relevant and ethically-minded ways" (Christen 2008, 2011, 2012, 2015). Founded by Dr. Kimberly Christen at Washington State University, Murkurtu began as a digital archive for the Warumungu Aboriginal community in the Central Australian town of Tennant Creek. Murkurtu, which means "dilly bag," or a safekeeping place for sacred materials, is inspired by the notion that "not all information wants to be free" (Christen 2012). The project began when Christen created a database that allowed the Warumungu to digitize their cultural information with user permissions that mirrored their restrictions based on cultural groups (e.g., women could only see certain assets, while only men could see others, elders could see more of the assets while younger generations could only view certain items). While this project is critical for the Warumungu, Christen realized it also addressed a broader need for Native communities. Thus, Christen and her colleagues worked to create the Murkurtu CMS and a set of intellectual property licenses to go with it. Like Omeka, Murkurtu now has a free hosting platform at Murkurtu.net. This project is an example of a community resource that has grown to meet a larger need, but only because Christen Withey and her team have carefully listened to the communities they work with and built something that meets their needs.

These initiatives take the collections out of storage and get them out into the community. Open access has a number of benefits including increasing engagement by enabling individuals and groups to search and use collections using their own creative methods. For K–12 educators, getting collections into the classroom, regardless of whether they are in physical or digital form, provides invaluable teaching tools (see Cruzado, Crosson this volume). For artists, teachers, and community members, collections provide a source of creative inspiration. However, an important expansion of such programs is getting community members and visitors to not only interact with collections but also create new content that becomes part of the museum's collection.

Crowdsourcing and Community Sourcing

Museums and cultural institutions seeking to make themselves more open must recognize that simply offering the information will not necessarily make it more accessible. Carefully designed engagement tools and strategies that facilitate interaction must accompany collections data. Museums and cultural institutions cannot expect the majority of visitors to interact with raw, messy collections or collections data (Frankle 2011). Instead, it is necessary to create interfaces for people to connect with collections and associated data to put them in context, make the interaction meaningful, and enable visitors to contribute their own ideas. Crowdsourcing and community sourcing (Ridge 2013, 2014) are examples of initiatives that encourage individuals to contribute their ideas and talent to improve collections. Crowdsourcing, or obtaining information or services by soliciting input from a large number of people, is generally thought to draw from a larger, more anonymous user group, while community sourcing has a set of known users who perform more tasks and tend to stay involved in the projects.

In the digital realm social tagging, or folksonomies (Beale and Boast 2012; Cairns 2013), open possibilities for multiple visitor and descendant communities to create and implement their own ontologies for ancestral collections that allow them to be open to a variety of ways of being organized. Additionally, a number of museums have opened their doors to edit-a-thons to make their collections more accessible. Edit-a-thons bring interested individuals together to edit Wikipedia articles of predetermined topics to improve the scope and depth of Wikipedia. For example, the Peabody Essex Museum in Boston, Massachusetts, held an edit-a-thon[1] to get visitors to engage with their Native American and Chinese collections by creating articles on identified areas that needed help.[2] Other projects include Citizen History[3] and Citizen Science[4] initiatives, which provide opportunities for interested individuals to explore and analyze a museum's data in a structured user framework, or gather data to assist researchers with scholarly research projects. In this volume, Cruzado and Alejo and Solis demonstrate that getting communities involved in content generation also has the added benefit of building important skill sets for participating individuals, especially students.

Besides projects that get collections out of storage and into the hands of the public (digitally and physically), institutions have opened their doors to companies and individuals who have taken the initiative to create nontraditional programming that enables members of the public to interact with the physical museum space and associated collections in nontraditional ways. Perhaps one of the best known is "Museum Hack."[5] Operating under the tagline "This Isn't your Grandma's Museum Tour," Museum Hack is a company that originally started by running untraditional tours out of the Metropolitan Museum of Art in New York. It has now grown extensively and operates in three different museums. These tours encourage visitors to interact with collections in spontaneous ways and, perhaps most importantly, feature team-building exercises that get visitors to interact with each other. By relating the art to everyday concepts and helping visitors connect with each other the company seeks to make museums more engaging and fun.

Empowering communities and individuals to engage with collections and contribute information and data is an important aspect of Opening Authority. The final part of this discussion moves to another level in the spectrum to focus on projects that aim to engage communities beyond participation. These projects fall more into the co-creative or hosted realm.

Getting Outside the Museum Walls and Giving Communities Space to Express and Create According to Their Own Interests

Beyond creating opportunities for user-generated content and new methods of engagement, museums are implementing Open Authority on the participatory/co-creative end of the spectrum by getting out of the museum space and going out into their local communities. In this volume Cruzado and Alejo, Moore, Price, and Young and Sekaquaptewa demonstrate the critical importance of *going out into communities* and learning about their needs in order to implement programs that work best for them. These case studies, although they focus on very different geographic and cultural regions, demonstrate that active and deep listening is a critical part of Open Authority. Moreover, physically leaving the museum and meeting community members in an area that is comfortable for them is vitally important. To paraphrase Moore, in order to build trust, museum professionals have to be willing to meet communities on their own turf. Young and Sekaquaptewa provide an example of an interesting and inventive way of connecting students with a source community using videoconferencing technology. In this digital age there is little to no excuse for not getting out and connecting with communities near and far.

Serving as a Space to Consider and Discuss Difficult/Politically Contentious Topics

While museums have long been held up as bastions/temples of learning, their roles as institutions with regular operating budgets, revenue goals, and high-level donors can sometimes put them at odds with missions to educate and engage. One of the most well-known examples of this challenge was the controversy over the *Enola Gay* exhibit at the Smithsonian Institution (Kohn 1995). When museum officials tried to create an exhibit that presented multiple viewpoints on the role of nuclear bombs in World War II they were met with staunch opposition from veterans and political groups. Not surprisingly, many large museums have tended to be more conservative in their choice of exhibit topics, as the politics of exhibiting culture and race have proven to be risky ventures (Butler 2000). Consequently, more difficult or controversial topics have traditionally been relegated to small or niche museums (Wood 2013, 217). However, museum professionals (Brown 2015; Brown and Russell 2015; Cameron 2007; McKensie 2015; Phillips 2013; Smith et al. 2011; Tate 2012) have carried forward Cameron's (1971) efforts to push museums and cultural heritage institutions to serve more as forums where difficult and politically contentious topics can be addressed head-on and discussed.

Recent efforts have shown that museums can become a space where dialogue and conversation around these difficult subjects is possible. Case studies that have covered such efforts demonstrate that museums can serve as both digital and physical spaces to discuss difficult topics such as immigration (Harden et al. 2015), gun violence (Jennings 2015), and race (Brown 2015; Tayac 2009). Adams's case study in this volume provides valuable insights into how the Missouri Historical Society became a place for a community to come together and begin a dialogue about the difficult issues brought up by the shooting of Michael Brown.

Moreover, this is not an area where only niche museums can contribute; large museums have also successfully taken on controversial topics with the goal of engaging and educating audiences. For example, the Children's Museum of Indianapolis has successfully mounted an exhibition with the goal of educating parents and children about the difficulties faced by children all around the world (Wood 2013). Additionally, perhaps one of the most difficult topics—race—was addressed head-on in a recent exhibit called *Race* put together by the Science Museum of Minnesota and the American Anthropological Association. The exhibit has traveled to over forty-one museums including large venues like the Smithsonian Museum of Natural History and Museum of Science in Boston (http://www.understandin grace.org/about/tour.html). The *Indivisible* exhibit at the Museum of the American Indian (Tayac 2009) addressed the particularly difficult issue of intermarriage between American Indian communities and African American communities.

A less contentious example of dialogue in the digital space is the opportunity the Rijksmuseum has created for audiences to interact with each other through mobile applications and tours (http://augmentingmasterpieces.eu/). The museum has created a mobile app that allows visitors to see multiple scholarly and visitor interpretations of different pieces in the museum's collection. This project helps visitors to see the multilayered types of interpretation that are possible and contribute their own ideas to the discussion.

These exhibits and programs indicate that museums best address complicated topics not by serving as authorities on the subject or subjects but by acting as facilitators or informants (Cameron 2008; Cameron et al. 2013). A fruitful way forward for museums to address the challenge of sharing authority is to embrace their ability to facilitate and show a variety of perspectives, rather than serving as the authority and proponent of one viewpoint or interpretation. In this volume, Moore's case study is a powerful example of how a museum can act as facilitator to discuss complicated issues.

What Have Museums Learned?

The implementation of participatory and collaborative engagement will no doubt continue to impact how museums operate. It is a slow process—persistence is vital, as is patience and an open mind. However, the past decade has seen a good deal of movement toward a more participatory/collaborative model. By way of conclusion, this last section summarizes some of the major findings of these types of efforts.

Museums Need to Go Outside of Their Walls to Engage Communities and Individuals

While there is always a need for museums to keep revenue generation in mind, there is also the very real fact that the majority of the population likely will not be able to physically set foot in any particular museum whether because of distance, lack of funds, or time. Making collections available either online or through traveling/mobile programming increases the reach of museums. Moreover, these programs engage communities who may not be comfortable visiting a museum. As Moore eloquently argues there is evidence that certain populations (namely minorities) do not feel comfortable in museum spaces. Consequently, it is necessary for museums to meet communities on their terms to demonstrate their desire to actually engage and show that they care about these populations.

Opening Authority Takes Time

As noted by Adams, Connolly, Moore, and Price in this volume and others who have discussed collaborative and Open Authority initiatives (Ames 1999; Bria and Cruzado 2015; Connolly 2015; Simon 2010) engaging with communities can be a slow process. Sometimes timelines or deadlines will need to be extended to accommodate changes introduced by bringing in new individuals or groups as partners. Additionally, the maintenance and sustainability of community projects and interest is time consuming and can be challenging.

Successful projects have community managers who put either most or all of their time and effort into cultivating and sustaining the community (Zeitlin 2011). There will be ebbs and flows to engagement, not all community members or museum practitioners have the time and energy for active engagement, for long, extended periods. But ultimately this work is worthwhile because the products that are created are more valuable and sustainable than those created by experts operating under assumptions of what they think audiences want.

Increasing Access Does Not Put Collections at Risk

Initially museum experts were worried that increasing access to collections and collections data would put museums and the collections at risk. However, the results of projects summarized here demonstrate that it is not the case. In fact, it is likely the opposite. Making collections more accessible and the processes of interpretation more transparent and inclusive creates a larger community that genuinely cares about the collections and the museum. Making the information available for others to explore, collect, and interpret increases engagement.

Evaluation Is Critical but Complicated

An important part of moving Open Authority forward is having data to demonstrate that such initiatives are engaging audiences either in new or beneficial ways. Evaluating community engagement is no easy task. A number of museum professionals have noted the projects that may have the most impact don't necessarily have straightforward metrics (Rice 2013). In fact, at times museums and cultural institutions can be fooled by metrics of the easiest things to measure, such as the number of users, visitors, hits, or clicks. These metrics may seem to be valuable but may mask or divert attention away from more important aspects that are more difficult to evaluate or measure. Audience research must strike a balance between qualitative and quantitative measurements to understand communities, their needs, and how to successfully implement changes.

This is not to say, however, that evaluation isn't warranted. In fact, for nonprofits and for-profits alike, evaluation is critical to understanding whether goals are being met and fortunately we are in an era of digital tools that make evaluation easier in many ways. Starting small with Google Analytics and SurveyMonkey surveys can help provide useful feedback that is certainly better than no feedback at all. A report by the UK organization Culture 24 (Finnis et al. 2011) demonstrates that more cultural institutions need this kind of help to connect to their communities. Getting a baseline of information on audiences is vital before more complex questions can be asked and change over time can be measured. Moreover, as demonstrated by all of the case studies in this section deep and active listening also needs to be part of the evaluative process. Perhaps most importantly, it is necessary to provide environments in which community members feel safe providing honest feedback. Finally, museums must start developing longitudinal data sets to track change over time (Stein 2014).

Museums Need to Work to Ensure Everyone Is Onboard

While Open Authority practices may seem like a no-brainer to some, they understandably can be considered quite radical in the eyes of staff who have built their careers and reputations by serving as experts on a particular subject. Furthermore, donors who have given money or objects to a museum for the specific purpose of keeping them safe and having them curated by experts may also be hesitant to put the collections in the hands of the wider community. While enlisting community support is a critical step to cultivating Open Authority so is ensuring that staff members and donors are comfortable and supportive of the process.

Shifting focus to the larger level, museums and cultural heritage institutions need to work together. While we are in a sense competing for visitors, one aspect of Open Authority is that museums can better understand what unique opportunities or value they can bring to the table by working together. Despite the variety of terms that describe this process many museums are facing the same issues and working together can help ensure the long-term survival of museums in this constantly changing world.

Conclusion—Where Are We Going?

In many ways museums are not alone in this challenge—experts across the board, in the natural and social sciences, and humanities, are being held accountable to communities and the public. Consequently, a variety of institutions are being called to be more inclusive and make their results understandable to a wider audience. Major public and private funding agencies, including the National Endowment of the Arts, National Science Foundation, National Endowment for the Humanities, and Institute of Library and Museum Services, require plans for making research results accessible to the wider public. As a result, museums and cultural institutions have had to find new ways to engage and educate but don't have to reinvent the wheel. We should look to our colleagues in other disciplines such as libraries (Waibel and Erway 2009; Zorich et al. 2008) for help and ideas. Ultimately, building or maintaining silos will only lead to isolation, and in an increasingly interconnected world, that is the last thing museums and cultural heritage institutions should want.

Notes

1. https://en.wikipedia.org/wiki/Wikipedia:How_to_run_an_edit-a-thon.
2. http://connected.pem.org/join-our-edit-a-thon/.
3. http://futureofmuseums.blogspot.com/2011/07/more-crowdsourced-scholarship-citizen .html.
4. Zooinverse, http://zooniverse.org.
5. http://futureofmuseums.blogspot.com/2014/09/museum-hack-we-love-people-who-dont .html.

Oral History for, about, and by a Local Community

Co-Creation in the Perúvian Highlands[1]

Elizabeth K. Cruzado Carranza and Leodan Alejo Valerio

THE RURAL VILLAGE of Hualcayán is the first community in the central highland Andes of Perú to publish a local history book co-created by their residents. The village high school students recorded and compiled the oral histories on which the book *La Historia de Hualcayán: Contada Por Sus Pobladores* (*The History of Hualcayán: as Told by Its Inhabitants*) is based. Not only is this project the first of its kind in the Perúvian highlands, but the model used is simple and can be replicated by any cultural heritage institution, large or small, urban or rural, throughout the world.

A Co-Created Oral History

The project began in July 2014, when a group of archaeologists and museum professionals from outside the region met with local teachers from the Hualcayán community school. The purpose of the meeting was to discuss the needs of the school and village. The first need the teachers mentioned was a written record of the modern history of the community. After a brief discussion, the group decided to implement an oral history project that would be created and administered by residents of the village to address their expressed need.

The most significant aspect of this project was that from start to finish, the project relied on a co-creative approach. By co-creative, we mean a project where the cultural heritage professionals from outside the community partnered with the community members in carrying out a project based on the expressed need of the local residents. In this case, the expressed need was for a recorded history of the modern community.[2]

The primary researchers for the project were students at the secondary school in Hualcayán. The students conducted interviews with the village residents that focused on the origins of the community, lifestyles, important events, traditions, meanings of words in the Quechua language, and information about the present-day community. When the interviews were collected, the cultural heritage professionals transcribed and organized the interviews, which served as the basis for a narrative published as a forty-page book. One hundred copies of the volume were delivered to the community on Perúvian Independence Day in July of 2015.

Rural Community Hualcayán

Hualcayán is located in the highlands of Ancash, Perú at an elevation of 3,221 meters above sea level in the Huascarán National Park. Those who live in this area are mainly engaged in agriculture and domestic livestock. Before the 1970s, the area was largely uninhabited and was used for grazing of small animals with only occasional human occupation. Because of the increasing agricultural interests in the Hualcayán area, the land gradually became inhabited by the residents from the nearby communities of Cashapampa, Colcas, and Caranca of the Santa Cruz district. (We note that this very information about the village origins was obtained and recorded by student interviews of their elders in the oral history project.)

In addition to a rich landscape the Hualcayán community has a rich cultural heritage included in many modern traditions. However, only a few of the 300 residents know the details of this cultural legacy because there was no written record of their past. The oral history project was an opportunity for the details of that cultural heritage to be shared broadly with all residents. In the region, not sharing cultural traditions with the next generation is particularly problematic as more indigenous cultures put aside their customs and adopt lifestyles they see portrayed in the mass media.

The Co-Creative Method in Hualcayán

Why a co-creative project? In 2013 students in the Museum Practices graduate seminar at the University of Memphis produced a suite of products including educational programs for the school and small museum in Hualcayán. The project goal was to promote and preserve the local patrimony of the community. The programs were installed in Hualcayán in July 2014 by a combination of outside cultural heritage professionals and area residents. Some of the programs worked very well in the school, such as one based on a prehistoric accounting system that used quipus. However, other projects were less enthusiastically received. We recognized the poor reception was not a result of the program quality. Rather, the limited reception was because we had not engaged with the local teachers to determine the interests and needs of the Hualcayán students. As a result, some of the projects were based on our perception of the interests and needs that were not necessarily valid. Based on that experience, we learned that an important part of any future project must be based on the expressed interests and needs of the community. Therefore, we prioritized including the community voice and opinion in all future planning.

In co-creative projects, community members work closely with professionals from the start to build a project based on the interests and needs of the community. Thus, all participants define project goals, respond to the concerns, suggest solutions, and are constantly involved in the development and implementation. In Hualcayán, Professor Leodan Alejo, the high school teacher, expressed the need for a written record of the community's history. To meet this objective, Professor Leodan and his students had an equal voice with the cultural heritage professionals in determining the scope and tools needed to meet the project goal.

The Student Role

From the beginning, all participants agreed that the participation of high school students was vital for the success of the oral history project. We trained eight students in the use of video cameras so they could conduct the interviews. With considerable enthusiasm, the students participated in the training sessions. Next, teachers, students, and the outside cultural heritage professionals created a list of more than thirty interview questions to solicit information from elders and leaders of the Hualcayán community.

Students practice interviewing with each other. Photograph by Robert P. Connolly.

Initially, some of the residents of Hualcayán were hesitant to participate in the project. However, when the intent of creating a published volume on their community history was made clear, the hesitancy was largely removed. Despite the nervousness over video recordings, between August and December of 2014, the students talked with a number of residents and documented many events in their community's history of which they had no previous knowledge. In carrying out this work, students enriched and strengthened their own cultural identity with a pride in the land of their birth and their native Quechua language.

Book Preparation and Presentation

We were very pleased with the enthusiasm, interest, and work the students devoted to the project. The time and dedication of the students, led by Professor Leodan Alejo, was essential to collecting the oral histories. When we met in January 2015 to evaluate the interviews, the results were outstanding. The students had collected nearly two dozen ten- to fifteen-minute interviews from individual community members.

Elizabeth Cruzado Carranza then transcribed and compiled the histories collected by the Hualcayán students into a narrative format. This latter part of her work was completed as an internship in the Museum Studies Graduate Certificate Program at the University of Memphis. The project culminated with the publication of the book *The History of Hualcayán:*

Community residents reading the published oral history at the Independence Day Celebration. Photograph by Elizabeth Cruzado Carranza.

As Told by Its Inhabitants, a small but significant book that tells the history of Hualcayán in the voice of its own people.

The book launch took place on July 28, 2015, Independence Day in Perú. The date now has further significance for the people of Hualcayán, as an event when the documentation of their history, written and based on research performed by the community students, was officially published. At the Independence Day celebration, each member of the community who participated in the oral history project took several hours, break from their work in the fields to share a meal and receive their own copy of *The History of Hualcayán*.

At the celebration several community members gave emotional statements about the importance of the oral history project and book publication for their community. Attendees acknowledged the advantages of the co-creative nature of the project and thanked all participants. Several parents expressed joy for their children's participation in conducting interviews with community members. Professor Leodan Alejo, who was the chairperson for the celebration, spoke passionately about his commitment to such projects. Then switching from Spanish to the local Quechua idiom, he spoke of the need to continue with the project and include additional interviews and documentation of the community traditions.

Assessing the Project

Co-creation proved a successful method because the two cultural heritage professionals, working in concert with local teachers and students, were able to provide technical support and expertise to meet an expressed need of the local community—a written record of modern history by the Hualcayán community.

As a result of this work, students strengthened their understanding of the past and also developed a greater appreciation of the archaeological heritage located in their community. Additionally, students improved their skills in the Quechua language while interviewing members of the community. The interviews served as a means to preserve the native Quechua language.

Such co-creative projects can also have a positive impact on cultural heritage management by involving local residents in the preservation of their patrimony. This factor is particularly relevant in Hualcayán as the modern village is located in the midst of substantial prehistoric archaeological resources and at the entry to a UNESCO World Heritage natural area.

This oral history project was a unique occurrence in the municipality of Huaylas. No other published volume in the region has been written by and for its inhabitants and tells the story of a community solely from their perspective. Of importance, the project can readily be replicated elsewhere. For the cost of an inexpensive video camera or audio recorder, the recruitment of community stakeholders, and the participation of local students, any museum regardless of size or location can host such a project. Publication venues for oral histories can also occur online (see Solis this volume), or printed as e-books. We published our volume for about $3 per copy. Larger bulk orders can be printed for considerably less.

Expanding Co-Creation to Other Communities

In March 2015, Professor Leodan Alejo began to teach in Huallanca, a town known for the Canyon Hydroelectric Program. Huallanca, like Hualcayán, is a location that has rich prehistoric archaeological cultural resources that are largely uninvestigated.

In following up on his previous oral history work, Professor Leodan Alejo, along with the high school students from Huallanca, are committed to researching, conducting oral history interviews, writing, and then publishing the history of Huallanca, using Hualcayán as a model. The initial work in Huallanca has proven important for documenting little-known aspects of the town's history and particularly the role of the Canyon Hydroelectric Program.

The renewed interest in modern Huallanca history has also prompted residents to visit local archaeological sites such as Mallcush, Gibraltar, Cuchicorral, Pampa de La Libertad, and Pueblo Viejo, among others. During these site visits and with the support of local residents, Professor Leodan Alejo and his students have documented previously unrecorded prehistoric archaeological structures, such as platforms, tombs, walls, and channels. These findings provide a link from the past to the present for the Huallanca district. The students learn firsthand the true depth of their cultural heritage outside the classroom.

We note that what started off as a small project to interview people about their recent past provided the seeds to expand the scope dramatically and extended into the prehistoric past. But most importantly, co-creation was shown to be a method where cultural heritage professionals can partner with local residents in any location in the world to record and preserve their past. We, as cultural heritage professionals, are only intermediaries providing the resources and tools needed to do this work.

Acknowledgments

We thank the following individuals and institutions for their assistance in this project: high school students and teachers from School No. 87009 of Hualcayán, members of the community of Hualcayán, the C.H. Nash Museum at Chucalissa, Robert Connolly, and Rebecca Bria.

Notes

1. A Spanish-language version of this article is available at www.museumcommunities.com.
2. For more detail on this project see Robert Connolly, Rebecca Bria, and Elizabeth Cruzado. "Co-Creation and Sustainable Community Engagement." In *Collections Care and Stewardship: Innovative Approaches for Museums.* Rowman & Littlefield, 2015; and Rebecca Bria and Elizabeth Cruzado. "Making the Past Relevant: Co-Creative Approaches to Heritage Preservation and Community Development at Hualcayán, Ancash, Perú," *Advances in Archaeological Practice*, 3 (2015):208–222.

Working with a Private Collector to Strengthen Women's History

Sewall-Belmont House & Museum

Rebecca L. Price

MUSEUMS DON'T HAVE EVERYTHING. All that other "stuff" is out there in private collections. There are gaps and voids in many museum collections for this reason. A critical outcome is that a comprehensive understanding of history is in jeopardy. How can the public get access to that history and a more complete and fair understanding of our past? Can a museum be a bridge between these communities, the private collectors, and the public? The Sewall-Belmont House & Museum addressed this challenge by collaborating with a private collector without having acquisition as the goal.

The Sewall-Belmont House & Museum, located in Washington, D.C. on Capitol Hill, has stood for over 200 years. Early occupants of the house participated in the formulation of Congress and witnessed the construction of the U.S. Capitol and the Supreme Court. It's most famous, and last, occupant was the National Woman's Party (NWP), led by Alice Paul, which purchased the house in the 1920s. It became the fifth and final national headquarters for the political organization and soon evolved into a center for feminist education and social change. For over sixty years, the trailblazing NWP utilized the strategic location of the house to lobby for women's political, social, and economic equality. The NWP ceased to be a lobbying organization and became a 501(c)3 educational organization in 1997.

Today, the Sewall-Belmont House & Museum is one of the premier women's history sites in the country. It currently employs a staff of four and is open two days a week for scheduled tours. The museum seeks to educate the public about the women's rights movement and to use and preserve the Sewall-Belmont House & Museum—with its outstanding historic library and suffragist and ERA archives—to tell the inspiring story of a century of courageous activism by American women. The museum celebrates women's progress toward equality and explores the evolving role of women and their contributions to society through educational programs, tours, exhibits, research, and publication, and houses the archives for the NWP.

The Challenge of Suffrage History

The Suffrage Era represents at least seventy-two years of history that played out on the national and local levels, and is quite diverse and still underrepresented in many collections. In the case of the Sewall-Belmont House & Museum, the collection and archives are rich in suffrage history pertaining to the NWP but lacking in objects related to the other threads of the movement. As the nation approaches 2020, the centennial of the 19th Amendment and woman suffrage, a comprehensive and inclusive telling and understanding of the suffrage era is still missing from the field.

Compounding this predicament, a majority of suffrage objects and material are still in private and family collections. Furthermore, many of the private owners have no immediate plans to donate. This is not uncommon, and understandable; these are very personal objects from their mothers and grandmothers. Owners want their collections to be known and available for research and exhibitions; they are just not ready to part with their cherished family memories.

Planning and Implementing the *Circle of Suffrage*

In 2015, private collector Ann Lewis put her collection of suffrage objects and artifacts into an online database.[1] This collection includes more than 1,200 books, periodicals, pamphlets, fliers, leaflets, broadsides, postcards, correspondence, buttons, playing cards, ribbons, ceramic and porcelain figurines, and much more. The collection presents a well-rounded account of the varied voices within the social and civil movements of the time, including suffragists and antisuffragists, temperance workers, working women, political and religious leaders, abolitionists, advocates for birth control, and teachers.

Jennifer Krafchik was the private consultant who worked with Ann Lewis for one year to process and digitize the collection. Now at Sewall-Belmont House & Museum as the deputy director and director of strategic initiatives, she recognized the incredible opportunity this online collection presented to the museum and its mission-driven work. Ann Lewis's collection contained many parallels to the NWP collection as well as stories the museum did not have represented in their collection. Through collaboration with other key museum staff and Ann Lewis, the museum created the *Circle of Suffrage* campaign, with the goal of sharing and building a more robust and complete story of suffrage and presenting a "broader circle of women's suffrage work, the tactics and strategies, the places, and the language that contributed to winning the fight for women's suffrage in the United States."

Because Krafchik had worked with Ann Lewis for a year on her private collection, a level of trust had been built between these two stakeholders. Having this trust between a private collector and the public institution was instrumental to the success of the project. Sewall-Belmont House & Museum needed to demonstrate to Ann Lewis that she could trust them with her collection and were not going to pressure her to donate. For Ann Lewis, Sewall-Belmont House & Museum offered a way for her to share her collection with more people, which she had always desired to do.

Circle of Suffrage launched May 2015 for Mother's Day on social media with curated content and images.[2] The museum paired an object from their permanent collection with an object from the private collection on themes related to motherhood and suffrage. At the same time, via social media, the website, and other forms of e-communication, the museum asked its supporters, visitors, and fans to share their stories and memorabilia online, thus continuing to widen the circle.

After the theme of motherhood, the online campaign moved on to cover topics such as suffrage postcards, Women's Equality Day, anniversaries, and even The New 10 (the U.S. Treasury Department's decision to place a portrait of a historic woman on the ten-dollar bill).

For the process, Krafchik conducted the research and curation of the themes. Once a theme was decided, she would consult with Ann Lewis on her collection to find pieces that would match/complement/supplement the museum's artifact. After this, Elisabeth Harper, the digital media and outreach consultant for the museum, would design the content and develop the media strategy. Ann Lewis receives the completed image at

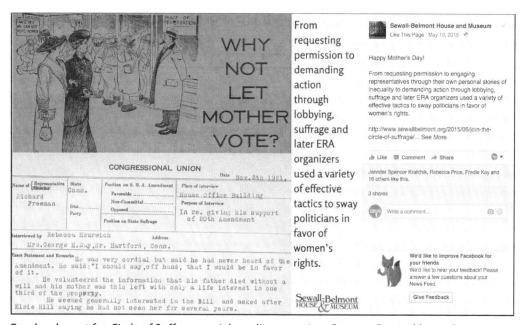

Facebook post for *Circle of Suffrage* social media campaign. Source: Created by author.

Sewall-Belmont
@SBHMuseum

Follow

Do you have any objects or records from the suffrage campaign? Please share them with us! #circleofsuffrage

Speaking tours aimed at swaying public opinion were presented in cartoons on the cover of *The Suffragist* to inform members.

RETWEETS
6

11:31 AM - 30 May 2015

Twitter post for *Circle of Suffrage* social media campaign. Source: Created by author.

this point, but is not involved in design and strategy. For all design work, Harper used a web-based program at www.canva.com. This software allows users to design, for free, images and content for social media platforms. Various templates make the image web ready, complete with the correct dimension for whatever social media account your organization uses.

Results and Lessons Learned

The first year of the campaign, described internally as the experimental year, has already received positive feedback. Staff have noted an uptick in online engagement, and on-site visitors and regular supporters of the museum provide anecdotal reviews. Another happy outcome, Ann Lewis—a high-profile political analyst and consultant—receives feedback from the public.

Now that the first year of the campaign is complete, staff will take what they learned and apply that to the next phases. The first year was planned as multiple pilot campaigns to test the successes and weaknesses, which could then be turned into the next phases of the campaign. Staff have learned that the social media component of the project works in ebbs and flows and was definitely a slow build. Engagement works best when the campaign is "fed continuously." To help this, Krafchik and Harper work together on an editorial calendar to plan and create the posts. They avoid creating an image and posting that image on the same day. They plan clear objectives with a target audience for each theme, and reach out to them online during the campaign to help with promotion and support.

Setting guidelines and an agreement between the museum and Ann Lewis was very important at the beginning of the project. The agreement established the goals and boundaries for what the museum would do and what the collector would do. Even small details, such as who was responsible for blogging, how many tweets, etc., need to be established and agreed upon. Additionally, a private collector may have very high expectations of what a museum—especially a very small museum with budget constraints—is capable of doing. Maintaining transparency and respecting the privacy of the collector are both very essential to a cooperative agreement of this nature. Most importantly, for the private collector, they need to feel that *they* still own their family history.

Next Steps and Moving Forward

As the year unfolded, the collaboration has opened new doors and opportunities. By working with Ann Lewis, the museum has been able to meet other private collectors and begin developing relationships with them. These relationships will prove fruitful in the coming years as the campaign grows and evolves, and other collection voids can be filled.

The trust between the museum and Ann Lewis has grown so much that the museum is now working on a temporary exhibition of her collection to be on view at the museum. Art museums have long practiced this type of lender cultivation. This collaboration between Sewall-Belmont House & Museum and Ann Lewis shows historic house museums can successfully think about these types of relationships to expand their public programming.

Ultimately, the museum wants to use the campaign over the next five years to build toward 2020 and the 100th anniversary of the 19th Amendment. They want to expand the *Circle of Suffrage* to include more narratives and to discover unknown stories, artifacts, and connections. As the project grows over the next five years and more people become aware of it, the museum is very excited about the possibility that iconic suffrage objects may be found in private collections. For example, the original draft of the *Declaration of Sentiments* written for the 1848 Seneca Falls convention and the famed Ratification Banner made by the NWP for the ratification of the 19th Amendment are both iconic suffrage artifacts whose present location is unknown. Could these unknowingly be in a family collection?

In order to sustain the *Circle of Suffrage*, Sewall-Belmont House & Museum knows several commitments must be made by the museum. A dedicated staff member to handle the design and social strategy is necessary. Jennifer Krafchik states that without Elisabeth Harper the project—as well as other social media campaigns—would not be possible. The museum is open only two days a week to the public for tours, not uncommon for many small historic house museums, and has made a commitment to reach people online as it looks for new ways to engage with the community. For the same budgetary reasons, the museum is not in an active stage of acquisition. Leveraging the private collection helps them meet their programming goals and has positively engaged with the private suffrage collecting community.

Krafchik also notes that while the campaign is fully supported by the executive director, it is a staff initiative. As the project grows and the museum enjoys more success and benefits, she hopes it will become an institutional initiative. This would be important if she or Harper left the museum.

After completion of its first year, museum staff and Ann Lewis consider the *Circle of Suffrage* a great success and both look forward to the evolution of this cooperation. By engaging with the public, working with private collectors, and not having acquisition as the goal, the Sewall-Belmont House & Museum demonstrates how museums can address a critical collection void in this particular time in American history.

Acknowledgments

I thank the entire staff of Sewall-Belmont House & Museum for sharing this project. In particular, I thank museum staff members Jennifer Krafchik and Elisabeth Harper for discussing their work and giving their time during the interview process for this case study.

Notes

1. See http://lewissuffragecollection.omeka.net/.
2. See http://www.sewallbelmont.org/join-the-circle-of-suffrage/.

Reconnecting a University Museum Collection with Hopi Farmers through an Undergraduate Class

Lisa C. Young and Susan Sekaquaptewa

Introduction

WHEN UNDERTAKING COLLABORATIVE projects, museums with anthropological collections face challenges because source communities are often located far away. Digital technology is being used by both museums and indigenous communities to share information about collections (Bohaker et al. 2015; Christen 2008; Rowley 2013; Shannon 2015; Srinivasin et al. 2009). Creating online catalogs of museum objects, however, involves investments of time to compile, digitize, and enter information and requires expertise to develop or use software created for museum purposes. For many museums and communities, time and the needed expertise are often scarce resources. In this case study we describe how a project in an undergraduate course created an online digital catalog of museum objects and then helped reconnect this collection with members of the source community using videoconferencing technology.

The Museum Anthropology Class

The Museum Anthropology class at the University of Michigan explores the changing role of anthropology museums from colonial collecting institutions to organizations that collaborate with contemporary communities. To learn about changes in museum practice, students work with a museum collection. During the 2014 and 2015 fall semesters, students worked with a collection of Hopi plants. These plants were collected from Hopi villages and households in northeastern Arizona between 1932 and 1935 and are currently curated by the University of Michigan, Museum of Anthropological Archaeology (UMMAA). For the class project, students contributed information on the plants to an online catalog (http://ummaahopiplants.omeka.net/).

Creating an Online Catalog of Museum Objects with Students

To prepare the collections and related museum information for this class project, Lisa Young, the course instructor, worked with UMMAA staff to select objects, digitize the museum records (e.g., field notes and accession records), and have photographs taken. She chose Omeka, an open source content management system, as the platform for the online catalog. Omeka (www.omeka.net) allows users to easily create a website to display information on objects from libraries, museums, and archives (Table 2.1).

Working in teams of three or four, students compiled information on the Hopi plants into a spreadsheet using Google Sheets (http://www.google.com/sheets/about/), which

Table 2.1.   Online Catalog

Google Sheets	Collaborative Spreadsheet
Omeka.net Resources on Omeka for educators: ◦ http://info.omeka.net/omeka-net-help/use-case-educators/ ◦ http://omeka.org/codex/Teach_with_Omeka	The free cloud-based version of Omeka includes 500 MB of storage space
Videoconferencing Meetings	
Logitech Conference Camera (BCC950)	Cost: $250
Jabra Speak speakerphone (510+)	Cost: $150
Laptop: ◦ need at least 2 USB ports to plug in speaker and camera ◦ up-to-date operating system	Used existing computer
Large-screen TV monitor	Used already existing to enhance visibility of people on other end of meeting
Internet connection	Used locally available (DSL) service
Videoconferencing service: Bluejeans (http://bluejeans.com/), which provided a more stable connection than Skype or Google Hangouts	Used University of Michigan contract

allowed multiple students to work on the same spreadsheet during class meetings. These spreadsheets were downloaded and checked for standardization and accuracy. The information was then batch uploaded using CVS Import, an Omeka plug-in. Photographs of the objects were added to each record.

Omeka uses the Dublin Core Metadata Element Set, a vocabulary of standardized descriptive categories. Only those elements that were most useful for the purposes of the online catalog were chosen, although the use of some was modified. For example, the "description" element in Dublin Core typically includes the physical information of an object. For the Museum Anthropology project, the taxonomic classification, the Hopi name recorded by anthropologists in the 1930s, and other information from the field notes (e.g., plant use, the source of the seeds, and farming techniques) were included in the description.

In Omeka, objects can be grouped into collections and tagged. One of the goals of this online catalog was to create a resource that was organized in ways that were

---

Title

Gray Blue Corn

Subject

UMMAA cat #15386

Description

Scientific name: *Zea mays*
Hopi name from 1935 field notes: Ma-si-ka-3 or ma-sis-kwa-pï
Source of seeds: Old Hopi type. Pure Strain
Crop management: Grown in sand dunes, back of Si-kya-tï-ka, separate field. Harvested a week before interview.
Harvesting and Storage: Husked in field, left tops there, in place. Trampled down. Good keeping corn, about same as white. Dried on roof and piled in house for storage. For disposal or crop, trade. or feed stock when worked.
Properties and use: traded or fed to stock when worked. Food as a corn meal, Piki or any other bread.
Hopi classification: More closely related to other blue corns than to white corn

Example of the use of Dublin Core elements in the Hopi Plants online catalog with information from museum records and field notes shown in regular type. Source: Created by author.

meaningful to the Hopi community. Based on suggestions received during a planning meeting with Hopi community members, museum objects were organized according to the Hopi Mesa where they were collected, rather than the taxonomic organization used in the museum. Similarly, tags were used to sort items by the Hopi village where the object was collected.

During two semesters, students collected information on over 175 items. By working with the objects, the museum records, and the anthropologists' field notes, students learned about the history of collecting for museums and the types of information available in museum archives.

Learning from Source Community Members

After working with the collection, students learned about the cultural context of these plants directly from Hopi community members using videoconferencing technology. Lisa Young developed the class project, especially the videoconference component, in collaboration with Susan Sekaquaptewa,[1] a Hopi museum professional. Videoconference meetings took place in Susan's home on the Hopi Reservation. Based on over a decade of experience working on Hopi cultural projects, she selected individuals who were knowledgeable about Hopi farming and plant use and who were comfortable discussing aspects of Hopi culture. In preparation for the meetings with students, she introduced community members to the project and the museum collections through the digital catalog and a notebook containing copies of the original field notes. The meetings used locally available Internet service (DSL), a big-screen TV, and a videoconferencing camera and speaker phone attached to Susan's laptop to enhance the audio and visual quality of the meetings (Table 2.1).[2]

Individual student teams met with one or two Hopi community members for an hour to an hour and a half. Students led the conversations by asking questions that were vetted by Lisa and Susan ahead of time. Questions focused on community members' experiences, rather than specific objects in the collections. Community members also asked the students questions about their backgrounds and experiences working with the collections, as well as their knowledge of gardening.

Using videoconferencing technology, each semester fifteen to twenty Museum Anthropology students met with five Hopi community members, as well as a Hopi elementary school class. The conversations with the elementary school students highlighted that these children already have a strong sense of tradition and identity based on Hopi farming, plants, and foods.

Impact

Sharing information about a museum collection using these digital technologies created a dynamic intercultural learning environment. Students gained experience discussing museum objects with members of the source community, and Hopi people learned about the plants collected from their ancestors without having to travel to Michigan.

Museum Anthropology Students

Throughout the semester, students wrote blog posts (https://ummuseumanthro.wordpress.com/) reflecting on what they were learning. As the blog posts below show, students learned how vital the perspectives of source community members are for understanding museum collections:

> To us, informed by the voices of the Hopi community, each plant in our archive has transformed from "just another bean" into something much more—a child of the Hopi community.
>
> If we had not communicated with the Hopi community, our observations about the seeds would probably have been based on their functions instead of on their importance to the Hopi way of life.

Students were also able to apply theoretical knowledge about changes in museum practice learned through course readings and discussions of a real-world situation.

Hopi Community Members

After their participation in the videoconferencing meetings, Hopi community members shared their thoughts with Susan through informal conversations. They commented on

- their interest in the information about the family and village history recorded in the anthropologists' field notes and
- the diversity of crops grown in the past and the need to continue to grow a variety of crops.

The conversations with the students also sparked discussions among Hopi community members about more general issues, including

- the importance of passing on information about Hopi farming and related cultural values to the younger generation and
- the need to protect Hopi heirloom seeds from contamination by genetically modified crops.

What We Learned

The most common place for source communities to see and discuss collections is at museums and with museum staff. Student interns may be present, but usually as bystanders. In the Museum Anthropology project, students led the conversation. The structure and topics also differed from the typical conversations about museum objects during community consultations. These differences include

- Hopi people were teachers, not informants.
- Conversations focused on Hopi farming and individual life experiences, rather than discussing specific museum objects.

- Videoconference meetings occurred in a neutral and familiar space for community members.

We also noticed that many Hopi community members who participated in the project did not look at the online catalog until after they discussed the collection with the students, in part due to limited Internet access on the reservation. As a result, the conversations with the students were critical for reconnecting the museum collection with Hopi community members.

Next Steps

For any project involving collaboration between a museum and a source community, information sharing about collections is a critical first step. However, partnerships with source communities are most successful when they address community needs. The next step, which we have begun, is to share our experiences in the Museum Anthropology class and the online catalog with additional members of the Hopi community. They, in turn, will help identify how best to utilize this collection for continued education and cultural learning by Hopi people. This project's focus on farming and food complements the mission of several nonprofit organizations and programs created by Hopi people, such as the Natwani Coalition, the Hopi Tutskwa Permaculture and Institute, and the Hopi Food Co-op. These organizations may also help identify future opportunities for educational collaborations. Many Hopi people have become increasingly concerned about the impact of genetically modified crops and the contamination of Hopi heirloom seeds. They are also concerned about high food insecurity and sustainability. This collection could be used to help address some of these issues as well. This project can also serve as a model for future projects within the Hopivewat Cultural Resource & Learning Center, which is at the beginning stages of development and planning. Digitally accessible objects and archives, such as the ones the Museum Anthropology students worked with, are envisioned as an important tool for Hopi community access and use.

The Museum Anthropology class project illustrates an innovative way to use museum objects to teach students about changes in museum practice that intertwines collaboration with a source community and the use of digital technology. Omeka provided a relatively easy-to-use platform for creating the online catalog. For museums located on or near university campuses, this type of project also provides opportunities for students to contribute to the digital records of a museum and, in the words of one of the Museum Anthropology students, "do something real."

Acknowledgments

We gratefully acknowledge resources at the University of Michigan, including the Museum of Anthropological Archaeology and grants from the Global Teaching with Videoconferencing program and Instructional Support Services, as well as Hopi community participants.

Notes

1. Lisa and Susan began working together on educational and exhibit projects in 2006 at the Homolovi State Park, which contains several ancestral Hopi villages.
2. Lisa received funding for this project from the University of Michigan Global Teaching with Videoconferencing grant program through the Office of the Vice Provost for Global and Engaged Education and the LSA Instructional Technology Faculty Project grants. These funds were used to purchase a videoconferencing camera and a speakerphone, as well as for honorariums for Hopi community members who participated in the project.

Our Stories, Our Places

Centering the Community as Narrative Voice in the Reinterpretation of an African American Historic Site

Porchia Moore

Overview

HISTORIC COLUMBIA (HC) is a nonprofit organization dedicated to preserving the history of South Carolina's capital city, Columbia, along with the surrounding heritage sites in Richland County. The Woodrow Wilson Family Home, the residential home of fourteen-year-old would-be President Woodrow Wilson, is the most known and valuable property HC maintains. In 2005, HC, which preserved six historic house museums and gardens, was forced to close the Wilson Home and initiate major renovations due to structural issues associated with the physical building. The HC organization began to have significant internal conversations about the future of the site and the relevance of historic house museums in the twenty-first century. HC decided that researchers would embark upon a reexamination of the Reconstruction Era[1] by exploring how the narrative of the Woodrow Wilson Home could be told through a new, more dynamic interpretation. The interpretative framework would be more racially inclusive and reflect the varying ways in which multiple social identities experienced oppression and domination in the new economic system.

In February 2014, the Woodrow Wilson Family Home reopened to local and national acclaim. A recent example is Jennifer Schuessler's August 2015 *New York Times* article,

"Taking Another Look at the Reconstruction Era."[2] In the article, Schuessler congratulated the team for drastically shifting the Woodrow Wilson Home narrative and their unique interpretation of Reconstruction, which is now told from the perspective of the formerly enslaved. This radical shift in interpretation was directly correlated to the internal decision to be more culturally responsive and relevant to new communities while reestablishing a commitment to the promotion and preservation of African American heritage.

At approximately the same time in 2015, HC commenced a multiyear archaeological excavation of another property, the Mann-Simons Site. Located a few miles away from where the Confederate flag once flew on the grounds of the South Carolina State House, the Mann-Simons historic house museum symbolizes black resistance and entrepreneurial success. The archaeological excavations, led by Dr. Jakob Crokett from 2006 to 2012, uncovered 60,000 artifacts from 2,200 square feet during four field schools. While the Woodrow Wilson Home and the Mann-Simons Site are within a few short blocks of each other, these properties could not be more different in terms of interpretation, visitor appeal, and historical narrative. The former interprets the childhood home of one of America's most venerated presidents. The latter seeks to interpret the domestic and commercial properties owned by formerly enslaved Africans: Celia Mann and her husband, Ben Delane, and their descendants. HC wanted to increase awareness of the site and foster deeper engagement with its story as a result of the new information from the archaeological excavations.

On the heels of the success of the reinterpretation of the Woodrow Wilson Home, HC realized the newfound discoveries from the multiyear excavation of Mann-Simons that provided a plethora of new information that would inherently impact the existing story of the house and the way the house's narrative was framed. There was concern regarding the ways in which the new archaeological knowledge would impact the local African American communities who perceived the Mann-Simons site as a revered cultural space telling a specific story of ownership. Would the communities whose traditions had evolved around a single, known interpretation be amenable to a new, more complex interpretation? Under the incomparable leadership of HC Executive Director Robin Waites, it became clear that any reinterpretation had to be community driven as this property has been perceived by African American community members as a space for and about black people and thus considered their own and a vital part of their neighborhood.

Planning

A plan for the reinterpretation of the site was established in the fall of 2014 with a six- to eight-month timeline for completion. Phase I included closing the site to the public and removing the furniture. Next, a small committee of HC staff, volunteers, and local scholars was put together to operate as a task force to think critically about the following overarching issues:

1. What necessary changes needed to be made to the current interpretation based on the new information revealed by the analysis of 60,000 artifacts?
2. What role might technology play in the interpretation?

3. Would this new information alienate African American community members who had based their own organizations on affiliation with the site?
4. How would the reinterpretation benefit the African American community?
5. How would the reinterpretation strengthen community engagement?
6. How would the reinterpretation reinforce the mission for both the site and the organization as a whole?

Once the larger-scale issues were identified the task force focused on specific challenges including

- Challenge 1—An awareness of subtle tensions between the organization being perceived as a white organization in control of that site and the need to maintain and reinforce trust from years of relationship building. The nearly all-white staff felt it imperative that the reinterpretation of the Mann-Simons Site should not center on what the *organization* felt was the significant story. Instead, they wanted to privilege the expressed desires and cultural knowledge African American community partners possessed to ensure this group's influence on what the narrative could and should be. The staff hoped maintaining the focus on the community would enable them to continue the decades-long legacies of deep engagement and participation.
- Challenge 2—The need to honor the two main groups—the Links and the Wisteria Garden Club—that have been among the strongest advocates for over two decades for Historic Columbia and a part of the original group of community members who actively advocated for HC to purchase and preserve the property. Members of both groups volunteered as docents for the site. Moreover, members of the Wisteria Garden Club, one of the oldest African American garden clubs in the country, traditionally decorated the home for Christmas as part of a longstanding southern custom. These groups, as well as Calvary Baptist Church, one of the oldest African American churches in Columbia, have the longest standing relationship with the Mann-Simons Site. When the committee came together to discuss a vision for the Mann-Simons Site from a historical and academic perspective, it became clear that in order to dismantle any notion of hegemony and promote community agency at the deepest levels these community assets and what they deemed culturally and functionally relevant had to serve as a guide for the project.
- Challenge 3—To reopen the house and execute the new interpretation in time for the Jubilee festival in September 2015. Jubilee is an annual celebration of African American history held on the grounds of Mann-Simons. The celebration features tours and interactive historical demonstrations at the site as well as performing arts, genealogy workshops, music, dance, and other cultural arts.

Implementation

Phase II of the plan called for a process of co-creation. HC utilized a grant from the National Trust for Historic Preservation to fund a community event entitled *Our Stories, Our*

Places: The Role of Historic Sites and Museums in African American History in May 2015 at Calvary Baptist Church. The National Trust for Historic Preservation is a privately funded nonprofit organization that works to save America's historic places.

Designed as a roundtable discussion, the event was led by Bob Beatty, vice president for programs at the American Association for State and Local History; Dina Bailey, director of educational strategies at the National Center for Civil and Human Rights; and Porchia Moore, PhD candidate at the University of South Carolina (USC) School of Library and Information Science and the McKissick Museum Management program. The program was meant to instigate a conversation about national, regional, and local trends in African American interpretation, programming, and ownership at historic sites and museums. Dr. Bobby Donaldson of the USC Department of History moderated the panel discussion with curated questions that sought to help both panelists and community members think critically about the role of historic houses in their communities. To assess what the public understood about historic house museums and to gain insight about how the organization is perceived and what they can do to bridge those gaps, Director of Cultural Resources John Sherrer, III devised these fundamental questions for the community listening session:

1. How can or how do people talk about the divide between historically African American (or otherwise) sites that may be preserved and administrated by predominantly white-associated agencies/organizations?
2. How can institutions build trust with communities whose members feel the organization's members, staff, and supporters "don't look like them"?
3. How can meaningful support for historic properties/collections be garnered from groups that are hesitant to offer it when they perceive or realize an actual historical imbalance in power/cultural currency?

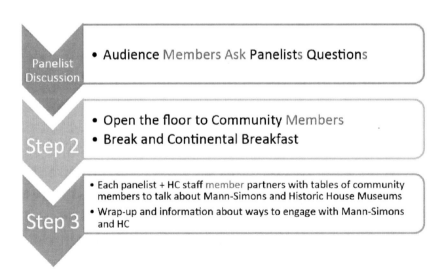

Three fundamental steps of *Our Stories, Our Places* community event. Source: Created by author.

4. How can/should communities for whom sites/collections were preserved and interpreted "step up" and how should/could the organizations that have desperately sought to engage said communities "step aside" to make stewardship, cultural ownership, and educational programming reflect more of a community focus and be more effective?
5. In what ways can such interaction lead to a model site/experience that proves to be a place of healing/understanding/forward thinking?

The *Our Stories, Our Places* community event comprised three fundamental steps:

Believing that true community engagement is connected to the practice of being a story-catcher and not a storyteller[3] Director Waites participated in the event by sitting on the floor on the far right of the room to blend in and record audience feedback on her laptop. The practice of storycatching was a lesson learned in past years when the organization attempted to collect histories from community members in an effort to "Catch it. Record

Six components and three pillars for community engagement with the Mann-Simons project. Source: Created by author.

it. Share it" so that HC could serve as a repository for neighborhood stories. She quickly learned from these communities that they were hesitant to entrust HC with their stories because they did not believe the organization had earned their trust or that the stories would be correctly told. As a result, Waites approached the Mann-Simons project with the philosophy that Community Engagement consists of six components with three pillars:

1. Community Engagement from Deep Listening
2. Community Engagement from Active Listening
3. Community Engagement from Advocacy for Participation

The audience commentary and recorded feedback from the break-out sessions (see figure on page 82, Step 3) that the panelists and HC staff facilitated were reviewed after the *Our Stories, Our Places* event was complete.

Results

The results from *Our Stories, Our Places* were unexpected. It became evident that the timeline for the project required an extension. Although the initial goal of the project was to gather the community's thoughts on how they would like to see the interpretative narrative for Mann-Simons shifted, it immediately became clear that this was the beginning of a much larger discussion. Historic Columbia realized communities were describing how the HC could shift to better meet local needs. Consequently, to responsibly listen to that information and be genuine and congruent to the values of deep engagement, the organization discarded their timeline and instituted a continuation of the *Our Stories, Our Places* as a long-term community listening series. The extended timeline project privileged these communities' ways of knowing, cultural needs, and focused on assessing how this feedback might impact institutional changes. The decision was made by Waites and HC staff to reopen Mann-Simons to the public during the Jubilee festival in September 2015. This allowed new and returning community members to take a tour of the unfurnished site, participate in a survey regarding the types of objects and participatory interactives that might be of interest by dropping their votes in strategically placed buckets around the house, and sign up for facilitated *Our Stories, Our Places* conversations that would take place in the house at predetermined dates. HC organized a series of these sessions through February 2016. In April 2016, an artist created original works about the site and the Mann-Simons home to serve as an exhibition space. Upon the closing of the exhibit, the house reopened to the public officially in the fall of 2016 during the annual Jubilee festival.

Lessons Learned

One of the most meaningful aspects of the project is the amount of data collected by the sessions. I facilitated these discussions without HC staff present. Each session provided refreshments and was recorded for later transcription. This Open Authority model helped create dialogue without the pressure of community members performing "Blackness" or feeling that honesty and transparency were hindered by staff presence. Several community members stated that my being African American provided them a comfort because I could "safely translate" their meaning to HC and that they could drop their "double consciousness" and speak with greater freedom. The latter is both a success and a challenge because it highlights the work that needs to be done to erase racial tensions and continue to strengthen relationships and promote racial trust. The most significant success was the community enthusiasm and support for *Our Stories, Our Places* because community members felt valued as genuine assets to the organization and all enthusiastically vowed to urge others to sign up for future listening sessions. The HC organization felt that it was better to have more listening sessions than too few.

Next Steps

Now that substantial data have been collected, HC is entering Phase III of the project, which is to invite local African American groups to utilize the Mann-Simons as a free meeting space. The only caveat is that a portion of the meeting be reserved to hold more listening sessions. This idea partly derived from suggestions made by community members in listening sessions. Not only does this allow new visitors the opportunity to learn about the site but also allows them to experience the potential of the site as relevant for contemporary community members.

Acknowledgments

Special thanks to Historic Columbia Executive Director Robin Waites for her incomparable leadership and tenacious efforts to value and privilege community voices, stories, and histories. Love and appreciation for the members of First Calvary Baptist Church for their support and rich, historical legacy. I would also like to acknowledge the dedicated Historic Columbia staff and the communities who courageously and enthusiastically participated in the listening sessions.

Notes

1. The Reconstruction Period is an era of American history recognized from 1865 to 1877 that followed the Civil War. It marks a period during which mandated regulations from the U.S. government dictated the terms of reconciliation between the northern and southern states. A major part of the terms of reconciliation was the institution of full political and civil rights for blacks in addition to the denial and termination of rights (politically) for all whites involved with the secession of states.
2. See http://www.nytimes.com/2015/08/25/arts/park-service-project-would-address-the-reconstruction-era.htm.
3. Based on Christina Baldwin's *Making Sense of Our Lives through the Power and Practice of Story*. Novato, CA: New World Library, 2005.

Part III

ADVOCACY FOR HERITAGE PROFESSIONALS DURING THE CRISIS AND THE CALM

Sarah E. Miller

LTHOUGH CRITICAL to the health and sustainability of museums, advocacy is often considered a task that the small museum does not have time for. In this part I explore why advocacy is everyone's responsibility and how the work can be done by any institution, no matter the size. Advocacy is the art of garnering support, encouragement, backing, and promotion for a cause. There are many kinds of advocates, those who support medical, educational, and environmental causes, to name just a few. When working with first-time advocates some have asked, "Aren't you just preaching to the choir?" Yet choirs take assembling. They need direction by a conductor; they need practice before a performance. The role of a heritage advocate is to first raise a choir, then provide the best possible sheet music.

The existing heritage advocacy model suggesting education leads to appreciation that leads to preservation leaves a lot of action to be detailed (Tilden 1977, 8). Too often advocacy is synonymous with working with elected officials; however, this is just one spoke of the overall advocacy umbrella. Advocacy requires skills, tools, and building upon lessons learned by others. Many of the examples in this part come from the field of archaeology and my own experience as director of a Florida Public Archaeology Network (FPAN) center. The advice that follows and case studies by Connolly, Farber, and Prycer will, however, speak to broad advocacy concepts that can be applied by those working in museums, historic sites, or organizations.

Planning

The need for advocacy is triggered by threats beyond an advocate's control. Whether a museum will close, a position will be eliminated, or a site slated for development, there is generally a catalyst that throws people together in an organic and often reactionary rushed manner. Therefore, planning requires proactive building of skills during the calm and reactive tools to apply in a crisis.

Developing Your Advocacy SkillSet

Advocacy is an ethical obligation for heritage professionals and very often part of their employment. Unfortunately, Advocacy 101 is more often offered by professional organizations, like the Florida Trust for Historic Preservation workshop of 2006 or the Society of American Archaeology's recent 2015 webinar, but not a course offered as part of undergraduate or graduate training in academic degree programs. Thus, advocacy skills are developed on the job by observing others and very little assessment or evaluation of advocacy for comparative efforts exists. Opportunities for heritage advocacy should exist in the form of clubs or interest groups that mirror social justice or environmental activism on campuses, as well as directed internships in cultural resource advocacy.

For the time being, beginner advocates can think of themselves as conductors in training. Conductors need to listen and give clear direction. They need to be able to advertise and audition new choir members and know the strength of each singer. They need to be able to book venues and plan concerts. Unlike an army that is aggressive and directed to think in terms of offense and defense, a choir is a community effort; they contribute to a community's quality of life, practice, and have fun. An experienced conductor is an enthusiastic leader that instills confidence. Look for opportunities to improve and practice communication, social media, networking, and observing local government.

The first necessary skill is communication. For this, Certified Interpretive Guide (CIG) training offered by the National Association for Interpretation is an excellent opportunity to consider. Training takes place over several days as participants learn to build interpretive presentations based on themes and subthemes. CIGs build programs on the notion that people remember themes, not facts (Ham 1992). Heritage advocates must provide facts, but effective communication for a cause requires editing down to the most salient points to inspire an emotional connection to your resource. The course will help define themes and subthemes with related tangibles and intangibles that will serve the advocate in written and spoken tools to follow. Communication is also two-way; a conductor must listen to individual members of a choir to understand their strengths and to gauge audience interest. Alternatively, the National Park Service hosts Interpretive Development Program training modules online for no cost that similarly develop interpretation skills.

Next, hone social media skills. The Florida Association of Museums, for example, offered a workshop facilitated by a marketing consultant to train heritage professionals to be more effective in using online platforms. The National Association for Interpretation, Society for Historical Archaeology, and Society for American Archaeology have all offered similar workshops or webinars in the recent past. Facebook and Twitter are proven tools for advocacy. As the case studies by both Melissa Prycer and Ember Farber that follow point out, social media is the gateway tool for first-time advocates. Most are familiar with personal use of these platforms, but for professional use, attending a workshop will help you transition from one online world to another and provide you a credential critical to training your own future choir.

Networking is another essential skill. Attending conferences is expensive and exhausting but essential to staying current and developing a support collective. In addition to the annual meeting, volunteering on committees provides opportunities for developing long-term communication over great distances, relevance to national trends, and colleagues to add to your support network. As alluded to in the paragraphs above, workshops offered by professional societies, and preservation groups in particular, are the only formal training in advocacy currently available to heritage professionals. Using the choir analogy, a conductor needs to find gifted singers but also listen for the best arrangements being sung by other choirs.

Finally, brush up on your civics knowledge and study local government procedures in your area. Every government entity has its own culture, its own way of doing things. Make a point to observe and when appropriate participate in procedures at city and county commission meetings. Be aware of districts, committees, and term limits of elected officials. Elected bodies are dynamic; diligence is required to stay current.

Tools for Advocacy

A variety of tools are at an advocate's disposal including written, verbal, and integrated types (Table 3.1). Be mindful across all tool types to craft legal, ethical, and emotional arguments for your cause. Better yet, if you are part of a united effort, delegate separate writing assignments to those with the greatest potential to deliver the legal, ethical, and personal statements. Think of them as your three-part harmony to fill out the spectrum of notes that can be heard. If the catalyst of your cause violates federal, state, or local laws, ask those that enforce the laws to help you communicate that message. Laws also have their limits, and here the ethical arguments can be explained by a respected academic in the area or a representative from your professional organization. Emotional arguments are best made by descendants or longtime residents. These arguments for your cause can then be transmitted via written tools, such as letters, press kits, social media platforms, mass emails, and petitions. Similarly, crafted messages can be spoken in public meetings, presentations, and discussions with elected officials. Finally, some advocacy tools take a combined effort to culminate in events or communications on a larger scale, such as workshops, festivals, and resolutions.

Written Advocacy: Putting Pen to Paper to Support Heritage

Letters remain one of the most effective written tools to express an advocate's views. They are the ultimate sheet music. Many kinds of letters exist: letters to the editor, public comment put into writing, and letters of support for grants or appeals. Letters allow the writer to provide the larger context and history of a given issue, name experts involved, or provide facts in support and should include a call to action. The same can be said of a coordinated social media effort,

Table 3.1.   List of Advocacy Tools by Type

WRITTEN	VERBAL	INTEGRATED
Annual report	Civic organizations	Awards
Article	Classroom presentation	Awareness Day/Week/Month
Blog	Conference paper	Display
Bumper sticker	Elevator speech	Festival
Clearinghouse	Meeting	Proclamation
Contacts/mass emails	Presentation—adult	Protest
Dropbox	Public comment	Resolution
Google Docs	Public service announcement	Seminar
Google Groups	Radio interview	Summit
Handout		Televised news
Impact statement		Video
Letter of support		Workshop
Letter to the editor		
listserv		
MailChimp and other EMS		
Newsletter		
Petitions		
Postcards		
Poster		
Press kit		
Press release		
Proclamations		
Public comment (written)		
Slideshow		
Social media: Facebook, Twitter		
Stickers		
Survey		
Webpage		
Wiki		

which has become the most popular way to advocate. Blogs, Facebook, and Twitter are proven mainstays, but heritage organizations are increasingly turning to Instagram, Tumblr, and even Snapchat for advocacy. As all forms of government have their own culture, so do social media platforms. It's best not to link platforms to automatically share the same message across all accounts, if only not to annoy regular users of that application. Social media as an engagement tool will be further discussed in Part V of this volume, but for advocacy purposes take the time to pause and plan hashtags and links to optimize your cause. Use a blog post so that you can update as needed, yet the URL address stays the same. You can't control what other people will share and forward, but you can control the content if yours is the initial call to action. Or if you are supporting a larger call to action, reshare what already exists and join the ongoing conversation with links to your partners to give them a boost as well.

Not all direction from a conductor is related to musical composition; often they need to communicate rehearsal times, what to wear, or announce a concert. Email is less interactive than social media but still a good tool considering you can use contact lists, mass email, email marketing software (EMS), and finally listserv or email groups. The variables to consider when using email for advocacy are administrative control and time. All require written communication skills and diligent editing. However, email only allows one-way or single-responder communication, which is ideal for announcements but limited for discussion. Same goes for EMS services, such as MailChimp or Constant Contact, which help manage mass emails where people subscribe to your email feed but cannot post content. Both contact lists and EMS allow for categories that for advocacy help you target media outlets, elected officials, or those with a specified interest in advocacy. Improved tools for advocacy include listserv and groups that increase chances for dialogue between the subscribers via threads by subject but take more administrative effort. Yahoo! and Google Groups are similar in that all subscribers can post to the group, yet different in that they do not require the listserv application. While we still use email tools, FPAN's Cemetery Resource Protection Training (CRPT) Alliance and EnvArch Facebook groups result in a notably higher number of individuals posting content compared to the initial Yahoo! and Google groups for the same causes because subscribers hesitated initiating threads.

Another written tool for advocacy are petitions. Traditional paper petitions can be powerful to present in front of an elected body, but popular online petitions can damage effective advocacy channels. They create confusion if not administered properly, as anyone can fill out the template and vetting or duplicate checking process done by Change.org. In a recent example, at FPAN we found three different Change.org petitions fighting the same bill—in this case House Bill 803, to be described in a later section—but all used different content, they were different in who would receive the petition emails, and social media users freely shared the petition but did not send in traditional letters or make public comment when action was crucial. We asked one representative if she received any of the petition emails, and she had not. Another local official shared she had to once block Change.org when she was incorrectly targeted on a previous petition; thus, she receives no Change.org emails even if it's for another issue. Images were also used without permission, meaning someone can inadvertently become the poster child for an issue without granting permission. Online petitions are easily shared to a national audience, but they distract from effective local actions, such as writing letters and making public comment.

Verbal Tools for Advocacy: Speaking Up for Heritage

Verbal advocacy tools require the same attention to crafting legal, ethical, and emotional arguments. They should also similarly reuse and recycle content generated from other tools. When done well, speaking in a public forum appears to be done on the fly, but in truth requires preparation and practice. Choirs never spontaneously burst out into perfectly choreographed numbers without sheet music; in truth the performance represents tens if not hundreds of hours practicing and breaking down the measures to perfect pitch and tempo. Verbal communication requires oratory skills and overcoming the prevalent fear of public speaking. Standing up in public makes the speaker more vulnerable and the experience more personal, which is why it's so effective.

The mainstay of spoken advocacy is public comment in government body meetings. Public comment can be found on council agendas published before the meeting, is regulated by template and time allotment, and requires observation in advance of participation to be effective within the council's culture. For example, in Florida, at St. Johns County commission meetings you sign up on a paper list at the start of the meeting, the clerk calls speakers up one at a time by name, and a large three-minute countdown is displayed to keep comments to the time allowed. Other meetings allow more time; for example, St. Johns County allows eight minutes for invited experts or up to fifteen minutes if a presentation is requested as part of a commission workshop. It is also standard to ask speakers to introduce themselves and give their address; be prepared to insert your title, and if you don't live in the jurisdiction of the body you are addressing, let them know how your work relates to their municipality. To fill three minutes draft a double-spaced page and a half of what you plan to say and practice. Record yourself and listen to the playback. For larger meetings keep a checklist of themes to address and cross them off as speakers before you use these arguments, to eliminate redundancy. A conductor knows when to crescendo the sopranos forward and dim the altos.

Presentations are often overlooked as an opportunity to insert advocacy. Standard lectures for heritage professionals tend to focus on a historical event or artifact type but fail to include a call to action. Consider adding an advocacy slide at the end of standard talks. What would you like your audience to do now that they are more informed on what you do or study? Same can be said for school visits. Heritage as a whole would be better served if students received potential solutions to heritage issues along with the subject matter content.

Working with elected officials may be the number one thing that comes to mind when taking on advocacy but in many respects they are not the choir; they are the audience or regional judges. Relationships with the audience take time, require charm to develop rapport, and are best delivered as informal interpretation between set pieces. Good ways to foster relationships with elected officials include scheduling an introductory meeting, giving presentations to civic groups where elected officials are also members, and attending local events. Volunteer to serve on preservation or planning committees for local government. Elected officials often sit in on preservation board meetings, or in rare cases a city commissioner will be appointed to a county preservation board, which is the case in St. Johns County where St. Augustine City Commissioner Nancy Sikes-Kline is a member of the county's Cultural Resource Board. The case studies to follow have advice for speaking to elected officials. Keep in mind as a heritage professional, elected officials need to hear your opinion especially during the process of evaluating future legislation. Resources for defining the line between lobbying and advocacy are provided at the conclusion of this part, but in most cases advocating for heritage is invited and your professional opinion is necessary for officials to make informed decisions.

Integrated Advocacy Strategies

Some advocacy activities are difficult to categorize because they depend on a combination of written and verbal tools. Meetings, workshops, mass media, and organizing conferences require multiple lines of communication and opportunities for promotion. When you don't know where to start in advocacy, call a meeting. Meetings are like rehearsals that afford face-to-face time between partner organizations, the opportunity to distribute minutes and follow up on action items, and help maintain traction on an issue. Workshops help the singers develop their skill. They generate public interest through publicity and have the potential to include others for a multidisciplinary approach, and they also put pressure on the organizer to set firm dates and help define ways people can help as training will be required. Televised news coverage reaches a large population but requires developing relationships with individual reporters and press kits for effective content to be altered into brief transcripts. For heritage stories the camera tends to favor person-on-the-street interviews over the experts and the overall message is difficult to control.

Festivals and public days are excellent integrated events to generate larger numbers while maintaining control over your message. They are the Macy's Day Parade and large benefit concerts that bring multiple choirs together. Beginners can start by offering to provide an information table or activity for an existing festival. Later, volunteer to serve on the planning committee for a festival to better understand the full-year commitment to organizing such an event. Ultimately, host a festival to promote your site or concern. Festivals require unprecedented time for preparation, organization, and promotion. At FPAN we found success in developing bumper stickers, buttons, stickers, and postcards for advocacy as handouts (see below). These freebies were initially designed for festival tables but are also useful when putting together press packets, inserts for folders we prepare when meeting with elected officials, and branding archaeology advocacy in our region.

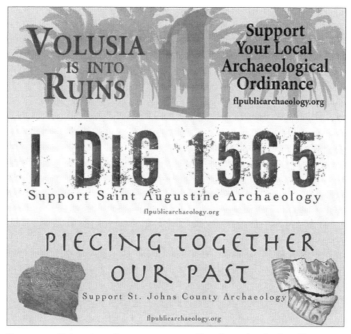

Bumper sticker to raise awareness of archaeological ordinances.
Source: Created by author.

Building on written and verbal tools for working with elected officials, proclamations and resolutions are integrated tools to advance your cause through local government. If your issue has an awareness day or month, ask your local government to do a proclamation, as we do every year for Florida Archaeology Month. During the writing of this section the opportunity arose to draft a resolution against Citizen Archaeology Permits (CAPs), which will be described later. In short the resolution required technical writing and verbal introduction, provided an opportunity for public comment, and garnered local media coverage for opposition against a proposal that would harm submerged heritage sites. The resolution also allowed the city to add fighting CAP proposals to their legislative agenda, meaning lobbyists would now be in Tallahassee tracking and actively working against the proposal's adoption. Proclamations and resolutions therefore go beyond raising awareness and create documents publicly adopted and with measured action.

Some of the most memorable events in advocacy of any kind are protest. The footage of the mall during Dr. King's "I Have a Dream" speech or recent sit-ins by students advocating for their teachers in Madison, Wisconsin, come to mind as powerful, life-changing events. In the choir analogy this may be the only case where people do start spontaneously singing music, moved by the lyrics behind "We Shall Overcome" or "Give Peace a Chance." Recently in Wisconsin, advocates of Native American cultures protested against a bill that would issue permits for landowners to investigate their own property for burial remains and if none were found in the area, including previously recorded burial mounds, could then be leveled for development. Archaeologist Elizabeth Reetz (personal communication, 2016) participated in the Save the Mounds protest in Madison and advised future advocates to (1) be aware of professional and political boundaries, (2) harness the power of social media—in this case search #savethemounds on Facebook to see the array of supporters and supplementary information

Advocacy at the 2016 Save the Mounds protest in Madison, Wisconsin (left to right: Jacki Rand, Elizabeth Reetz, Brianna Hoffmann). Photograph courtesy of Elizabeth Reetz.

provided, (3) stay positive and remember the demonstration is a celebration of culture. If you work for a government agency, be mindful you may not be able to take a supporting or opposing view, only offer information. Ask your supervisor in advance of action in case there is a conflict of interest that could endanger your employment. Links to library and literacy organizations that publish advocacy guides and have previously organized peaceful protests are provided in the Resource Guide.

Advocacy Action Plan Implementation and Results

With the skills and tools acquired, the next step is action. Draft an Advocacy Action Plan with the template provided or use a poster board folded into three sections (Table 3.2). The first step to filling out the chart is defining the Issue, which is the heading of the left-hand column. Be specific to limit your scope while also addressing what is the larger issue behind your localized problem. For example, climate change is too large an issue to address, but as an archaeologist I can define the issue as sites endangered by sea level rise. Next label the center column Desired Outcome. How will you determine action and know when the mission is accomplished? The previously noted CIG training gained as an advocacy skill will also help define measurable objectives and how to write outcomes. Before you amplify your position on the issue, you need to know what solution you want to work toward. Finally, brainstorm what tools are the best fit for your desired outcome. Tools may organically arise, but if you can settle upon a few to start it will help as you develop the content needed for those platforms. Know who makes the decisions impacting your issue and be efficient by using tools that target that audience or that your choir can use to get the attention of your

Table 3.2.   Template for Advocacy Action Plan

ISSUE	DESIRED OUTCOME	TOOLS

target audience. Consider a combination of written and spoken tools, and select one of the integrated tools to work toward sustainability of your short-term efforts. Communicate with partners and set a launch date. You want your tools—blog post, hashtags, service announcement—whatever they may be ready as an organized package for the launch.

Advocacy Plans in Action: Examples from Ten Years at FPAN

Advocacy Action Plans were not in place when I started as director of the Northeast Region for the FPAN but were first developed five years ago as an activity for an advocacy workshop. They now help describe past advocacy efforts and are used as a planning tool. FPAN's mission posted on our website (www.fpan.us) is "to promote and facilitate the conservation, study and public understanding of Florida's archaeological heritage." The organization is small in that it employs less than twenty full-time staff but large in that FPAN serves the entire state through eight regional centers. By advocating for cultural resources we are already achieving the initial network goal to provide education and outreach, regardless of the result. After ten years of advocacy in action FPAN illustrates what can be accomplished by other small-scale museums and heritage centers. Here I highlight FPAN's advocacy on reoccurring issues surrounding abandoned cemeteries, illegal metal detecting, sites impacted by sea level rise, and proposed CAPs detrimental to submerged resources (Table 3.3).

Fighting Illegal Metal Detecting on Archaeological Sites

Metal detecting on archaeological sites is a felony on state land and is not allowed on many county and municipally owned lands in Florida. Advocacy efforts are triggered when citizens persuade local governments to reconsider ordinances against the activity, when looting is reported on social media or becomes a feature in the local news, or when treasure hunting off shipwrecks is celebrated in the news. The issue escalated when two separate reality shows contacted our office seeking assistance in filming metal detector series, on both protected city and county land. Fortunately, we were not alone as the Spike TV show *American Diggers* and the National Geographic Channel show *Diggers* targeted a diversity of sites around the country, raising the ire of an estimated 5,000 members of professional archaeological societies (Society for American Archaeology 2015). Locally we issued press releases, held workshops, managed paper petitions by printing our Change.org documents and collecting local signatures (see figure on page 98), and presented a united social media front. While we had faced metal-detecting issues in the past, this round we focused on serving as a clearinghouse and centralized resources for our choir to a single blog post, which was updated as new articles and advocacy resources became available. We learned to integrate this targeted advocacy effort into programs already in progress. The culminating event was a public advocacy workshop conducted at city hall in St. Augustine that was later repeated for heritage professionals at the Florida Trust for Historic Preservation Annual Meeting. We gained seventeen official partner organizations that supported our cause and provided speakers including county historic resource specialist and the chief of police, who delivered

Table 3.3. Advocacy Action Plan Examples from FPAN

ISSUE	DESIRED OUTCOME	TOOLS
Metal detectors in the media endangering archaeological sites.	Demonstrate that the public does not want this attention on our archaeological sites and provide enough public awareness to block access to sites on public and private lands.	• Speak at city commission meeting. • Speak to professional and non-professional organizations. • Organize community workshop. • Editorial. • Blog post. • Petition. • Social media. • Official thank you to city hall.
Abandoned cemetery without an owner of record, case of demolition by neglect.	Local government take ownership and responsibility of abandoned cemetery.	• Speak at county commission meeting. • Speak to neighborhood association. • Organize community workshop. • Blog post. • Video. • Cemetery a Day in May #CADIM blog posts. • Facebook posts, CRPT Alliance Group. • Official thank you.
Sea level rise is endangering sites in coastal and inland areas.	Have cultural resources integrated into state and local action plans related to sea level rise and increase reporting and monitoring of sites in high threat zones.	• Include in strategic and annual planning. • Speak to professional and non-professional organizations. • Organize community workshop. • Serve as clearinghouse for topic. • Blog posts. • Video. • EnvArch Facebook group. • Lecture series. • Official thank you to host organization and site monitors.
Citizen Archaeology Permits (CAP) proposed despite long history of failed attempts and feasibility.	End proposition of CAP program by state legislators.	• Blog posts. • Letters to the editor, press release. • Mass email requests. • SurveyMonkey by state. • Webpage to serve as clearinghouse. • Social media #HB803 #BS1054. • City resolution.

legal messages; archaeologists from the Florida Museum of Natural History and the Society of Historical Archaeology's Ethics Committee, to speak to ethical messages; and the retired state psychologist for Florida who is a member of a displaced community and delivered very moving statements as to why heritage matters. When a new metal-detecting issue arises, we are able to transition rapidly by updating the blog and relying on the tools that worked in the past.

Petition Summary:	The show "Diggers," as described by your network—"unless you're in a coma, it's impossible to find treasure hunting...anything less than exhilarating"—celebrates the exploitation of OUR heritage at multiple sites across the United States. This is not acceptable. We will not watch shows that show the illegal and unethical looting of historical sites for the economic benefit of your network and the hosts your shows.	
Action Petitioned For:	We the citizens, residents, and visitors of St. Augustine, Florida petition you (National Geographic Channel) to cease production and do not air episodes of "Diggers."	
Name	Signature	Email Address

	Petition Summary:	The show "American Diggers, as described by your network—"led by former professional wrestler-turned-modern- day relic hunter Ric Savage as they scour ... battlefields and historic sites, in hopes of striking it rich by unearthing and selling rare pieces of American history—celebrates the exploitation of OUR heritage in northeast Florida. This is not acceptable. We will not watch shows that show the illegal and unethical looting of historical sites for the economic benefit of your network and the hosts your shows.
	Action Petitioned For:	We the citizens, residents, and visitors of St. Augustine, Florida petition you (Spike TV) to cease production and do not air episodes of "American Digger."
	Name	Signature	Email Address

Stop exploitation of OUR shared heritage by Spike TV and NatGeo

Petitions modified to collect signatures against metal-detecting reality shows. Source: Created by author.

Abandoned Cemeteries

Abandoned cemeteries and endangered sites are another major and reoccurring issue. We began with a goal to provide a Cemetery Resource Protection Training (CRPT) workshop in every county we served—seven at the time—and found our list of partners and resources expanded with each offering. In one specific example, the San Sebastian Cemetery in St. Augustine was featured repeatedly in the news as a target for vandalism and became a standard backdrop for civil rights leaders to stand before and acknowledge institutional racism illustrated by abandoned African American cemeteries. We participated in several cleanup days and brought the cemetery to the attention of local officials, who were ready to implement a solution. We asked the county to use an existing state law to declare the cemetery officially abandoned, whereby after a length of time the cemetery would become county property. What we did not anticipate was the county then transferring a deed-restricted title to the local neighborhood association, which made sense geographically, but the association was not in our opinion prepared for its long-term care and maintenance. Our desired outcome has shifted to adoption of these sacred places by trained advocacy organizations.

Impact of Sea Level Rise on Cultural Resources

Climate change is a worldwide crisis with very real local consequences that need sustained evaluation and planning as macro drivers of climate change are addressed at national and global levels. Such evaluation and planning is hampered by a state government that denies the reality of climate change. FPAN advocacy helps to mitigate inaction by developing tools to protect sites and assist local players in protecting their vulnerable resources. We aim to engage the public in monitoring and recording sites at risk, as well as assist local governments as they integrate sea level rise into coastal planning documents. Integrated tools used to produce sustained results include organizing panels, EnvArch Facebook group, and we have completed three Sea Level Rise workshops, with more scheduled across the state. This issue had challenged our ability to engineer discussions and activities toward cultural resources without diverging into private property and homeowner issues beyond our desired outcome. We found the abundance of information available overwhelming and as a result organized an SLR Workshop Resources DropBox folder.[1] In that folder we maintain an annotated bibliography of written resources related to cultural resources and sea level rise that are listed and continually updated.

Citizen Archaeology Permits and the Reoccurring Nightmare of Isolated Finds

During the writing of this part, Florida endured not one, but two waves of the CAP propositions. The titles of these programs are confusing as you would think FPAN would want to partner with the public in any archaeological endeavor. However, CAP proposals are not about education or engaging the public. They in fact run contrary to the mission of FPAN to protect the state's buried past. CAP programs would allow individuals to apply for a permit, remove artifacts from state-owned lands, then transfer ownership of the artifact so it can then be sold, which is currently against the law for state-owned artifacts. The affordances and constraints of CAP propositions and the previous Isolated Finds program are complex, but as FPAN published on a webpage dedicated to this cause (http://flpublicarchaeology. org/resources/collecting.php), the issue is a well-documented failure. In terms of advocacy, archaeologists successfully wrote letters, posted blog articles, and submitted letters to the editor that helped reverse the Isolated Finds program. Unfortunately, every year it seems a legislator is approached by constituents wanting to revive collecting permits, and bills are annually submitted with some form of the CAP included. As this section was first drafted, the state published a survey to collect public responses and published a 237-page feasibility report to squelch support for CAP from one direction, only to have HB 803 and its companion SB 1054 submitted a few months later. Same advocacy issue, same desired outcome, but we needed to rethink our tools. We learned from the metal-detecting issue that clearinghouses work to centralize advocacy efforts. We learned to brand the opposition to the bill and to specifically target sponsors of the bill. As previously mentioned, the city of St. Augustine asked FPAN to help draft a city resolution against the proposed state legislation, which has opened up a new avenue for advocacy.

Conclusions and Recommendations

After ten years in advocacy, the most important lesson learned is the role of a museum or organization as a clearinghouse. Small issues may come up year to year, but as a museum or cultural center the stability that comes with storing institutional knowledge is valuable and greater than a single individual or site. Success in advocacy depends upon ceaseless education efforts, that heritage matters and places are worth preserving, and that heritage contributes to the economic health of the community. Take heart when facing adversity over and over; there is great efficiency to be found when combating an issue multiple times. If the choir is already assembled, they just need the updated arrangement of an already familiar tune.

Another major lesson learned was the importance of a thank you. After metal-detecting producers cleared the area, one of our professional colleagues noted that after all we asked from the public, he never saw us issue an official thank you. He was right. Conductors must know a concert isn't about them; it's about the music and after every song they call for recognizing the performers with applause. We then made a point to celebrate when *American Diggers* was officially canceled, email those who signed the petition to let them know they made a difference, and publicly stood up to thank St. Augustine's city commission for their support. For abandoned cemeteries we took another route and nominated stewards for established statewide awards to recognize their positive contributions. When that proved positive, we developed our own "Cemeteries Are Safer Because of You" (CASBY) awards, now presented annually. Look for awards and other opportunities to publicly thank your choir for all the work they do.

When it comes to advocacy tools, reuse and recycle. Once you have selected and practiced a set of music, take it on the road to schools, nursing homes, YouTube videos, or organize a flash mob. A letter to the editor can be reworked into a blog post with additional prompts and links to social media platforms. Bumper stickers for festival tables can be brought to public meetings, used as a thank you to those filling out your petition, and branded as an advocacy logo used in presentations. Workshops for the public can be repeated for professionals, and vice versa. Maximize your effort by repackaging the same content and combining written, verbal, and integrated tools to maintain traction and sustain support.

Finally, something alluded to in the case studies to follow, be patient and establish your network now. You can't activate what's not there. Take time assembling the choir using the tools available to steadily grow your audience and remember it's a two-way relationship. As the heritage professional, you must provide the content the audience comes to you for to keep them engaged, and in return when you need them they can help amplify your message to new audiences and elected officials.

The following case studies employ a variety of advocacy tools to accomplish their goals. The American Association of Museums and Robert Connolly provide good templates and tools to open up dialogue and expand museum relationships. The impact statements described by Connolly provide the perfect example of the music those who make the decisions want to hear. Ember Farber's article also features resources for improving the relationship with elected officials by first assisting you in locating them. The importance of social media in advocacy is highlighted by both Farber as the way first-time advocates become engaged and by Melissa Prycer, who shares her experience in getting familiar with elected officials by their social media accounts. Prycer also highlights the importance of being in the room, in a sense representing all heritage professionals by being present at meetings. Connolly, Prycer, and Farber all reinforce that advocacy, like a choir, takes patience and practice, and well-composed sheet music works.

Note

1. For link, see https://www.dropbox.com/sh/o34ss9gvgbrcoxx/AAD95qRg0ZIiObF_fB5OHY o8a?dl=0.

Making Advocacy Everyone's Priority

Ember Farber

Introduction

THE AMERICAN ALLIANCE of Museums (AAM) is committed to barrier-free, year-round advocacy and to being the voice for museums on Capitol Hill and beyond. We believe museums are essential, and that everyone who works for, with, or simply loves museums is an advocate for museums. As the field-wide voice for museums of all types and sizes, we strive to provide all the tools and information needed to be an effective advocate for museums. From the annual Museums Advocacy Day and Invite Congress to Visit Your Museum initiatives, to our online advocacy campaigns and resources and the practical tools in our *Speak Up for Museums* book, we can help empower museums to make the case for their institution and all museums at the national, regional, and local levels. This case study examines how easy and important it is for everyone to Speak Up for Museums.

Overcoming Broad Misconceptions: EVERYONE Is an Advocate for Museums

Do legislators understand the value of museums? What museums do and the services they provide? Who are the right people to advocate for museums? Do my advocacy efforts make a difference? These are questions we field weekly, if not daily, since I joined the AAM back in November 2003. The answers in short order are No, No, Everyone, and YES. But I'll expand a bit further in this brief case study.

I've had the pleasure of being part of AAM's Government Relations & Advocacy program for a dozen years. My role, of course, has evolved some over that time, but its primary focus has always been helping museum professionals and supporters engage in *effective* advocacy for museums. In this time my colleagues and I continue to be struck by the misconceptions legislators and advocates sometimes have. Lots of legislators throw around that they "love the arts," but we know museums are so much more than that. And, experience shows, loving the arts doesn't necessarily equate to supporting public funding or favorable policies for the arts or museums. Moreover, I would argue that few people who work outside of museums understand the vast and varied resources required to hold, interpret, and share our nation's art, history, culture, science, and more in the public trust.

For our part, as savvy advocates, we must understand that talking *at* agreeable staff or elected officials doesn't wholly equate to a successful meeting or a nod of support. We must always be prepared to share the facts, tell a story, and *make an ask*.[1] And that is where the fun really begins!

As my time at AAM has grown, so has the experience, expertise, and engagement of the field. But I think we all know there is still a long way to go. When I started at AAM, it was a regular occurrence to have to convince museum professionals of the need to engage in regular advocacy, and that it was appropriate for them to do so, whatever their official role at their museum. Thankfully, now I'm much more likely to hear from museum professionals and supporters who love museums and want to know what more they can do to join the larger effort and advocate for them. I'm so proud to be part of this movement we have created together. I hope the following information encourages and empowers you to engage, whatever your role in the field may be.

Launching a Year-Round Advocacy Program

So, what does it take to build a movement? Would you believe it if I said practice, practice, practice?

All kidding aside, it has been a slow-and-steady, practice-makes-better undertaking over the last several years as we have all worked to make advocacy for museums a habit. First, we transitioned from fax-based (yes, fax!) communications to broad email communications.[2] Then we built an advocacy website (www.aam-us.org/advocacy)[3] that is accessible 24/7 and provides barrier-free access to finding your state and federal legislators, getting contact information for their offices and staff, and finding them on social media. The website also offers extensive legislative and policy information and resources for engaging in advocacy at every level—federal, state, and local. Tools include book and magazine chapters/articles, webinar recordings and slides, economic and educational impact statements and samples, and much more.

We helped make sure that advocacy was a habit and a practice by regularly communicating with advocates, pushing out legislative and policy updates, identifying the best way to take action (email, phone call, joining a broader effort, etc.), and providing the tools needed to take those actions.

We launched Museums Advocacy Day,[4] a day each February dedicated to ensuring that at least once a year museums and museum advocates from around the country take the message about the value of museums to the congressional offices that represent them to make the case about their significance and museums' essential roles in their communities. Of course, we realize not everyone can make that trip to Washington, D.C. And you don't have to be here in person to be an effective advocate. We developed an Advocate from Anywhere[5] toolkit so that advocates around the country can participate in conjunction with the activities on Capitol Hill, making Museums Advocacy Day a truly national day of advocacy for museums.

But advocacy is, and needs to be, a year-round activity. And aren't elected officials home in the month of August? As Museums Advocacy Day moved beyond its infancy, we had the strong desire to truly empower—not just urge—museum advocates to fully engage with their elected officials, at all levels of government, during the annual congressional recess. And to me, that meant providing an in-depth how-to guide and template tools far enough in advance of August for museums to actually take advantage of them. In 2012, Invite Congress to Visit Your Museum Week[6] was born, and in 2014 #InviteCongress[7] was born on Twitter. To me, this is the feather in the cap of our year-round advocacy initiatives. In fact, in the last four years I've heard and seen several times that this is the effort through which many museums engaged for the first time with AAM, advocacy, and their local, regional, and federal elected officials and influencers. (Thinking about that actually takes my breath away!)

Building a Movement: Creating a Cadre of Museum Advocates

Obviously, there are lots of different ways to measure advocacy success. Does it include the number of actions taken over our online advocacy website? Sure. Does it include the number of visits made and states/elected officials reached during Museums Advocacy Day and Invite Congress to Visit Your Museum Week? Yes. Does it include tracking the use of #InviteCongress and how much legislators like, share, and post about museums on social media? Of course. Should it include the simple acts of engaging your board in advocacy or bringing elected officials into the museum and starting that relationship with them? Absolutely. (You can see some of your peers' success stories on our website.[8]) And legislators are taking note, too. They have begun to notice when their colleagues get museum visits if they aren't scheduled to see museum advocates from their own state or region. Legislators and staff look forward to seeing their museum folks in February and know to prepare for those visits. They ask the museums that have developed relationships with them about how policy decisions would affect them. And they seek out the museums they represent for opportunities to visit them during in-district work periods, in August and throughout the year.

We also see how the field especially responds when there is a distinct, disarming threat, such as unfavorable votes in Congress, the near exclusion of all museums from federal stimulus packages, or budget decisions that lead to the closing of state museum systems (re: Illinois State Museum system, October 30, 2015). Those responses are powerful. But they are also good indicators of the long-term work left to be done—educating decision makers over the long haul, and hopefully someday preventing such decisions from getting made. So we persevere.

It has been truly humbling and inspiring getting to work with museums and museum advocates of all types and sizes from all backgrounds and parts of the country these last several years. Museums really are amazing places, and the multitude of people and effort it takes to keep them running is nothing short of awesome.

Writing It Down: Tell Them What You Want Them to Do, Tell Them How to Do It, and Tell Them What They Did

Advocacy may be a personal, passionate endeavor in some ways, but one thing I've learned in this time spent helping build a field-wide initiative is how much process matters and helps to turn a fleeting instinct into a feasible, regular, powerful habit and practice. I suppose this is part of what experienced yogis have come to understand about their practice, too.

What does this look like? It means that internally and externally people appreciate being given direction. And tools. And the knowledge that lets them know that they are doing the right work in an effective way. As we have built our advocacy initiatives and campaigns we have gone to great lengths to record internally the steps and resources needed (templates, guides, articles, webpages), to provide the advocacy programs and support we are committed to providing to you, the field.

This concept also drives another tenet of our advocacy program that is very near and dear to me—if we ask advocates to take action, we provide updates on the status or results of that effort. This is a critically important step both for continually educating advocates about the process, and for providing advocates a return on their investment of having responded when asked to weigh in. This is also a good practice to keep in mind as you engage your colleagues at your museum in advocacy locally, regionally, or nationally.

For our advocates (including you!) this means the more we can provide truly turnkey tools and instructions for when and how to take action, the better response we get and the more advocates get engaged. This is also where having your year-round advocacy plan and educational and economic templates in place helps reinforce the creation of a practice of advocacy, or even a culture of advocacy, at your museum. And it's a powerful thing to watch.

Keys to Success: Making Advocacy a Habit and a Call to Action

My call to action to you is to engage. Pick the one thing a month or week you feel like you can take on, and commit to making it a habit. This may be "liking" and "following" your elected officials (mayor, state representatives, senators, governor, school board, or zoning office) on social media, which will give you great insight into their positions, policies, and interests. If your museum is on social media, begin tagging your local partners and elected officials in your posts, sharing your news with them, and inviting them to participate in the museum's events.

Some museums put a standing agenda item on monthly or quarterly board or staff meetings to visit our Contact Congress online action center and send emails to their legislators on current issues affecting museums. Offer your museum as a space for elected officials or local councils to hold events or meetings, or even as a regular work space. Volunteer as a local polling place or to host naturalization and citizenship ceremonies in your community. Or you could use our Advocacy Inventory[9] to assess the advocacy assets you have to tap into. You can also use our Year Round Advocacy Plan[10] to help you get started planning.

Activity begets activity. Advocacy begets advocacy. You might be surprised by the range of results you see, whether it be more deeply engaging with your museum and community or solidifying your museum as an influencer and resource to local and regional partners and elected officials.

Notes

1. Make an ask/communicating with legislators: www.aam-us.org/advocacy/resources/communicating-with-legislators and www.aam-us.org/advocacy/resources/making-the-case-with-elected-officials.
2. Broad email communications: www.aam-us.org/advocacy/take-action/advocacy-alerts.
3. Advocacy website and advocacy resources: www.aam-us.org/advocacy and www.aam-us.org/advocacy/resources.
4. Museums Advocacy Day: www.aam-us.org/advocacy/museums-advocacy-day.
5. Advocate from Anywhere: www.aam-us.org/advocacy/museums-advocacy-day/advocate-from-anywhere.
6. Invite Congress to Visit Your Museum: www.aam-us.org/advocacy/resources/invite-congress.
7. #InviteCongress on Facebook and Twitter: https://www.facebook.com/media/set/?set=a.10152914314492364.1073741835.74952697363&type=3 and https://twitter.com/search?q=%-23inviteCongress&src=typd.
8. Success stories: www.aam-us.org/advocacy/museums-advocacy-day/success-stories.
9. Advocacy Inventory: http://www.aam-us.org/docs/default-source/advocacy/chapter3_advocacyinventory.pdf.
10. Year Round Advocacy Plan: www.aam-us.org/advocacy/resources/year-round-advocacy and www.aam-us.org/docs/default-source/advocacy/year-round-advocacy-plan.pdf.

Impact Statements— Demonstrating a Museum's Public Value

Robert P. Connolly

WHAT IS THE RELEVANCE of your museum to the community? Why should funds be provided to support this museum? These are questions that a diverse group of individuals including governing boards, grant funders, and the general public routinely ask small museums. Or as my mentor of many years ago, the late Dr. Patricia Essenpreis, told our group of assembled students during the first day of an archaeological field school, "If you cannot explain to the public why their tax dollars should support this research, you might as well go home."

At the C.H. Nash Museum at Chucalissa, a set of impact statements is one way that we answer these questions. By 2010, our governing authority, the University of Memphis (UM) experienced very serious funding cuts of up to 25 percent from the state of Tennessee. The UM administration was searching everywhere to cut corners and save money. Departments scrambled to justify their piece of the available economic pie of funding. At Chucalissa, we had the advantage of being a fifty-year-old UM institution, but the disadvantage of being in a location that is rarely visited by administrators as the site is a thirty-minute drive from the main campus. Also, the museum had been an economic drain on the university for a number of years. However, since 2007 we revamped and expanded all of our programming and became a true asset and stakeholder in the underserved community of Southwest Memphis. We also reversed a deficit economic trend, resulting in a budget surplus at the end of the 2010 fiscal year.

We needed an effective way to tell our story to the administrators who were making decisions on budget allocations. Since taking over as director at Chucalissa, I had dutifully published articles in peer-reviewed academic journals on our museum's research and community outreach. I also regularly produced the reports that our governing authority mandated. However, the UM administrators likely were not going to read my published articles and our reports were shuffled in with those of all other departments. We needed to stand out for our unique contribution to the UM mission. Ultimately, concise impact statements provided the answer to that need.

Making a Hard Copy of an Elevator Speech

I began by searching for a method to tell our story in a manner that addressed our communication needs directly. As in all else that we do at our museum, that method needed to align with both the mission of the C.H. Nash Museum "to protect and interpret the Chucalissa archaeological site's cultural and natural environments, and to provide the University Community and the public with exceptional educational, participatory, and research opportunities" and the UM's mandate "of providing high quality educational experiences while pursuing new knowledge through research, artistic expression, and interdisciplinary and engaged scholarship."

In 2010, the idea of transparent website "dashboards" of museum operations as quite popular, as exemplified by the Indianapolis Museum of Art (http://dashboard.imamuseum .org/). Although an efficient method of communication, these dashboards are typically limited to total economic and visitation trends and do not directly address mission mandates.

Flowing from the dashboard example, we produced a graphic that showed trends in regular and irregular staff hours at Chucalissa (see figure below). This graphic allowed us to present a couple of important ideas relevant to our mission. First, Chucalissa provided educational opportunities to both UM and high school students in the Memphis area,

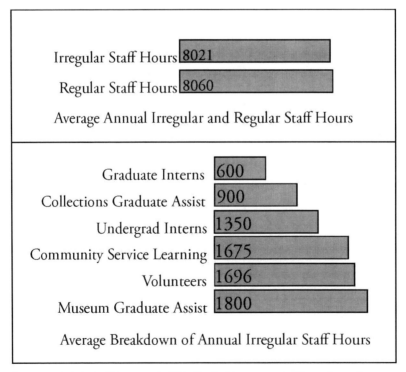

Average total staff hours at C.H. Nash Museum at Chucalissa. Source: Created by author.

along with volunteer opportunities for the general public. Second, we demonstrated that our "irregular" staff were as integral to the operation of the museum as the "regular" staff made up of full-time paid employees. Creating the graphic was simple and only required that we keep track of who was doing what at the museum—information we already collected. Since 2011 our ratio of irregular to regular staff has remained at about one to one. The impact of this graphic was significant. When the UM provost called on several top-level administrative personnel to visit the museum to make recommendations about our future, he began the meeting by saying, "I want everyone to know from the start that Chucalissa is a model for volunteerism and student engagement at the university." Obviously, these opening comments set a positive tone for what could have been an otherwise rather stressful meeting.

I began showing the regular/irregular graphic in other meetings as well. We printed and framed a copy and placed the image in public view near the museum front desk. The graphic told a good story, but it was not enough. We had a lot more to tell beyond who was contributing hours at the museum. By 2011 the American Alliance of Museums (AAM) devoted a section of their website to advocacy and published the book *Speak Up for Museums*. Initially, the AAM website's advocacy section focused primarily on building Advocacy Day lobbying events in Washington, D.C. While important, as a small museum director I liked that the *Speak Up for Museums* book and website included tools that could be used on a local level. (Ember Farber's case study in this volume discusses that topic.) The tools I immediately latched onto were the Economic and Educational Impact Statement templates and samples listed on the AAM website. This tool seemed an effective means for telling Chucalissa's performance story to both our governing authority and the general public. Chucalissa's Economic (see figure on page 110) and Educational Impact Statements are now listed as samples on the AAM website (http://www.aam-us.org/advocacy/resources/economic-impact-statement/samples), the place where I got the inspiration to develop them.

We have perhaps five hours invested in collecting and composing the information for each of the two documents—the Economic Impact Statement and the Educational Impact Statement. The layout, review, and copyedit for each document took another three hours to complete. We use Adobe's InDesign software (under $200) for such projects but they can be completed in Microsoft's Word or Publisher, or online with free software at Google Docs.

The impact statements effectively contextualize our museum with national and the local museum trends. The national information is readily available from a number of resources, including the AAM website. The local information is typically available from the area chamber of commerce or visitor and information bureau. The information specific to Chucalissa was pulled from our regular reports. All of the information contained in the impact statements was readily available and did not require a significant investment of our limited staff resources to compile.

The Results

The expected outcomes for the two impact statements were achieved on several levels. We now have two single-page two-sided documents that speak directly to performance relevant to both our museum's mission and that of our governing authority. Instead of a single bar

2015 Economic Impact Statement at the C.H. Nash
Museum at Chucalissa. Source: Created by author.

chart graphic for each individual measure, as in the case of the irregular versus the regular staff hours, we have a considerably more robust tool that provides a comprehensive measure of our performance toward our mission.

The impact statements are available on our website. As well, copies are distributed to all of our public officials, key stakeholders, and UM decision makers. We also keep copies at our front desk information rack for all visitors to see. With the impact statements, in two minutes, one can obtain a considerable amount of information about our museum operation that would take at least twenty minutes to communicate in a PowerPoint type of presentation. The statements do not require the listener to take notes of key points on a presentation—the statements are the notes that they can take with them for review long after the meeting or museum visit is over. Impact statements are the printed equivalent of the two-minute elevator speech, and much more!

Our evaluation of the effectiveness of the statements is primarily anecdotal. For example, when the dean of our college first read our Economic Impact Statement he distributed a copy to the chairs of all departments and units and encouraged them to produce a similar type of document. That our statement is featured on the AAM website is also an indication that our small museum on the outskirts of Memphis has made a meaningful contribution to a national discussion. We regularly receive compliments from visitors and UM policy makers about the effectiveness in information communication of the impact statements.

Perhaps the best evaluation measure is that the statements have formed an essential part of our information package to UM administrators who make resource allocation decisions. We are able to provide ample justification of my former mentor's admonition to "explain to the public why their tax dollars are going to support" our museum. To that end, we have experienced no budget cuts and in fact have received resource increases over the past few years. The impact statements remain a critical tool in our ability to explain the value of what we offer at the C.H. Nash Museum to a diverse group of stakeholders.

What Worked and What Didn't Work

We have learned that impact statements are very effective tools for communicating a complex set of information in a very succinct manner. The format forces us to be very concise in our presentation. We find that the concise statements are very useful as conversation starters. For example, the simple line on our Educational Impact Statement "Since 2012, AmeriCorps teams contributed more than 3000 hours of service" prompts a broader discussion of our work with AmeriCorps in community outreach, and in 2013 our museum received the Sponsor of the Year Award from the ten-state AmeriCorps NCCC Southern District.

The impact statements also changed how the UM administration evaluates aspects of our operation. For example, UM graduate assistants (GAs) are typically allocated based on whether they conduct research in their assigned area. The four GA students assigned to the C.H. Nash Museum spend a significant portion of their time in visitor services leading tours, staffing the front desk, and in group programming. However, they do spend up to 50 percent of their time performing research and creating exhibits, programs, and other products.

Rather than entering into a discussion with the UM administration on whether research should be the basis for evaluating GA student assignments, we created a Graduate Assistant Impact Statement (see Resource Guide at www.museumcommunities.com). The statement contains critical information relevant to GA students and the missions of Chucalissa and the UM. For example, since 2007, twenty-two out of twenty-three Chucalissa GA students are now employed in the cultural heritage sector. Since 2012, nine GA students received scholarships to attend professional meetings and five published peer-reviewed journal articles. Chucalissa GA students receive national awards such as fellowships to the Metropolitan Museum of Art and the Smithsonian. And since 2007 our museum GA students expended over 15,000 hours in direct-research-related training and practice. This impact statement is directly responsible for a shift in how the administration evaluates the GA students at the C.H. Nash Museum and prevents any reduction in the assigned number.

We do not want to create so many impact statements that their utility is reduced. For example, we created a Scholarly Works Impact Statement that got very little traction as it was of limited interest and primarily relevant to UM administrators. A single line on our Educational Impact Statement about staff and GA research publications is sufficient for the general public, elected public officials, and most other stakeholders. As with the example about the single line on our AmeriCorps teams, a simple statement on publications by staff is the opportunity for a more detailed in-person discussion.

Sustaining the Results and Next Steps

As with any communication tool, the information must be kept up-to-date. We also act on understanding that the need to create or update impact statements is not something to do only during times of crisis when budgets are being slashed. Rather, as with all advocacy work, impact statements can be a tool to open up dialogue and build relationships with the visitor, community stakeholder, public official, or governing authority, who all play a critical role in the promotion and preservation of cultural heritage venues in both times of economic prosperity and downturns. Impact statements are ideal for a small museum on a limited budget looking for an efficient and cost-effective way to tell their story.

Small Fish, Big Pond

How to Effectively Advocate in Your Community

Melissa Prycer

IN 2013, shortly after being named interim executive director of the Dallas Heritage Village (DHV), I was sitting in a professional development workshop taking a quiz about how connected we were with the community. The quiz deeply frustrated me—DHV is located in one of the largest metropolitan areas in the country. Major institutions in the city routinely have close to a million annual visitors. Our annual budget is barely a million dollars. The second most visited history institution in Texas (behind the Alamo) is a few minutes' drive away. To better understand some of the daunting numbers at our neighbor institutions, be sure to look at the figures on page 114. And this quiz was asking me if the mayor had ever visited my museum. And how often other city officials attended events. I asked the facilitator: "If you're a small organization in a big city, how can you begin to make those kinds of connections?" They stared at me blankly.

A few months later, I had a meeting with Joanna, who is president of the Dallas Area Cultural Advocacy Coalition (DACAC). I had seen notices of their meetings but didn't think it applied to me because I assumed it was a bunch of arts people. And then she told me that while the Office of Cultural Affairs (OCA) received the first budget increase since the recession, an arbitrary line had been drawn and only organizations with budgets of $1 million or less got an increase. Technically, six institutions fell on the other side of that line, but two of them had advocates in the room so they saw an increase. DHV wasn't one of them. That's when I started showing up to meetings—and ultimately became an advocate. Over the last few years, I've learned quite a bit about how to navigate advocacy work as a small organization in a major city.

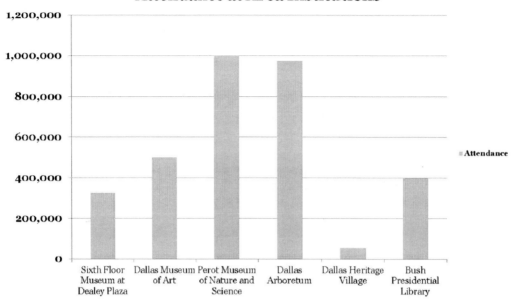

Attendance for select Dallas area cultural heritage venues. Source: Created by author.

DHV is a collection of thirty historic structures that were moved to Dallas' first city park. The park has been a central part of the Cedars Neighborhood since the 1880s (in fact, Dallas' first residential neighborhood grew up around the park), and the museum began in 1966. We are located just south of downtown, but because of a major highway, the museum and the neighborhood have never been considered part of downtown. In

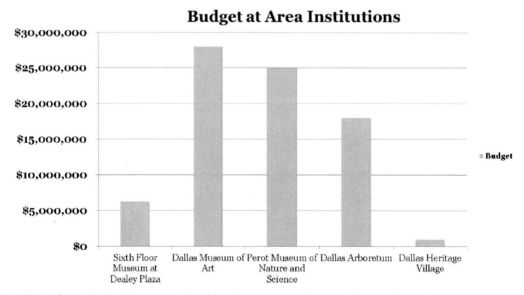

Budgets for select Dallas area cultural heritage venues. Source: Created by author.

addition, because we are south of I-30 (a perceived wealth dividing line), our concerns are often quickly dismissed. We have the blessing and curse of working with two different city departments. Our land is park land, and the Parks Department handles basic grounds care and trash. Our buildings are owned by the OCA. We also receive about $150,000 from the city for maintenance and general operations. In the past, we've had difficult relationships with these two departments and an ineffectual elected council member. We have often felt neglected simply because of our location. However, around the same time that I took over the leadership role at DHV, there was an election—and a few staff changes at the city as well.

In no particular order, here are a few stories from the last few years about our advocacy work.

Introduce Yourself and Your Institution before There's an Issue

When I returned to Dallas after attending the Seminar for Historical Administration in late 2013, one of my first priorities was to invite DHV's new council member, Adam Medrano, for a visit. However, I also wanted to properly time his visit. Winter is not a good time to visit an outdoor museum, so I waited until spring and timed his tour to take place during our annual Spring Break activities. He was able to see the museum in action on a nice spring day. During a public official's visit, make sure you spend plenty of time listening. As we talked, I learned that Adam was a former school board member, so I made sure to emphasize our educational programming. I also learned that he used to work for the Parks Department, so I made sure to point out concerns about our grounds.

Since that first meeting, Adam has visited the museum many times for meetings, fundraisers, and other events. I have also visited him at city hall. His friendship to both me and the museum has been invaluable. Currently, the Cedars neighborhood is undergoing massive redevelopment. The ability to work with Adam through these development projects will help ensure that our place in the neighborhood remains secure.

Keep an Eye on Local Politics

Even though our relationship with Adam is excellent, he is just one council member. Adam is part of a small, progressive group of council members who are trying to change the way things have always been done in Dallas. These changes are already being felt in conversations about the future of our city, and we are certainly sensing some changes in the way that we are able to work with city staff.

It is essential to keep up with the twists and turns of local politics. I rely heavily on social media, following key council members. We are also lucky enough to have an "anonymous" source, Wylie H. Dallas, who posts all sorts of interesting articles that spark conversation. Following Wylie's page has alerted me to all sorts of simmering issues, and later, I'm able to use this knowledge in conversations with other civic leaders. Even though I rely on social media, I still get the daily newspaper. Perhaps newspapers are dying, but flipping through the daily paper is still an excellent way to keep up with the local community.

The only way you'll be able to sense any kind of shift in local politics—whether for good or for ill—is if you're keeping up with the political scene. For example, if you're receiving money from the city, a conversation about deferred maintenance in the streets department may impact your funding. Keeping current will help you scan the horizon for potential threats or opportunities.

Keep an Eye on Your Neighborhood

Do you know your neighbors? Are new developers coming in? If you're in an area with a neighborhood association, become friends with the neighborhood association. Attend meetings. Offer to host meetings. Over a decade ago, Dallas Heritage Village helped found the Cedars Neighborhood Association (CNA). There had been an earlier association that had gradually faded, so they decided to start again. The executive director at the time, Gary Smith; a handful of the artists; and a visionary developer were the main organizers. Gary did not want to be a president of the group, but he agreed to "give" them a staff member for one year to help get things properly set up. At first, the main emphasis was on crime watch meetings. Then, the Cedars Open Studios (an annual neighborhood tour of artist studios) idea became more important. Though DHV's level of involvement with the CNA has varied over the years, we remain members.

Our neighborhood, the Cedars, is going through some massive redevelopment—six major projects within walking distance of the museum, including nonprofits, residential, and office space. Over the years, I've built a solid relationship with one of the key neighborhood advocates, Michael Przekwas. Because of that relationship, I find out things before anyone else. If a "For Sale" sign goes up on a building, I'm not surprised. I know who has an offer on something and who I need to reach out to. We have organized multiple meetings between these diverse new neighbors. Developers aren't generally known for their ability to communicate or talk to each other, but they can come together at DHV to discuss general neighborhood improvements, partnerships, and more. They see us as Switzerland—we're not hoping for one project to be more successful than another. We want all of the projects to be successful.

Keeping up with the changes in the neighborhood has also landed me in meetings at city hall (sometimes as the only female or nonprofit person at the table). In the last year, I've also been a part of strategic plan meetings with urban planners about the future of downtown and conversations with traffic engineers about the highways encircling our city. These aren't the type of meetings that museum directors typically attend, but as a part of the community, it's crucial that we are at the table. This work has also enabled me to help shape how people are talking about this newly discovered historic neighborhood. Because of our long relationship with the CNA, I'm not the only one at key meetings talking about the neighborhood gem. It has been incredibly gratifying to attend meetings and hear other voices talk about ways to strengthen Dallas Heritage Village.

Build Your Local Network

Five years ago, a colleague and I co-founded the Informal Educators of Dallas County. We did it out of frustration at seeing the same faces at meetings hosted by ArtsPartners but never getting time to network and build relationships. The simplest way to explain ArtsPartners is that it's the mechanism through which Dallas Independent School District (ISD) books and funds the vast majority of its field trips.

Fast-forward to fall 2014: Dallas ISD makes a decision that ArtsPartners-funded field trips have to be arts-related field trips, effectively leaving out history and science. Within days, we got a meeting together of educators from key institutions to start discussing advocacy strategy. We wouldn't have been able to do that if we hadn't already built that network.

I am the only executive director in town that is a former educator, so though I led the smallest organization, I was the one that wrote the letter to Dallas ISD and led the meeting with the superintendent. We got our funding back—and it was increased. Size of institution doesn't necessarily equal political power or advocacy leadership. That's certainly something I learned during this experience.

Show Up—Even if You Don't Think It Applies to You

In February 2015, I got an invitation to a transportation task force meeting to update a strategic plan from 2011. This group, Downtown Dallas Inc. (DDI), has historically ignored us because we're "not downtown." My first thought: This must be a mistake. My second thought: Well, I'm going anyway. After all, one of our major borders is an interstate.

So, I did my homework, pulled up the existing transportation plan, and discovered that there was a proposed streetcar line through the middle of our property—on a street that had been grass for several years at the time this plan was released. And with that, I had no problem fitting that meeting into my schedule.

It was good that I went—there were lots of voices besides mine that talked about the need to connect DHV with the rest of downtown. Since then I've been invited to a planning meeting for the Texas Department of Transportation and we've become a more integral part of the planning process for the new DDI plan. Their executive vice president joined our board in the fall of 2015. Never in my wildest dreams did I think I would get involved with transportation planning (and these are not meetings that my predecessor was ever invited to), but these conversations could have enormous long-term benefits for the museum.

Data Are Essential

In 2009, a severe hailstorm hit DHV. We later discovered major damage to four flat roofs on Main Street at DHV, and experts said all four should be replaced. We followed city policy on major damage and learned that the city had switched insurance (remember, the city owns our buildings and is supposed to be responsible for maintenance). As the new insurance deductible is $1 million, the city basically said, "Oh well. You fix it." Gary, my predecessor, fought the city response. The city recommended that we buy insurance on the buildings, but no insurance company will do that. Eventually, the city agreed to replace one of the roofs.

In 2011, the repair work finally happened, after much pestering. By 2014, as often happens, the roofs, especially on the Law Office, had become steadily worse. Two things happened in the lead-up to the approval of the 2014–2015 city budget: (1) DHV's council member publicly said "DHV is a pet project of mine and I'm trying to find some more money for ya'll" and (2) another council member (who is very good friends with my council member) started making deferred maintenance on city-owned cultural facilities an issue. Another point in favor of keeping an eye on local politics!

Shortly after the budget was passed, I asked for a meeting with Adam, DHV's council member. I gave him the entire list of deferred maintenance projects, complete with cost estimates and priorities. I highlighted the items I felt the city should pay for, namely roofs. I mentioned that the Law Office roof had reached the point where catastrophic structural damage was just around the corner. He said he'd see what the council could do. My hope was to maybe get some extra dollars in the 2015–2016 budget.

At the same time, the longtime director of the Office of Cultural Affairs (our department for city funding) finally left. She had always been very difficult to work with. An interim director for OCA was named. In 2015, the interim director called a meeting in January to discuss the future of cultural organizations in Dallas. The last time OCA called a meeting was in 2008. Deferred maintenance came up, so I chatted with the interim after the meeting, and he said that he was aware of our concerns. He agreed to meet with me. Two weeks later, he came to DHV with two colleagues. (His predecessor came to DHV twice in her nine years—and had to ask for directions. City hall is about six blocks away.) Conveniently enough, it was a misty, rainy day and the Law Office roof was actively dripping. He said he'd see what he could do. A few weeks passed. He magically found $45,000 and we were able to repair all three roofs. Ironically, once we received the money, the wettest May on record for Dallas happened, and delayed the work a bit. But, I'm very happy to report that we have completed the repairs!

First moral of the story: Lists and data work. I've had to drag my curator kicking and screaming into making real lists of our needs—and assigning costs to them—but now I can just point to our roofs when she complains again. It wouldn't have happened without that list—and the price tag.

Second moral of the story (and another lesson learned): Be patient and persistent. It can take a long time for advocacy efforts to bear fruit. Getting the roofs repaired took almost a year—and if you count from when the damage actually occurred, six years. At times, it can feel that all you're doing is planting seeds. Not all of the seeds will bear fruit, but you never know what opportunities might blossom.

You Don't Have to Be a Lone Advocate

At the time I became involved with the Dallas Area Cultural Advocacy Coalition in 2014, the economy was starting to bounce back from the 2008 recession. However, the funding for the OCA was the only line item in the entire city of Dallas budget that wasn't back at 2008 levels. That summer, I found myself at my very first Budget Town Hall meeting, advocating for the arts. Of course, I wasn't alone—we had a whole team of advocates spread across the city. Not only did we get the increase we were fighting for—OCA also got $50,000 over the amount we requested. In this last budget cycle, the OCA budget went up again, and for the first time in the city's history, the arts are getting a portion of the Hotel-Motel Tax revenue. (Previously, the entire amount had funded the Convention and Visitor's Bureau.)

Though I'm frequently the only representative of a history museum at these meetings, my presence reminds city hall of the full array of cultural opportunities in the city. It also helps me to keep up with what's going on in the larger community. And most importantly, my voice alone at city hall won't do much to garner an increase in our city funding—but the voices together can certainly make a difference. After about a year of regularly attending DACAC meetings, participating in advocacy efforts, and more, I was asked to join the steering committee for the organization.

Though you may not have an arts advocacy group in your community, remember that your board and staff can also play an important advocacy role. However, finding a group of local professionals, whether it's an arts group or nonprofit coalition, can be invaluable. We need to make sure we have friends, especially locally, that aren't part of the history museum world.

Closing Thoughts

As a former educator, my heart will always lean toward the warm and fuzzy stories of community engagement. But from a practical standpoint, community engagement is so much more than audience development—it also means advocacy. It means getting involved in local politics—not just making sure the local politicians are invited to your events, but making sure you're being included in the important conversations shaping your city. Sometimes it means showing up at meetings that may only have a peripheral connection to your organization. Most importantly, it means educating yourself on the issues, whether it's urban planning, homelessness, or traffic flow. My job has changed in profound ways as a result of these efforts, and it's also changing my museum. We're becoming more externally focused, more flexible, and more creative. We're becoming a community anchor, not just for the Cedars, but for all of Dallas.

This is work that will never be done. It is work that should begin immediately, before there is a crisis. By building relationships within the community today, it will be easier to weather future storms. As we at DHV deal with homeless encampments, neighborhood development, highway planning, and more, I know that we have an army of advocates with us, ready to fight when we need them.

Part IV

MUSEUMS ENGAGING WITH PEOPLE AS A COMMUNITY RESOURCE

Robert P. Connolly

A S THE DIRECTOR of the C.H. Nash Museum at Chucalissa (CHNM) and an instructor in the Museum Studies Graduate Certificate Program at the University of Memphis, I am in regular contact with a broad range of graduate and undergraduate students in both classroom and museum settings. I routinely pose this question to students: "Why do museums exist?" The answer I am looking for is "Because of the visitors," and the students understand my reasoning pretty quickly. I argue were it not for the visitor, our museums would be either artifact repositories or research facilities. The visitor who walks through the door is what makes a museum a museum. This understanding is explicitly or implicitly stated in all museum mission statements.

This part of the volume considers the ways that museums serve as a community resource for that visiting public. I use my experiences at the CHNM as a framework for presenting the range of engagement types. Chucalissa is an ideal venue to develop a model for a small museum's community engagement. The CHNM is located on the grounds of a prehistoric Native American earthwork complex. With an annual budget of under $250,000, a full-time staff of four, supported by about twenty-five hours per week of combined part-time staffing, the CHNM qualifies as a typical small museum. Founded in the mid-twentieth century amid Jim Crow era segregation policies, in the past the CHNM had been viewed as an enclave of white academic privilege. The University of Memphis has administered the CHNM and the Chucalissa archaeological site since 1962.

As a longtime tourist destination to learn about Native American prehistory, the CHNM had a public persona of passive public viewing of active archaeological research. However, in the past decade, Chucalissa evolved to serve as an incubator to involve students and the general public in a host of experimental and experiential opportunities beyond traditional archaeological research. Also, students are now drawn to CHNM through the University's Museum Studies Graduate Certificate Program, internships, and class projects. A wide variety of geographic and interest-based communities are now active at the CHNM.

At the outset of this part, I pose another critical question for consideration. In an article published in 2011, I asked the question "If there were an opportunity for an unlimited number of paid staff at museums would we still recruit volunteers to assist in collections work?" In this paper we answer that question with a resounding yes.[1] The response meant that museums do not engage with communities only to satisfy an institutional need, such as compensating for staff shortages. Rather, museums engage with their communities because their missions mandate that public service. When museums truly function as a community resource the relationship is reciprocal.

This part focuses on four ways that museums can function as a resource for their support communities. First, I take up how museums can serve the expressed needs of the local community. Second, the role of engaging with a community's student and volunteer needs is considered. Third, I discuss how museums can promote a movement for local cultural heritage presentation and preservation. Finally, the possibility of museums serving as a Third Place is explored. All four of these points are based in both the community needs and the institutional needs of the museum. That is, the relationship is reciprocal.

Taking Steps to Respond to Community-Expressed Needs

John Cotton Dana's clarion call in 1917 "Learn what aid the community needs: fit the museum to those needs" is of particular importance in planning local community engagement. Instead of second-guessing the type of engagement that a community might desire, an important first step is to ask the community of their interest and be prepared to act on the response. In a case study in this section, Allison Hennie details how interviewing community members about the very purpose and function of a proposed museum provided the board of directors with insights not considered when initially conceptualizing the institution's mission statement and strategic plan.

Taking a similar approach at the CHNM, several years ago we began to reach out to the community surrounding the museum. We asked community members, "What role would you like for this museum to play in Southwest Memphis?" We found the key was not just asking the question but acting on the responses that fell within our mission. In one instance, we revised our mission statement to better serve our community's needs. Below are two examples of acting on a community's expressed needs from our experience at the CHNM.

Initiating Black History Month

In 2010, after high school students created a community-based cultural heritage exhibit at the CHNM,[2] we held a meeting to discuss additional projects residents might wish to pursue. We hoped to continue and deepen the activity generated through the exhibit creation. About twenty individuals, composed of students, community stakeholders, and CHNM staff, attended the planning meeting. In initial discussion all attendees reported how much they enjoyed their roles in the exhibit project, and the importance of cultural heritage to their community identity. The meeting produced considerable intergenerational dialogue between senior citizens and the high school students in attendance.

After a forty-five-minute discussion, the conversation hit a road block. The community participants clearly wanted to see the cultural heritage process continue but did not have a clear vision on the next steps. A CHNM staff member asked if Black History Month events occurred in the community. The response was negative but sparked the idea of how to continue the cultural heritage project. The next February the CHNM hosted the first ever Black History Month Celebration in Southwest Memphis. The event consisted of a diverse set of presentations on aspects of cultural heritage that ranged from collecting genealogies to the legacy of the 1968 Memphis sanitation workers strike.

The Black History Month Celebration is now an annual event at the CHNM. Over the past six years, the museum has played an increasingly smaller role in the organization of the event. The community residents determine the theme and organize the program. For example, in 2015 community members chose the theme Women Who Led the Way. The event featured presentations by Bertha Looney, one of the Memphis 8 who desegregated Memphis State University in 1958, and Georgia Harris, a U.S. Air Force major who served in Thailand during the Vietnam War era. Following the speakers, a film was shown on the 1972 presidential campaign of Shirley Chisholm. In 2016, the celebration was co-sponsored with a local charter school (see case study by Abdalla and Pender, this volume). Since its inception in 2011, the Black History Month Celebration has grown in size with the complete responsibility for the coordination now resting with the community. The CHNM hosts the event and provides a light lunch.

Launching an Urban Garden

In the spring of 2011, the CHNM held several focus groups to obtain input on the pending redesign of the main hall exhibits. One of the focus groups was composed of community residents. The group noted that they were not particularly interested, nor did they offer much input on the redesign of the Native American main hall exhibits. One resident did single out the traditional food exhibit because it reminded him of his youth when traditional foods were grown in his neighborhood. He lamented that today because of vandalism and pollution, there was no safe place in the community for a public urban garden.

The Chucalissa complex is located on 100 acres of open and forested land in the southwest corner of Memphis and is adjacent to the 1,400 acres that comprise the T.O. Fuller State Park. The CHNM grounds would provide an ideal protected environment for an urban garden. Within days of the focus group, the CHNM proposed several spaces for an urban garden. The community residents chose a plot and started to work. The residents take full control and responsibility for the planting, maintenance, and harvesting of the garden. In exchange, the CHNM incorporates the garden as an exhibit of traditional foods to supplement the adjacent Three Sisters (corn, beans, and squash) Native American garden.

Since the urban garden's first season in 2011, the community residents have maintained the space. Participation has expanded to include AmeriCorps NCCC team members, area high school students, and other volunteers. In the summer of 2016, an intern from the University of Memphis centralized the programming and activities of the urban garden with five other garden spaces at the Chucalissa site complex. However, throughout the years, the community residents remain in complete control of the planting, harvest, and distribution of all the vegetables grown.

Being a Community Resource

The urban garden and Black History Month examples demonstrate the need to actively solicit the input of the community residents on how they wish to engage with a museum. Quite clearly, neither the Black History Month Celebration nor the urban garden would have occurred without following Dana's mandate to fit the museum to the needs of the community. In both instances, the fit was well within the parameters of the CHNM mission and the community interest.

Such co-creative processes most often do not occur naturally from community expectations of cultural heritage venues. Museums are often considered elitist institutions where visitors passively view what the venue chooses to offer. That is, the perception is one of a deficit model where the museum is charged with filling in the deficiencies in the community's knowledge on a specific issue.

In the two examples discussed above, the CHNM did not have the expertise in either Black history or in urban gardens that the community brought to the table. Ashley Rogers's case study in this section from the Whitney Plantation in Louisiana is another example of the essential need to base projects on community knowledge. Whitney directly captures the local community's experience to tell the history of the enslaved peoples from the pre–Civil War era to the sharecropper era of the twentieth century. This is not a story that Whitney staff can tell on its own without the input of the descendants of those enslaved people. In so doing, the Whitney becomes a resource for the community to discover and embrace their own cultural heritage.

Community Service and Applied Learning Education— A Win-Win for All

A museum's reliance on volunteers is often crucial to the very survival of the institution. But opportunities extend far beyond staffing just to keep the doors open and to administer programs. When I welcome visitors to the CHNM, I always note that whatever they see that is "shiny and new" was likely created by a student for a class project or internship, by a volunteer, or one of our graduate assistants.

When counseling students on their career paths, I encourage them to get a second opinion. I suggest that they solicit advice from a listserv such as Museum-L that is subscribed to by thousands of museum professionals. After all, these are the individuals who will hire the emerging museum professionals in their careers. A consistent response that students receive from these museum professionals is that employers are less concerned with an applicant's academic credentials compared to the hands-on experience they bring to the job. For this reason, students are well advised to seek out experiences where they can develop those skills. At the CHNM we have maximized the potential of community service learning for students.[3]

As any museum professional quickly learns, students and volunteers should not be considered "free" labor any more than grants should be considered "free" money. That is, to successfully incorporate students and volunteers into any task, the museum must be prepared to invest in the process. Volunteers who are brought into a chaotic situation with no guidance will quickly burn out and not return. Legal considerations aside, student participants and interns who are simply treated as unpaid or low-paid labor will perform thusly. Adequately determining the type of service-learning opportunities available at an institution ensures that adequate steps are taken to maximize the potential for success. Below are some points to consider in this process.

Recruiting Pre-trained or In-training Support

At CHNM we have hosted six NCCC AmeriCorps teams since 2012. In a unique combination of community outreach to perform repairs on the homes of elderly in need and projects directly at the CHNM, the AmeriCorps teams have proven very successful. In fact, because of this work in 2013 the CHNM was named Sponsor of the Year in AmeriCorps' nine-state Southern District. At the CHNM, AmeriCorps teams have built several structures including rain shelters and a thirty-square-foot pergola, repurposed and upgraded exhibit space, processed archaeological materials, worked with visitors, and much more. The teams consist of highly motivated eighteen- to twenty-five-year-old individuals who commit one year of their lives to national service. Of importance, for many assigned tasks, the teams are pre-trained either during their AmeriCorps orientation period or by skills the individuals bring to the project. Through the application process team skills are matched to sponsor needs.

The AmeriCorps process is an opportunity for the resource-stretched small museum. The museum must provide supervisory personnel, but the team is composed of individuals who hit the ground running. The museum must have a well-thought-out project, with a solid timetable and materials for completion. The AmeriCorps team brings the skills and personnel to complete the project.

The AmeriCorps NCCC is a model of an efficient and coordinated pre-trained service-learning crew available for museums. Other examples of service-learning opportunities include Boy Scout Eagle Scout projects, alternative college spring break groups, campus service-learning organizations, Master Gardener Associations, and Rotary Clubs, to name just a few. Advance planning by a museum to adequately define the needs and resources is needed to ensure success.

As Part of Total Staff

At the CHNM, we completely integrate all volunteers, service learners, and interns into the total staff of museum personnel. We refer to them as "irregular staff" compared to "regular staff"—but they are staff, all the same. (See case study by Connolly in Part III of this volume for details on this distinction.) We demonstrate that the irregular staff role is as integral to the success of the museum as that of the director. All staff positions require an application, interview, and orientation process. Expectations are clearly explained for all positions. The Resource Guide for this volume (www.museumcommunities.com) contains several links to organizations and forms on this process.

A key understanding for irregular staff members is the reciprocal nature of the relationship. At the CHNM—whether interns, volunteers, or students working on class projects—all individuals receive mentoring and training in all tasks they perform. No one is treated as unpaid labor. For example, graduate assistants are able to add two years of hands-on experience to their resumes through activities completed during their tenures at the CHNM.[4] All interns complete projects that can be listed on their resumes.[5] With some regularity, volunteers gain experience working with our collections that leads to entry-level positions with area cultural heritage employers.

Because of the reciprocal nature of these relationships at the CHNM, we have developed a regional reputation as a place where irregular staff can thrive, gain experience, and be personally fulfilled. At the same time, the irregular staff is absolutely crucial to the existence of the CHNM. Because of the commitment we make and our clear expectations for irregular staff, we are able to recruit and focus our attention on motivated learners in our community.

Community Cultural Heritage—Whose Voice?

Small museums in particular are natural links to promote their community's cultural heritage. In fact, most of the case studies in this volume either directly or indirectly are examples where museums play this role. This type of engagement demonstrates that it is not the museum that is telling the community story, but the community is telling its own story through the museum. This approach invites community ownership and support for the small museum. In addition to the Whitney Plantation example discussed previously, the case study by Suzanne Francis-Brown at the University of the West Indies Museum is an example of this opportunity. An example from the CHNM illustrates how empowering a community's voice can evolve over time.

Native Americans—From Actors to Directors

At the CHNM, Native Americans served as interpreters beginning in the 1950s. However, their original role was more of being actors on the stage with a script provided. The topics and the very words were set by the CHNM administrators, archaeologists, and anthropologists, to provide an experience deemed appropriate for Memphis schoolchildren and other visitors. The voice was not that of the indigenous people. The CHNM was certainly not alone in this approach, which has evolved considerably over the past fifty years. Today the indigenous voice is more prominent in museum exhibits and programs than at any time in the past.

Still, a significant distinction remains in creating exhibits and programs that are *about* Native American communities and those that are *by* those same communities. In 2008 at Chucalissa the Native American interpreters were asked to provide content for a new exhibit on the history of the Native American staff at the CHNM. The process was slow and initially unproductive. Ultimately, the interpretive staff noted they had never been asked to provide this type of information before and questioned the value of their histories. This sentiment is not uncommon. The same response was encountered when the CHNM approached the African American community of Southwest Memphis to tell their story.

For the Native American history, a solution to this dilemma involved first engaging the tribal cultural heritage professionals to obtain their direct input. Over the past decade at CHNM the scope of Native American cultural heritage representation has evolved. Initially, the CHNM drew largely on the prehistory of Native American lifeways, but now also includes the story of the contemporary communities. This shift aligns with the focus desired by the tribal authorities—that Native American cultures continue to this day and are not remnants of the past. In 2008 we asked the Chickasaw Nation to consider establishing an exhibit at the CHNM. Their director of museums asked what we wanted the exhibit to be about. Our response was, "What do you want the people of Memphis to know about the Chickasaw Nation?" The exhibit was produced thusly. That response has led to a solid and growing partnership with the Chickasaw Nation over the past decade.

CHNM exhibits about both the Chickasaw Nation and the Mississippi Band of Choctaw are now directly controlled and the content approved by those tribal authorities. In several instances, the respective tribal specialists fully produced and installed the exhibits. The relationship is reciprocal. Our CHNM staff and network includes anthropologists and archaeologists that are called on to consult on prehistoric interpretation and to provide scripts and cultural materials at tribal museums and cultural centers.

The sum of these experiences with the tribal authorities of the Native American communities has led to an increased commitment and engagement of local Native American individuals living in the Memphis area as well. We now have local contacts with tribal members who review and promote our exhibits. Local Native Americans participate in volunteer and other service activities. For example, local Native Americans were critical in tagging photos and identifying individual participants in festivals and other cultural events held at the CHNM over the past fifty years.

For the small museum, direct engagement with the communities interpreted in exhibits is not just a matter of broadening participation. Rather, the participation is necessary to best tell the story of the community. Local members are often the sole resource of the unwritten history of their communities. This fact is demonstrated in several examples presented in this volume (see case studies by Cruzado and Valerio; Rogers; Abdalla and Pender; Frances-Browne; Wildermuth and others).

Third Place

In his 1991 book *The Great Good Place,* sociologist Ray Oldenburg is credited with coining the term "Third Place," which is neither work nor home, but a place where people gather to socialize and be in community. A key element of the third place is being accessible to anyone in a community regardless of economic, social, or other status. But why is the third place an important discussion for museums? The third place idea is relevant to build more engaged relationships with visitors as a social asset to the community. The engagement is not just a matter of building attendance and revenue streams, but, rather, central to a museum's function as a community stakeholder and partner.

Numerous cultural heritage institutions have successfully developed third place environments. For example, at the Sunwatch Village, a circa 1200–1500 AD American Indian site and museum near Dayton, Ohio, site manager Andy Sawyer developed regular concert gatherings of the Native American community through the Miami Valley Flute Circle. These public concerts have a strong community-building component. Visitors are encouraged to bring their picnic dinners, visit, and turn the gathering into a true social event. The Flute Circle is different from a typical festival or powwow event in their regularity (monthly) and the community component of both Native and non-Native participants. Conceptually, the Flute Circle is similar to a series of Sunday evening concerts in the park or coffeehouse, only in a museum setting. Of added significance is the relevancy of a Native American musical form being played at a traditional Native American site.

Another example of the third place is at the Walker Art Center of Minneapolis's Open Field project that invites the public to use the space surrounding the museum building as a cultural commons. During a Saturday visit to the Walker Art Center, I found that the activities in the Open Field consisted of a coffee shop/lounge space for refreshments and visiting, an area for Hula-Hoop contests, drawing, lounging, WiFi, and art projects. There is no fee to take part in any of the Open Field activities.

The Sunwatch and Walker Art Center are two examples of how the third place concept is applicable to museums. Third places seem a logical direction for museums in an era of heightened demands for an engaged visitor experience. Pragmatically, as museum staff sizes either stagnate or shrink, developing venues as third places where visitors become more active as institutional stakeholders is an important step. In this capacity, the distinction between volunteer, visitor, participant, and stakeholder likely will develop more gray area. Mary Wildermuth's case study of the Muscatine History and Industry Center and Melanie Adams's discussion of the Missouri History Museum in this volume are also examples of third place opportunities.

Conclusion

In this section I have touched on just a few of the many examples in which museums can serve as resources for the specific needs and interests of the many publics that make up their communities. As the examples at the C.H. Nash Museum and the other case studies in this section show, the ability of the museum to engage with the diversity of communities is key to the survival of the cultural heritage institutions.

The key understanding in this work is the reciprocal nature of the relationship. In all of the examples reported in this section, viewed solely from the perspective of museum administration and function, the projects can be viewed as a one-way relationship where the museum receives what the community can provide. This could be the view taken for the examples of the NCCC AmeriCorps, students, and Native Americans. However, the reciprocal nature of the relationship comes in understanding that the NCCC AmeriCorps teams make a commitment to one year of community service for which a museum can provide the opportunities. The students have a need for applied learning experiences and museums can fill that need. Native Americans wish to tell their stories and break through public stereotypes about their culture and museums are ideally situated to fill that need. A wide diversity of volunteers desire to contribute their skills and energy to worthwhile projects and museums can provide those opportunities as well. However, as the saying goes, "There is no free lunch," and the reciprocal nature of the relationship means that museums must be prepared to provide the services that communities desire.

Notes

1. Robert P. Connolly and Natalye B. Tate, "Volunteers as Mission," *Collections* 7 (2011): 325.
2. Robert P. Connolly, "Co-creation as a Twenty-First Century Archaeological Museum Practice," *Advances in Archaeological Practice*s 3(2015): 188–97.
3. I have blogged extensively about service learning and applied experiences provided by students at the C.H. Nash Museum. For example see https://rcnnolly.wordpress.com/2013/09/02/thoughts-on-how-to-get-a-museum-job/, https://rcnnolly.wordpress.com/2012/02/13/students-as-irregular-museum-staff/, and https://rcnnolly.wordpress.com/2015/01/26/museum-practices-and-co-creation/. A session held at the 2014 AASLH Annual Conference discusses opportunities and the legal caveats for student internships. See http://resource.aaslh.org/view/big-impact-for-small-museums-internships-as-a-win-win-win-for-all-participants/.
4. See link for Graduate Assistant Impact Statement that details their role at the CHNM: https://rcnnolly.files.wordpress.com/2016/05/2015-chuc-ga-impact.pdf.
5. A session held at the 2014 AASLH Annual Conference discusses opportunities and the legal caveats for student internships. See http://resource.aaslh.org/view/big-impact-for-small-museums-internships-as-a-win-win-win-for-all-participants/.

Taking Steps to Make a Museum Special-Needs Friendly

Colleen McCartney

FOR VISITORS with special needs, it is critical that a museum or other cultural venue accommodate those needs to ensure a meaningful visit. One in five people in the United States has a special physical or cognitive need. To serve this substantive segment of the population museums must make adaptations to be inclusive and accessible. At the C.H. Nash Museum at Chucalissa, I created or updated programming and adaptations to make the institution inclusive for visitors with special needs. In this case study, I review the methods for creating these programs, the lessons learned, and some general guidelines for such a project.

First Steps in Developing a Plan

Before starting to make our museum more inclusive of visitors with special needs, I carried out a bit of background research on our museum's visitation. I needed to determine the exact special needs of visitors to Chucalissa. These needs were quite different from what I expected. For example, based on interviews with parents, teachers, and caretakers our visitors with special needs included a significant number of people who were blind, hearing impaired, or autistic. This background research proved to be critically important to the process.

Creating Programs and Experiences

After the initial background research, the remainder of our project was organized in three phases: literature and organizational research, interviews, and program creation.

Literature and Organizational Research

I began with a literature review on best practices for becoming an institution inclusive of individuals with special needs. The review covered topics such as current perspectives on disability theory; museum theory on special-needs visitor experience; educational programming in museums and school curriculums; and national, state, and local disability laws. One resource I found particularly helpful was *The Disabilities Studies Reader* by Lennard J. Davis, which contains material on the historical, political, and cultural perspectives about people with disabilities. I also found that our state's (Tennessee's) special education standards were very insightful. The standards gave me a clearer picture of the curriculum expectations, as well as the specific special education programs that teachers currently use in the classroom.

After my initial literature review, I focused on researching professional museum organizations with experience in addressing inclusivity in special needs. These organizations offered a broad set of guidelines and resources. For example, the American Alliance of Museums' (AAM's) website contains a page devoted to special-needs issues and links to articles and museums that have developed these programs.[1]

I then shifted my focus to organizations that advocate for people with special needs. A quick Internet search produced many results on the national, state, and local levels. These organizations include schools, nonprofits, group homes, parental support groups, social groups, and treatment centers. For example, the national special-needs advocacy organization Best Buddies' website contains descriptions, links, and local chapter contact information. Throughout my project the Best Buddies' local contact proved particularly helpful in developing our museum's plan. During my research I also consulted with local schools, after-school programs, caretaking, and rehabilitation centers.

Interviews

With my list of national and local organizations, I set up meetings with their representatives to gain insights into the next appropriate steps I should take in developing our inclusivity plan. I found that getting a variety of perspectives was extremely helpful. A teacher, a caretaker, a disability rights advocate, and individuals with special needs provided insightful yet different views on the process a museum should take to create a special-needs plan.

For my interviews I met with contacts individually to create a personal connection. Alternatively, a small focus group allows participants to bounce ideas off of each other. Importantly, I created my interview questions beforehand. Sample questions included:

- Have you visited the C.H. Nash Museum?
- Did you have a good or bad experience?
- What did you like?
- What should our museum change to better accommodate special needs?
- What do you look for in a museum to be inclusive of people with special needs?

I made sure the questions did not deviate from the project goals yet incorporated the different interviewee areas of expertise. For example, for the interview of a teacher, I focused on the educational aspects of special needs. These considerations allowed my interviews to gather a broad scope of relevant information.

Program Creation

After gathering information from the literature review and interviews I began to incorporate those data into a plan to make our museum programming and overall visitor experience special-needs friendly. I focused on the recurring themes of needs obtained from my research. Interactivity, flexibility, and staff preparedness were the three key points raised in all of my research phases. From these points I created a staff training resource guide, multiple hands-on adaptations to our existing educational programs, and a guide to allow staff and visitors flexible options while touring our museum. For example, with our visitors who are visually impaired, when participating in our hunting and sports program, we now are certain to allow additional opportunities for the tactile examination of prehistoric spears in preparing the visitor for the hands-on portion of the program. This option allows the visitor a more clear understanding of the size and material properties of the tools. This small change in programming has made a big difference in the experience of our visitors who are visually impaired.

We applied a similar approach to other museum projects such as the renovation of our Hands-On Archaeology Discovery Lab. During the design phase of the renovation, the room layout was calculated to ensure ready access to all hands-on exhibits and stations, to accommodate the needs of all visitors.

Lessons Learned and Results

Overall, the project to make our museum inclusive for visitors with special needs was very successful and provided many insights. A few of the lessons learned include:

- At least initially, we found partnering with a single special-needs provider, such as Best Buddies, proved most beneficial. Multiple partnerships early on can cause an institution to spread itself too thin and ultimately create superficial relationships. We found that working primarily through Best Buddies allowed us to build a solid foundation that we could later expand to other service providers. In so doing, we found the partnership that will best benefit the museum and the community.
- Staying connected with our interviewees proved invaluable. This strategy allowed a networking opportunity to spread the word about our accessibility project. Also, as the advocacy staff for service providers can frequently change, staying in touch on a regular basis is important to maintain an institutional relationship.
- A reasonable timeline for project implementation is important. Consider the need to prototype with small groups in advance of full implementation. Hosting a special event promoted among contacts obtained during the project is an ideal opportunity to showcase and test new programs.

- Although perhaps intuitive for the experienced interviewer, I learned the need for a quiet place and taking copious notes in addition to a digital recording proved critical to have a clear and well-documented interview for later consultation.

Guides for Training

Along with the guidelines discussed below, there are many resources for training staff to be inclusive of people with special needs. The Office of Disability Rights' website has several guidebooks, manuals, videos, and links on these topics. Local and state government agencies often provide resources. The Scope Company's #EndTheAwkward campaign created videos that with humor perfectly capture the dos and don'ts of interacting with people who have a special need. The videos feature examples of real-life situations that show how awkward things can get but also how easily a trained staff can accommodate special needs. The United States Office of Disability Rights has a similar training video. You can find links to these videos in the Resource Guide.

General Guidelines

Beyond some of the specific program applications noted above, a list of general staff guidelines will create a hospitable and inclusive environment for all visitors. This type of list works great as a worksheet in a staff binder so that everyone is aware of best practices for visitors with special needs. (In the Resource Guide you will find a link to a general guideline sheet I created in my project.)

Be certain to:

- Be patient—Remember that people with special needs might take a bit of time to respond to a question or move down a hallway or look at an exhibit. Just because they might take more time does not mean they aren't enjoying the experience. Being patient shows understanding and acceptance and is critical to making your museum feel inclusive to all visitors.
- Be flexible—The typical tour might need to be changed for a group of children with autism or a group of visitors in wheelchairs. Don't let these changes, even if they are a surprise, fluster you or distract from the tour.
- Proactively offer available special-needs accommodations—Do not assume a visitor with special needs cannot participate in a program. Discreetly, or in advance of the visit, ask the visitor of any special needs and offer the different adaptations you have available. In so doing, the visitor can feel comfortable and satisfied with their choices for touring the museum.
- Offer to assist—If the visitor declines assistance, respect their decision. Offering to help is appropriate but if you insist someone needs help, the visitor can be made to feel inadequate or frustrated.

- Use people-first language—People-first language is used to speak respectfully and appropriately to a person with special needs and focuses on the person and not the disability. (See Resource Guide for links to People-First Language guidelines.) For example:
  - People First—The man who is blind. Disability First—The blind man.
  - People First—The woman who has autism. Disability First—The autistic woman.
- Respect assistive devices—Consider assistive devices such as wheelchairs and walkers as a part of the visitor's body. If you handle the assistive device remember to be respectful.

Be certain you do not:

- Get agitated or frustrated—Remember that the person with special needs might be unable to help in what caused the frustrating situation, and they might be just as frustrated as you are. Your being upset over the situation won't help.
- Treat a visitor as if they are incapable of doing or understanding something—For example, a person who is nonverbal can still understand what you are saying so don't change the information you provide unless doing so is requested.
- Talk down to the visitor—Never treat someone who has special needs as if they are unintelligent or cannot comprehend the information normally provided. Talking down to someone is very disrespectful and, frankly, rude.
- Speak loudly or slowly—You should always talk to visitors age appropriately and at a normal volume.

Some of the above points seem quite obvious; however, they are often violated. Sometimes we violate them unconsciously, meaning no harm. The golden rule when working with special needs always applies: Treat everyone how you would want to be treated.

Conclusion

This case study outlines the process of making a museum more inclusive and accessible for visitors with special needs. Carrying out this project at the C.H. Nash Museum at Chucalissa demonstrates that you don't have to make large or expensive changes to your museum to be more inclusive. By being flexible, understanding, and offering other options you can make your museum accessible and inviting for all visitors. Making a museum more adaptive and inclusive can offer benefits such as increased satisfaction and visitation by visitors with special needs and provide a critically important service to your community.

Note

1. Digital links to all references included in this case study are contained in the digital Resource Guide (www.museumcommunities.com).

Incorporating Descendant Community Voices

The Whitney Plantation

Ashley Rogers

OUISIANA'S RIVER ROAD, a seventy-mile stretch of highway that snakes along the Mississippi River, is lined with plantation museums that focus on different aspects of the region's history. Some interpret Creole culture or architecture. Others serve primarily as event spaces and boutique hotels. Until recently, none took on the task of exclusively telling the stories of the enslaved men, women, and children who worked this land. The Whitney Plantation tells the stories of some of these hundreds of thousands of individuals. Opened to the public in 2014 for the first time in its 262-year history, the Whitney is also a resource for community members who have historically been disconnected from the museums that surround them. Engaging local African Americans, most of whom are descended from enslaved plantation workers, is essential to our mission.

Fifty years after the passage of the Civil Rights Act, plantations across Louisiana and other parts of the South still offer object-based tours, some in costume, which focus almost exclusively on the lives and fortunes of slaveholders. Whitney Plantation is a direct challenge to the "moonlight and magnolias" interpretation that dominated southern plantation tourism for the better part of the twentieth century. Within fifteen minutes of several other major plantation tourist destinations, Whitney is first a memorial to those enslaved; second, a representation of slave life; and, third, a glimpse at the enormous wealth built on the backs of enslaved laborers.

Beyond its interpretive scope, what makes Whitney significant is the fact that its location, on the west bank of the Mississippi River in St. John the Baptist Parish, is occupied by thousands of descendants of former slaves. Fifty-five percent of the parish's residents are African American. Whitney's community is a descendant community. Because of its rural location, one hour's drive between Baton Rouge and New Orleans, the vast majority of Whitney's visitors travel from outside the immediate vicinity. Visitors come from as far as Asia, Europe, and Africa to visit this cultural heritage venue. Yet, people from the nearby communities of Edgard, Wallace, Lucy, and Vacherie have traditionally had few interactions with Whitney or any of the other plantation museums in the parish. This case study describes the Whitney Plantation staff's efforts to change this situation and explains how incorporating the local community has improved our ability to engage all of our visitors.

Building a Memorial; Listening to the Community

John Cummings, a trial lawyer from New Orleans, purchased the Whitney Plantation in 1999 from Formosa Chemical Corporation. The company had intended to put a rayon plant on the site before complications—including an outcry from the local community—interrupted the plan. Cummings worked on the restoration of the property for fifteen years. Though he grew up relatively close by in New Orleans, St. John the Baptist Parish is so insular that Cummings was still considered an outsider who had to prove his intentions to the community when he purchased the plantation. From the first years he owned the property, Cummings made a rule to do business locally if at all possible, even if it meant paying more for products or services. He attended local church services and civic meetings. He listened to the needs and concerns of whoever would talk to him. The impetus behind his actions was to combat misunderstandings about the museum and its mission.

Cummings's first staff member was historian Dr. Ibrahima Seck, originally from Senegal, whom Cummings hired to be a research director. Seck's academic interest in Louisiana slavery stems in part from the cultural legacies of his native country that he sees still present in Afro-Louisiana culture. Together, Seck and Cummings created memorials to the enslaved years before the museum opened. The most impactful, perhaps, is the Gwendolyn Midlo Hall Alleés, a memorial field that gives names to 107,000 known individuals who were enslaved in Louisiana before 1820. The site has a significant effect on visitors, as most have never been given the opportunity to reflect on the individuality of enslaved workers. Seck's years of research about the history of the plantation and the Africans who contributed so mightily to Louisiana culture culminated in the publication of his work, *Bouki Fait Gombo: A History of the Slave Community at Habitation Haydel.*

When it became clear that Whitney was going to open to the public, some local residents were opposed, though not all actively voiced their concerns to Cummings. Their opposition mostly took the form of private murmur, occasionally boiling up to action. One African American Edgard resident said that a common sentiment in the years Cummings was restoring the property was that there was no need for another plantation museum, and that no one needed to talk about slavery anyway. A resident from the nearby town of Vacherie recounted that just before the museum's opening in 2014, some locals took to decrying the effort on social media and removed a highway sign that would direct visitors to the site.

Interior of 1870s Antioch Baptist Church at Whitney Plantation. Photograph by Ashley Rogers.

Throughout the course of the sixteen years that Cummings has worked in west St. John the Baptist Parish, he has formed crucial bonds with local politicians, policemen, and other stakeholders in the community. He actively works with community leaders on a range of civic projects. After the museum's opening, he became a board member of the west St. John Stakeholders, community leaders who work for the betterment of the parish. Together, he and Larry Sorapuru, councilman-at-large for St. John Parish council, opened a community farmer's market that operates on Saturdays. In 2015 when West St. John the Baptist High School significantly increased its performance ranking, Cummings and the Whitney Plantation hosted a celebratory dinner for educators and administrators. These projects, though ancillary to Whitney's direct operations, nonetheless have a significant impact on how community members view the plantation organization. Though some contentious feelings undoubtedly still exist, the museum is seeing increased interest from local residents, particularly those who have lived and worked at the property themselves.

From its first opening days, Whitney Plantation has used two operational practices to engage the community. First, residents of St. John the Baptist and St. James parishes receive a 30 percent discount on their admission tickets. No other plantation museum on River Road offers this kind of discount. We felt that local community members should not feel priced out of hearing about their own history. The second practice Whitney has engaged in is to hire mostly local staff. Apart from a small leadership team consisting of a director of research and a director of operations, the Whitney Plantation has a staff of two full-time visitor services personnel, two full-time tour guides, and seven part-time guides. Hiring local not only improves the plantation's standing within the community, but also enriches the visitor experience because a local staff is interpreting its own history.

The majority of tour guides at the Whitney are African American women from the small towns of Edgard, Wallace, Vacherie, and Lutcher in St. James and St. John the Baptist parishes. For many of these guides, when they tell stories of how enslaved workers on Louisiana plantations were treated, they are talking about the living conditions of their own ancestors. The majority of them are only one generation removed from plantation life themselves since rural Louisianans continued to live and work on plantations until the late twentieth century. The Whitney Plantation grounds include a Freedmen's church, built in 1870 by former slaves in Paulina, Louisiana. One of the Whitney's tour guides was baptized in that church. These kinds of personal stories help visitors contextualize and personalize information, and it has been one of the most successful programs we have initiated.

Adina, a woman in her early forties from Edgard, came into the museum on a whim one day to see about a job. She had no prior tour guide experience and she had not studied history in college, but she had an expressed interest. I hired her after only a brief visit and she has worked as a tour guide for close to a year. Adina is naturally curious with an infectious positivity, and over the course of the time she has worked at Whitney she has grown increasingly interested in the significance of her own family's history in Edgard.

On slow days at the museum the tour guides and I sit around and talk while we do idle side work. Adina told me that her mother was born on Columbia Plantation, just a few miles down the road from Whitney. As a young girl in the 1950s, her mother picked sweet

Segment of the Wall of Honor memorial containing the names, origin, age, and skills of enslaved peoples. Photograph by Ashley Rogers.

potatoes there. Adina told me she had never thought about the wider significance of her mother's experiences until working at Whitney. With her familial interest piqued, I sat with Adina and did some basic genealogical research about her family. She confirmed names and ages and we were able to trace her lineage back to her third great grandparents, people who were born enslaved in St. John the Baptist Parish. Every man in the line we researched was a plantation laborer, many in the sugar industry, according to census records. In 2015, Adina, a U.S. Army veteran with a college education, now works at the Whitney nearly every day, telling visitors about the lives that her direct ancestors lived.

When working in such a small and tight-knit community, talking with visitors and employees about their own histories is critical in forming bonds of trust and respect. These stories are enormously important in the ongoing work of preserving the history of Wallace and west St. John the Baptist Parish.

Planning for the Future

As a recently opened cultural heritage venue, the Whitney Plantation has a laundry list of tasks related to formal community engagement projects. These tasks include creating curricula with local high school teachers and holding workshops and volunteer days for local residents to learn about genealogy and archaeology. As the museum grows, we intend to bring in community members to help with the curation of artifacts and creation of rotating exhibits. We have launched a comprehensive oral history project of the surrounding area, which we expect to complete over the next several years. One of the Whitney's tour guides, Courtni, a native of Edgard and recent graduate from Xavier University, has pledged to lead this project and is working with us to develop questions, make contacts, and conduct interviews.

Every day we add to the story of the Whitney Plantation and what it represents by speaking to current and former residents of the area and asking them questions about their history. On Christmas Eve 2015, a man walked in by himself toward the end of the day and looked around slowly at the exhibits. I asked him if he wanted to take a tour and he said no, then paused a moment and added, "I used to live here." John, a man in his sixties, described the house where he had lived during the 1960s and 1970s, which the overseer, Maurice Tassin, tore down to plant more sugarcane. I recognized his surname from labor records, so I asked him to wait while I pulled the original payroll document from 1947 for him to see. I asked him if he knew anyone and he pointed immediately to four names—an uncle and three cousins. I took down his number and asked him if he'd like to participate in our oral history project. He smiled and agreed, but he seemed a little surprised. Most people need coaxing to be convinced that their own lives have historical significance.

Much of the time, the experiences I describe above is what community engagement at Whitney looks like. Successful community engagement, for us, is about recognizing that we do not know everything, and asking questions from the people around us. Currently, we are building up a roster of people who want to talk to us and who have stories to tell. We are beginning the process of scheduling and conducting interviews. Our goal is to build a history of west St. John Parish that can be accessed via the web and used by anyone interested, especially the local schools. While all public school students study Louisiana history at designated times, these oral histories will help students connect their own lives and their own families with broader events.

One year into operations, the Whitney Plantation still has a lot of room for growth and development. Yet we stand on a solid foundation because of the years of effort that John Cummings put into building trust and respect with local stakeholders. Through creating a positive work environment and steady income for local residents, Whitney Plantation is growing that trust and reaching out to numerous other locals who can help us fulfill our mission and research goals. Our practice of hiring local is also a service to our visitors, who repeatedly tell us in reviews, in person, or in our written reflection area that having a guide from the area enriched their experience.

Museums can often be insular in their own way, wary of bringing in non-museum professionals to do work or help with research. But engaging the community that surrounds the Whitney plantation in active research is a significant part of our success. The people who work on this project from outside the museum field bring fresh ideas and perspectives that might have never otherwise been raised. Without the local community interpreting this history, Whitney would not have the same impact. Community engagement helps us take what could easily become a scholarly pursuit and make it human, emotional, and real.

How Community Input Can Shape a Mission

The Proposed Eggleston Museum

Allison Hennie

Incorporating Multiple Community Perspectives

MUSEUM PROFESSIONALS may ask themselves, "Who is the community? How do I engage with the community? How can the community voice be incorporated into the museum?" For a small museum to survive, community input is increasingly necessary. Such input was sought to develop the mission and strategic plan for the proposed William Eggleston Museum.

Planning and Initial Steps

William Eggleston is a preeminent American photographer born in Memphis, Tennessee, and currently residing in the city. He is credited with elevating color photography to a legitimate artistic form. A group of Memphis civic backers who recognized the importance of Eggleston's body of work founded a nonprofit organization, not associated with the Eggleston family, to pursue a museum dedicated to Eggleston's photography. As part of this process, I was contracted by a board member from the nonprofit to conduct a market survey and target audience study to identify programming goals, priorities, and interests of the Memphis public concerning a proposed Eggleston Museum, along with a proposal for the next steps in the development process.

The original survey scope was only intended to incorporate input from local photographers and members of the museum community. I suggested adding another layer to the report—the community located in geographic proximity to the proposed museum's location. My goal was to create a final document that effectively wove the story of multiple community voices to influence the future identity of the Eggleston Museum.

The Eggleston Museum's current proposed site is located along the eastern edge of Overton Park, a prominent urban green space in Memphis, Tennessee. Within Overton Park are multiple civic and cultural heritage institutions. Each of these institutional voices is vying for ownership of the proposed museum's location or potential collection objects for use in their own venue. These institutional communities create a dynamic voice with the potential to deafen other community voices.

Adjacent to the proposed museum site is the residential Binghamton neighborhood, a target area for the expanded marketing survey to incorporate the community voice. Binghamton's physical boundaries include approximately three square miles and a population of 13,000 residents. The following data illustrate Binghamton's basic demographics:[1]

- Race: African American, 63 percent; White, 27 percent; Other, 10 percent
- Language: English as a first language, 77 percent
- Income: $25,000 or less, 50 percent; $25,000–$45,000, 21 percent; $45,000–$100,000, 21 percent; $100,000 and above, 8 percent
- Education: high school, GED, or less, 61 percent; bachelor's or associate's degree, or some college, 29 percent; master's, professional, or doctoral degree, 10 percent
- Housing: rent, 57 percent; own home, 43 percent
- Access to a vehicle: no, 24 percent; yes, 76 percent

Following John Cotton Dana's directive (see introduction to this volume) of the importance of community engagement, the Binghamton community input should be a source for establishing the Eggleston Museum's mission and strategic planning efforts, including educational programs and exhibits.

Implementation

The nonprofit board member and I started by reviewing a report assessing the practicality of researching precedents, discussing the board's vision, and actually creating the proposed museum. After the initial background research, the majority of my work focused on completing the market survey objectives. Rather than making guesses about the goals, priorities, and interests of the Memphis public concerning an Eggleston Museum, we created a survey that directly solicited their response. This process took 150 hours over a three-month period.

Initially the board member viewed the project as a top-down initiative and that the interviews should focus on museum professionals. Given my training and professional experiences, I countered the board member's interests and suggested a wider community-based approach. I proposed we follow the words of John Cotton Dana by expanding the list of potential stakeholders and interview community residents and business owners located within the vicinity of the proposed Eggleston Museum site. This expanded approach proved to be a worthwhile exercise. The board member was eventually convinced to follow a community-based approach based on our conversations as well as the board member's own independent research.

We used a word-of-mouth approach to create a list of candidates for community interviews. The board member wrote the initial questions and I revised the wording with the goal of talking with the community rather than at them for the interviews. Questions were phrased in order to gauge items such as the Binghamton community's knowledge of William Eggleston, the community's current level of engagement with Overton Park, and how the future museum could fulfill the needs of Binghamton's community.

Prior to beginning this stage of the project, the proposed interview questions were submitted to the University of Memphis's Institutional Review Board (IRB). The purpose of the IRB process is to ensure the rights and welfare of individuals participating in a research project are protected. All information gathered during the interviews was anonymous. Interviews were conducted in two separate rounds. Each interview was recorded and then transcribed for analysis. Handwritten notes were also taken during this process in case the recordings were lost. The first round included twelve semistructured interviews with community members who worked or lived within Binghamton's boundaries, along with local photographers familiar with William Eggleston's work.

After analyzing the transcripts from the first round of community interviews, I conducted a second set of seven unstructured interviews with local professionals. This round of questions had a different focus. We asked museum professionals to explain how they conduct visitor engagement, to describe examples of successes and failures of engagement, and to define the community served by their specific museum. The interviews indicated different understandings or interpretations of the term "community engagement" by each of the two groups. The interviews also provided insights into the differences held by the two groups for expectations of the role of a museum within a community.

Results

In general, the interviews indicated a disjunction between outsider perceptions of community needs and those expressed by the residents of the Binghamton community. The process uncovered the fact that the Binghamton community is informally divided between Binghamton (without a *p*) and Binghampton (with a *p*), a fact unknown to many of the museum professionals. This divide occurs along a pair of north-south–running railroad tracks, located approximately at the center of the neighborhood's geographic area. The overall demographics of the communities are similar in terms of income, level of education, access to a car, and home ownership. When broken into two separate communities, however, there is a noticeable difference in racial diversity: Binghamton is 40 percent African American, 46 percent White, and 14 percent Other; Binghampton is 72 percent African American, 20 percent White, and 8 percent Other. As one community leader noted, the two Bingham(p)ton communities "don't do a good job of bridging those two [races]." Ongoing revitalization efforts are taking place along the commercial strip of Binghamton, known as the Broad Avenue Arts District. Broad Avenue attracts people from surrounding neighborhoods, but not those from within Binghampton. A local artist observed, "Binghamton is Broad Avenue versus everything else," widening the divide within the geographic area.

Interview responses also revealed the Binghampton community has little knowledge of William Eggleston's accomplishments as an artist, or that he is a Memphian. During the interviews, community members and museum professionals listed obstacles that museums need to overcome to engage with their surrounding communities, including traditional museums carry a stigma of being exclusive, some residents feel they need to be personally invited into a museum, the architectural forms of museums are not always welcoming, and museums are intimidating if one has never been previously exposed to similar cultural institutions.

A qualitative analysis of the interviews resulted in a list of recommendations and next steps that influenced the proposed Eggleston Museum's mission statement and strategic plan. The recommendations included:

Establish a Museum Identity Relevant to the Community

Museums cannot manufacture relevance within a community, but they can openly assess how to appropriately serve community needs. The community input provided insights on what the museum should and should not be. Key themes from the interviews included focus exhibit themes on inclusivity rather than exclusivity, educate visitors on differences and commonalities between digital and analog photography, and extend the museum's indoor exhibits to outdoor environments in the immediate vicinity of the proposed museum and Binghamton.

Provide Effective Leadership, Educate Staff, and Reward Volunteers

Effective leadership will invite a community perspective. The Bingham(p)ton community urged the museum to have a "face" within their community. Museum professionals underscored the importance of volunteers as a way to reach the community because of the effectiveness of word-of-mouth awareness.

Write a Mission Statement and Strategic Plan

Mission statements provide clarity of purpose and show how the proposed Eggleston Museum will make a difference for the Bingham(p)ton community. Throughout the interviews, local museum professionals spoke to the importance of aligning museum programs with a museum's mission and putting the strategic plan into action. Rather than the standard five-year strategic plan, museum professionals commented that a shorter two-year strategic plan could be more useful.

Create Public Awareness

Museum marketing efforts need to be strategic and mirror the organization's beliefs and values as stated in the mission statement. Otherwise, museums often rely on a "throw it against the kitchen wall and see if it sticks" mentality. As illustrated by the interviews with museum professionals, many floundered when asked to explain their marketing strategies. Some museums lacked general knowledge about the culture in areas where the museum puts forth marketing efforts, or lacked information about current visitors.

Community Collaboration

Community needs do align with those of museums. When interviewees conceptualized the Eggleston space as a museum, many described hands-on and interactive exhibits. Another emphasis was the potential to connect museumgoers with the outdoor landscape. This potential indoor-outdoor connection was given more importance than displaying William Eggleston's work. Responses from interviewees also emphasized the role the museum could play in the community—for example, as a photography-based museum, one potential service could include providing school portrait services at a reduced cost.

Cultivate Relationships with Community and Institutional Partners

Think geographically. Consider establishing an advisory council composed of members of the different communities. Discovering a leadership role for the community at the proposed Eggleston Museum is just as important as the museum becoming active in the community. Interviews with the Bingham(p)ton community identified essential characteristics of community engagement such as being proactive and making a long-term commitment.

Next Steps in the Process

The work conducted on behalf of the nonprofit for the proposed Eggleston Museum expanded beyond the boundaries of the museum's site and engaged with the larger geographic community known as Bingham(p)ton. This community appreciated being involved in the process to articulate their needs; however, many were skeptical that their input will be included in the final vision for the museum. As one interviewee noted, the proposed Eggleston Museum has the potential to "cross the boundary of . . . artistic photography and authentically enter a community." Based on insights gathered from the interviews, the nonprofit board gained an understanding of how the proposed Eggleston Museum will best fit not only in the fine arts community who have a specific interest in his work, but also the community adjacent to the site. The board did not consider the importance of understanding the latter component prior to the market survey. Of particular interest in these findings was that there had been no consideration of how the museum would be an attraction to the local geographic community. As discussions move forward on furthering the proposal for the William Eggleston Museum, all parties are now equipped with the results of a marketing survey that can lead to a cultural venue that will be contextually more attuned to the needs of all potential users.

Note

1. See http://midsouthgreenprint.org.

Building a Community History at the University of the West Indies Museum

Suzanne Francis-Brown

MANY INSTITUTIONS draw their histories mainly from written administrative records: correspondence, meeting minutes, event coverage, and news media. Mining the recollections of past leaders, visitors, staff, and other associated individuals, however, can add detail, texture, and depth to an institutional narrative. But for organizations more than fifty years old, the clock is ticking on engaging aging individuals capable of nuancing the origin story. Moreover, younger sources must be conscientiously pursued if the history is to be multilayered.

This case study focuses on a project at the University of West Indies (UWI) Museum created to reach and engage these aging communities. To negotiate resource challenges and still reach an aging population, the museum devised a low-tech way of engaging and collecting information that centered on a 1953 UWI promotional film. This case study demonstrates that despite slim resources, the museum was able to enhance our knowledge of the film's content, while simultaneously engaging pioneering alumni and increasing our institutional reach.

UWI Museum

The UWI Museum was established in 2012, fifty years after UWI became an independent, degree-granting institution and sixty-four years after it was founded as the University College of the West Indies (UCWI) in 1948.[1] Since its establishment, the museum has focused on building its small collection and on connecting with communities of interest. These communities include a wide range of people who have had a connection to the development of this unique institution. UWI was established through a fading British imperial power to provide leadership and expertise for the West Indian region, which once was expected to become a federated country.

As we began our efforts to engage communities of interest we first identified pioneering students and staff, now alumni and retirees, as important resources for increasing or nuancing our store of knowledge and gaining voices and personalities with life experiences of the early university. We are, however, challenged by realities: these alumni and retirees are a diminishing asset, many are scattered across the Caribbean region and across the world, many are not technologically savvy, and the museum has severe resource limitations. Our solution to this problem was a project we called Freeze Frame & Annotate.

The Project: Freeze Frame & Annotate

Freeze Frame & Annotate was the title given to an exhibition mounted in February 2014, elements of which have since been retained within the body of the museum's semipermanent exhibition. The title was quite literal: visitors were invited to annotate mounted images from a 1953 promotional film. The film had been shot in 1952 or early 1953 by the Jamaica Film Unit,[2] and provides a literal peephole to the university's past. Moreover, for the decreasing number of early alumni, the movie presents a glimpse into their personal pasts, a point made by retired Mona campus principal Elsa Leo-Rhynie in opening the exhibition. We hoped that making the film available and giving alumni an opportunity to not just watch but also interact with the film's content would provide us with invaluable information about the people, places, events, and experiences originally captured on a reel of celluloid to which we no longer have physical access.

Genesis of an Idea

Late in 2012, just months after the museum opened, two elderly alumni, one still living in Jamaica, the other visiting from North America, sat watching the grainy film and began pointing out old friends, eventually also spotting themselves. Some months later the UWI's chancellor, Sir George Alleyne, himself a medical graduate of UWI's first decade, spent some minutes watching the film and recognized some of his older colleagues. Observing our visitors sharing their recollections introduced a challenge: how to capture this rich source of information without the requisite technological capacity that would allow watchers to somehow pause the film, annotate appropriately, and continue watching without affecting the prior or future notations of other viewers. The very simple answer was to freeze frames from the film and, using computer technology, blow them up to a size that could be easily seen but wasn't so pixilated as to make them unrecognizable. Finally, the frames were mounted so that persons with insights to offer could easily record them.

Creating and Using the Stills

First, we had to determine how to capture and showcase a fairly comprehensive range of images from the film, including images that would engage a casual viewer and were clear enough to be relatively identifiable. We initially tried loading the digitized film into the free Windows Movie Maker program, freezing frames and saving them for later printing. Eventually, though, it proved easier and as effective to play the film, pause it appropriately, and capture the imperfect but recognizable images using the computer's "print screen" option.

Having obtained the stills, the next issue was how to cost-effectively use the freeze stills while balancing image size and clarity. Since the images were not high resolution, we mainly used letter-sized prints, a decision that allowed us to capitalize on access to a regular office color printer. We mounted the images in close physical proximity to the television where the film was playing so that viewers could easily watch the original footage, which helped to compensate for any shortcomings in image quality. Ultimately we chose just over 100 images—enough to make a strong exhibit—and mounted them in groups related to their place in the film. We gave each mounted image a unique letter/number combination so that anyone offering information could precisely identify the subject.

Creating Engagement

Once the stills were printed we created an exhibition flyer that provided instructions for interested participants:

- Look at the images.
- If you recognize someone or remember a place or experience, write the number from the frame and whatever information you have on the paper provided.
- Repeat the process for as many photos as you can.
- Leave the sheets with the museum along with your name and contact information if you are willing.

We provided clipboards with paper and pens so that our visitors could provide the requested brief biographical information, especially their names, country of origin, and subjects studied while at UWI along with any further relevant material. More extensive notes left by the visitors were then typed up and posted in the exhibition. But we went further, announcing that we were inviting visitors to engage quite literally with the images by annotating the mounted copies. This allowed visitors to contribute directly, and also to verify, correct, or supplement information left by others. On one photograph, for instance, a name was suggested, with a question mark; a later visitor crossed it out and wrote another name, which subsequent viewers seem to accept as correct.

We launched the exhibition during the university's annual Commemoration Week, with an informative recollection by our guest speaker, Emerita Professor Elsa Leo-Rhynie, the UWI's first female principal. She had worked where she studied, at the Mona campus—though not, as she emphasized, so early as the 1950s.[3] Our invitations and promotions targeted alumni of the 1950s and 1960s, and retirees who worked within that period. We

► FREEZE FRAME: A
SINGLE SHOT PRINTED TO
GIVE THE IMPRESSION OF A
STILL PHOTOGRAPH

► UNIVERSITY COLLEGE
OF THE WEST INDIES
(UCWI): THE PRECURSOR TO
THE UWI WE KNOW TODAY

Freeze Frame
& annotate!

ENGAGING WITH IMAGES FROM A 1953 FILM ON THE UCWI

*FROM THURSDAY FEBRUARY 13, FOR TWO WEEKS, an exhibition
that sets out to learn about the people and places in a 1953
film on the UCWI, produced by the Jamaica Film Unit—
perhaps the earliest colour film produced in the West Indies.*

Help us identify the people,
places and events...

The photo quality won't be great. In fact we can promise you that some of the photos look a bit like impressionistic paintings. But like the film from which they are drawn, they give viewers a peek into the early years of the University (College) of the West Indies.

We're sure that between the film and the frozen images, persons who were there will still recognize who's who. We hope that people with valuable memories will come and share them. And we hope that others will just join us for the fun of being part of a game of remembrance.

UWI Museum
Regional Headquarters Building,
Mona, Kingston 7

Opening hours: 10am-4pm weekdays except public holidays

Tel: 876 977 6085
Email:
uwi.museum@uwimona.edu.jm
Blog:
www.uwimuseum.wordpress.com

Flyer announcing the Freeze Frame Project. Source: Created by author.

were pleased to see that they formed the bulk of attendees. We also sought collaboration of the UWI's Institutional Advancement Division (IAD), which manages alumni engagement. Through them, Ms. Minna Israel, the special advisor on resource development, and members of the UWISTAT (UWI Students Today Alumni Tomorrow) Corps became involved. These engaged students helped visitors as needed, took photos and videos, and conducted brief interviews with willing alumni, relying on available smartphones. Conversations between the current students and much older alumni created an atmosphere of sharing that all appeared to enjoy and pointed to a potential future cross-generational project.

Results

Between February 13, when the exhibition was launched, and April 23, when it was dismantled, more than 150 persons signed the museum's visitor's book, some of them on behalf of family or other groups. The first ten signatures were from the launch event, which was attended by over thirty people.

Several other pioneering alumni visited the exhibition in subsequent weeks and provided a half dozen additional smartphone-recorded interviews. Transcriptions were created of these interviews and other written texts submitted by alumni. The transcriptions were also posted within the exhibition. Material from the launch and later visits was used to compose blog posts, which generated additional comments.

An idea to produce a short YouTube video on the engagement experience at the launch using material (digital images, audio, and video footage) recorded by the students did not come to fruition mainly because of insufficient video footage. For the future we recognize that such a video project requires a dedicated producer who can ensure effective deployment of the available interviewers, photographers, and equipment.

In the months following the exhibition, an informal assessment of the output revealed the following:

- A high response rate to the annotation invitation (81 of 112, or over 70 percent, of mounted photos have at least one name inscribed).
- A willingness to share recollections, especially in person, but a general disinclination to produce extensive written texts, even via email exchanges.
- A need to arrange and facilitate interviews expeditiously, despite limited museum personnel. One idea is to involve student interviewers, which would enable us to gain information while underscoring the connection across generations of UWI students.
- In the meantime the list of alumni contacts is growing and we have occasionally called on pioneers to clarify specific points related to UCWI/UWI history. Where the human and technological resources align with the availability of alumni, full-fledged interviews are also being recorded.

Follow-Up

As it was clear that there was still information to be gathered, several of the exhibition boards were remounted around the monitor where the film continues to be shown on a loop. Visitors occasionally add to the annotations. In a few instances, we have also targeted older alumni to watch the film and see if they can help identify people, places, or events depicted. In one instance, a visitor cheerfully identified her ex-husband. A family group also called to request a viewing and contributed information on the relative who briefly appeared twice in the film.

Trying to engage the many UWI alumni scattered across the Caribbean region and farther afield remains a challenge. Discussions with Internet technology colleagues on a user-friendly methodology led to the development of a Google Docs template with photos and spaces for input. However, initial tests of this process with two of the pioneering alumni garnered no responses. A more recent suggestion to post the images in a Facebook gallery is being considered, though we recognize that the target demographic may not necessarily respond well to social media or technology in general.

Based on the Freeze Frame experience, a few other low-tech and low-cost initiatives have been explored to engage with and capture information from such communities.

Targeted Requests to Individuals

Some known alumni and retirees have been targeted for information requests. Responses, whether concise or expansive, are moved to a research folder for further action.

Year Groups

Some experiences are common to groups by year that they attended UWI. Year Groups are composed of students who entered UWI in the same class, shared hall (dorm) life, or belonged to the same faculty or club. We believe capturing these experiences may help to flag periods of change in the university's history. For instance, students who attended the UWI in the mid-1960s appear to characterize their experiences as a calm before a storm of union and political activism and greater insecurity that began to affect many Jamaicans in the mid-1970s. As a result, an effort has begun to encourage Year Groups to pool their recollections.

Email correspondence with a follower of the UWI Museum's blog recently sparked a suggestion that she facilitate such a group recollection. While this did not emerge, she did initiate an email conversation with several fellow alumni on one particular aspect of their joint experience at UWI: Carnival. That conversation generated a new file in the growing research folder.

Lessons Learned

The initiative to engage with and collect written and recorded memories from the pioneering group of alumni has significant unmet potential and remains urgent due to the natural decline and disappearance of this aging population. The most positive outcome is that these audiences are willing to be engaged, though always within the limits of their convenience and ability.

Follow-up to the Freeze Frame initiative is also important for building community. The identification of volunteers willing and able to assist the curator with foregrounding the memory project is an unmet need. However, recognizing its urgency has sparked discussions with UWI's alumni organization toward another round of collaborative effort. Despite resource constraints, collected material can and is being used for simple activities such as posting individual recollections within exhibitions and the museum blog or creating Power Point-type productions.

Notes

1. The UCWI started at the Mona campus on the northern outskirts of Kingston, Jamaica, on a square-mile site leased by the government for 999 years. Until 1961, all students from

across the region came to Mona, which is now the site of the museum. A second campus, St. Augustine in Trinidad & Tobago, was added in 1961; a location in Barbados was opened in 1963 and an Open Campus in 2008. The geographic spread of the university, resulting from nationalist and economic imperatives, poses inevitable challenges that the museum must also seek to meet.

2. The Jamaica Film Unit, established in 1950, was part of an initiative to decentralize film-making specifically for the British colonial market. It began life in a surplus building at the nascent UCWI.

3. Coverage of the Freeze Frame exhibition and response and discussion of the film are posted on the UWI Museum blog: https://uwimuseum.wordpress.com/2014/02/12/freeze-frame-annotate/; https://uwimuseum.wordpress.com/2014/02/20/age-renew/; https://uwimuseum .wordpress.com/2014/12/17/historic-film-feedback/; among others.

Telling Our Town's Story

The Muscatine History and Industry Center

Mary Wildermuth

THE IDEA OF PRESERVING Muscatine, Iowa's, history took twenty-five years to come to fruition. Various iterations of the Pearl Button Story and collections were found in several locations in our downtown, the oldest historic segment of our town. A committee eventually evolved into a board of directors who created a vision to combine the 100-year-old Pearl Button Capital of the World Story with the fifty-year later story of the industrial manufacturing entrepreneurs who created the next generation of employment for the town.

The idea of the Muscatine History and Industry Center (http://www.muscatinehistory.org) took hold with the purchase of a museum building that housed two floors. The first level would be dedicated to the Button Story. The second floor would showcase the town's homegrown industries that had put their roots down in the 1940s and 1950s and became very successful international companies with their corporate headquarters still located in Muscatine.

Today, ten years since the doors opened, the center contains a beautifully choreographed Pearl Button Capital of the World exhibit located on the first level and eight homegrown manufacturers showcasing their stories on the second level. Second-floor exhibits include: HNI, Bandag, Monsanto, Kent Corporation, Musco Lighting, Muscatine Power and Water, Carver Pump, and Stanley Consultants.

Planning for the Center

The center building was a gift from a local philanthropist who believed strongly in Muscatine and the importance of telling our town's story. The building was renovated and a director was hired. The director, along with the connected leadership of the board of directors, began a major campaign to raise $600,000 to create and install the Pearl Button Capital of the World permanent exhibit, which is showcased today on the first floor. Local artifacts combined with pictures and audio became the backbone for the Muscatine History and Industry Center.

As the museum evolved over time, various local iterations and locations housed the Pearl Button Museum. Early exhibits were based solely on artifacts and treasured family memorabilia that were loaned or given to the museum to tell the local story of how pearl buttons provided a livelihood for families in our town. As a more permanent museum was created and the current building secured, the original button machines, buttons, and treasured family mementos became foundation pieces for the current exhibits found on the first floor. Family stories were shared and placed on audio tracks for visitor enjoyment and reminiscing.

Because Muscatine was the Pearl Button Capital of the World and button manufacturing was, by nature, a cottage industry, everyone in town is somehow connected or related to someone who was involved in the button industry's heyday. Today, visitors come from all over the world to learn our town's story. Relatives visit during holidays, funerals, graduations, vacations, or just a day trip to capture a bit of the past and enjoy what grandma, grandpa, sister, brother, or mom and dad did to be a part of the Pearl Button Capital of the World.

Innovative Community Partnerships

The originating committee did a lot of the groundwork with community partners to generate interest and eventually engage them in supporting the new entity monetarily. This legwork paid off by providing them information about vision for Muscatine History and Industry Center. The initial contact also allowed the community partners to understand and be a part of the original goals and objectives, understand the financial needs for the facility, and be a part of the marketing plan.

Today, company exhibitors on the second floor each partner with the Muscatine History and Industry Center to rent an exhibit space. Annual partnership fees are assessed based on the square footage of the exhibit spaces. The annual partnership fee is a win-win for the Muscatine History and Industry Center and for the eight partner companies. For a very nominal financial investment the partners get to showcase their companies to museum visitors. The Muscatine History and Industry Center uses the partner fees as a source of annual operating income.

A True Community Resource

The Muscatine History and Industry Center has become an engaging place for tourists but because of the nature of the facility and its architecture the space itself is used by our business community as a location for events. Individual corporate partners are able to use the space for after-hour events for member recognition or networking time with business customers or employees who live in Muscatine or travel from somewhere else to here on business. Additionally, a diverse set of community interests utilize the museum venue itself for events such as Cocktail

Hour Wine and Cheese, and other community gatherings. Our mayor's China Committee has seen the value of sharing Muscatine's story from the Pearl Button Capital of the World Days to the entrepreneurs of the twentieth and twenty-first centuries with many dignitaries and guests from China for tours and lunch and dinner meetings as business is discussed. The Mayor's Community Attraction Team also utilizes the Muscatine History and Industry space for workshop meetings with local partners from business and government, as well as facilitator expertise from our regional universities of Iowa and Iowa State.

The Greater Muscatine Chamber of Commerce and Industry also partners with us to share the town's story and the venue with economic development folks from our state and those from major cities, such as Chicago. Annually Muscatine Community College and the center partner to showcase and discuss the many entrepreneurs and their talents in the center that are representative of the spirit in Muscatine. The community appreciates our story and our venue so much that we are often asked to be the entertainment space for business visitors from all over the world. In the near future we will be hosting a luncheon for the Chinese Symphony, who will be performing in Muscatine.

Younger generations also use the center. Our Young Professionals Network (YPN) often uses our space to showcase our town. The space provides a venue for YPNers' family and friends when they visit Muscatine and serves as a historic place for younger persons or those new to town to understand the richness that is Muscatine. Additionally, fourth-grade students from the Muscatine Community School District make their annual visit to the Muscatine History and Industry Center to learn about the Pearl Button Capital of the World Days and about the second evolution of entrepreneurs who came in the 1950s. For many of the students these companies are still their parents' workplaces.

A Sustainable Result

The vision of the original board of directors was to create a museum for Muscatine that would showcase the Pearl Button Capital of the World story and to acknowledge the industrial entrepreneurial giants that contributed to the second evolution of our town. The Muscatine History and Industry Center has had its nonprofit doors open as a museum since 2006. The past ten years have not been without the normal struggles. Building upkeep, exhibit management, and fiscal responsibility keep the director and assistant director busy, as well as the pleasure of continually engaging the public and tourists in the venue. The board of directors planned well and the museum today continues as a thriving entity telling the town's story.

The robust fundraising campaign that allowed the implementation of the Pearl Button Capital of the World exhibit carried the museum well into the immediate future. Our board contains members with strong financial backgrounds enabling a strong repertoire of skills to lend to the project. Strategies continually need to be developed to sustain the museum. Changes in directors and perhaps little future planning after the initial museum's opening were problems that needed to be overcome. Initial structure in regard to staffing had to change in order to maintain the building and to keep the exhibits up to date. We are fortunate that the museum carries no debt and that the board of directors had the foresight to completely pay off the Pearl Button Capital of the World exhibit prior to installation.

Our charitable benefactors are critical to our success. We have three benefactors who are always looking out for us and making grants available to assist with our needs. Wall repair, tuck-pointing, and replacement of our ten-year-old awning have all been done with grants that have been graciously gifted. Our corporate partners, who understand the value of working with the museum and the community, are looking out for the needs of the Muscatine History and Industry Center as they install new exhibits or tweak existing ones.

Into the Future . . .

Our next steps are to enhance the museum exhibits and to hire more staff to address the expansion and future exhibit needs and developments. We are fortunate that we are located in the hub of growth in our historic downtown. A $40 million hotel complex is being built across the street from the Muscatine History and Industry Center. We envision utilizing a building adjacent to our current museum to expand our operations and exhibit space. We are definitely exploring our options and will capitalize on opportunities presented to us. The future is very bright for us. We are fortunate to have partnered with creative entrepreneurs who are passionate about the growth of our town as a tourist destination. We are a tourist site currently and will capitalize on the future expansion in our downtown!

Working to Address Community Needs

The Missouri History Museum

Melanie A. Adams

IN AUGUST 2014, a young African American man was tragically killed by a white police officer in Ferguson, Missouri. This event set off weeks of unrest that gripped the entire St. Louis region, and everyone watched and wondered what to do next. Only hours after Michael Brown's funeral, the Missouri History Museum, in conjunction with Kevin Powell, president of BK Nation, hosted a town hall meeting where almost 400 people came together to have a voice during this turbulent time.

Why did the History Museum become a place for the community to come together and begin a dialogue about the difficult issues brought up by the shooting of Michael Brown? How did the museum prepare to serve as a vital community resource during times of conflict? What will the museum do to sustain and grow its community connections? The answers to these questions can be found in the museum's Community Partners program.

Planting Seeds of Community Engagement

The Missouri Historical Society (MHS) was founded in 1866 and for 150 years has developed into a nationally recognized institution that uses historical events and figures to provide context for current-day events. The MHS is the umbrella organization for the Missouri History Museum and the Library and Research Center. These two organizations work as one to produce exhibitions, develop programs, and collect and preserve artifacts. Functioning as a public-private partnership, the MHS receives funding from regional taxes and private donors, which allows it to provide free general admission to all visitors.

In 2010 the MHS was scheduled to host the exhibition *Race: Are We So Different?* This exhibition, developed by the Science Museum of Minnesota and the American Anthropological Association, looked at the biological aspects of race and the social construct society places upon it. From housing to education to economics, race has played a pivotal role in maintaining the country's imbalanced status quo.

The MHS knew that this exhibition would be an opportunity to engage diverse communities and that many organizations would want to contribute to the conversation. When the exhibition was announced, the staff member in charge of community programs began receiving phone calls from organizations to schedule meetings to talk about program ideas. This barrage of calls and meetings quickly became overwhelming, and we knew we had to find a better way to work with organizations. After a few weeks we decided to have a meeting that would include all the organizations that had contacted us as well as a few others the museum felt were important to include in the program planning and implementation. This first meeting was the start of the Community Partners program.

The Community Partners program allowed museum staff to meet with a large group of organizations who were interested in working with the MHS on a specific series of programs related to one exhibition. This structure was not only beneficial to the MHS, but also to the organizations because it introduced them to the program planning process and timeline necessary to develop a successful program.

Growing the Engagement

The Community Partners program began with monthly meetings focused primarily on the race exhibition but quickly turned into meetings about the MHS's entire exhibition schedule. To help maintain the momentum and provide continuity, we developed a yearly schedule that included the exhibitions that would be discussed at each meeting. This was important because it allowed organizations to decide which exhibitions would showcase their expertise and which ones would not. This schedule also formalized the relationship with community organizations within the MHS's program planning process to create better avenues of communication and the building of trust.

The two most important resources needed to develop the Community Partners were time and staff. There was one staff member who was responsible for facilitating the meetings, while other staff members were always encouraged to attend to get to know the organizations. The staff member responsible for the meetings spent time marketing the meetings to both current and potential community partners in addition to working with the exhibitions staff to prepare the presentations. In the beginning the MHS relied on technology to promote the program but has since developed print materials as well. We started out providing light refreshments but have since transitioned to providing a meal since our meetings take place right after work, from 5:30 p.m. to 7:00 p.m.

In addition to the regular meetings, staff meets with community organizations to work through the program proposal form and, if a program is developed, the memorandum of understanding (MOU). The program proposal is available online, and many organizations fill it out even before the meeting to begin developing their ideas. The program proposal allows both the MHS and the community organization to have a starting point for discussion. Once a program is approved, the next step is the creation of the MOU. The MOU is based on the needs of the program and should include a breakdown of responsibilities by organization, any specific organizational policies (catering, safety, etc.), and all financial arrangements related to the program costs. The MOU then becomes a reference to clear up any possible conflicts that arise during the planning process. Without a written document it is hard to remember what was said and what promises were made.

During the early years the biggest challenge was to keep community organizations involved if they thought the exhibition content was not directly connected to their organization. This was especially true of organizations focused on issues of diversity or related to specific cultural groups. We worked hard to show organizations the different ways they could be involved in programs even if they thought there was little connection because we wanted organizations to think beyond traditional history narratives. We also utilized organizational representatives for documentary panel discussions as a way to keep them connected when they were not working on a specific program. The goal was to keep them connected to the institution for a sustained period and not just for one exhibition.

Sustaining the Engagement

The Community Partners program is now entering its fifth year and continues to serve as one of the MHS's strongest resources for engaging with the community and remaining relevant. While there have been no formal evaluations completed on the program, there is some anecdotal evidence of success. The main goal of the program was to find ways to more efficiently and effectively work with community organizations. The development of the program has allowed that to happen through its monthly meeting and newsletter designed specifically for community partners. The program has also created sustained relationships that have lasted beyond one or two exhibitions as well as some partners that have been with us for the entire five years. Finally, the most important outcome of the program is the way the MHS is viewed in the community. It is now seen as a community gathering space that welcomes discussions on difficult issues. Before the Community Partners program, the MHS worked with a few select organizations on specific anniversaries, exhibitions, or events for short-term impact. The Community Partners program has shown the region that the MHS has a vested interest in using its resources to create a climate that welcomes everyone and is willing to talk about the difficult issues that brought us to this place and time.

Lessons Learned

In order to even begin thinking about creating a community partners program it is important to assess your organizational mission, goals, and your intended outcomes. We started out developing the program as a way to streamline our communication with community organizations and quickly realized it was the perfect way to create positive collaborations and opportunities for shared resources. Over the past six years the program has ebbed and flowed as staff has changed (both at the MHS and in the partner organizations), but there are some concrete lessons we have learned along the way:

- Be open to new ideas that may stretch and challenge your institution. Some of the best partnerships started with staff uncertainty.
- If you realize some communities are not coming to your museum, reach out and specifically invite them to a Community Partners meeting. Even now, we continue to call both current and potential partners to make them feel included and welcome.
- Relationships are built on trust over time. Do not get discouraged if a program idea does not come to fruition on the first try. It is important to continue working together to find the right fit for everyone.
- Communication and clear expectations are vital to a successful partnership. It is important to put expectations in writing and to check in on a regular basis.
- Schedule meetings during a time when smaller organizations can attend. Many have few staff and cannot always get away for daytime meetings.

Future Engagement

The MHS recently went through a leadership change and developed a new strategic framework. This new framework recognizes the importance of community partnerships to the mission of the organization, and it is specifically mentioned as one of the key goals moving forward. In conjunction with the new strategic framework, the Community Partners program is being revamped to strengthen its impact on the community and the MHS's role as a community resource. The changes include a revised program proposal form that allows more in-depth explanation of program ideas, how they relate to the MHS's mission and goals, and their benefit to the larger St. Louis community. There has also been a change to the content of the partner meeting to include opportunities to learn about Historical Society collections and not solely focus on exhibitions. This change is in line with the new strategic framework to better utilize the MHS's collections and make them relevant beyond traditional exhibitions.

The Community Partners program is adaptable to all types of institutions regardless of size. The program can be as small or as large as the needs of the institution. The financial resources required for the program can be adjusted to fit any size budget. The Missouri Historical Society works with about 150 community organizations each year to develop and implement 400 to 450 programs. Based on the MHS's size, staffing structure, and financial resources, this is a reasonable number of organizations. In the future, in order to sustain the Community Partners program, the MHS will continue to assess the program to make sure it fits the needs of the organization as well as those of the community. The program has created a strong foundation for diverse community engagement and allowed the MHS to use its resources to become an anchor in the community. Because of the Community Partners program, the MHS was able to serve as a safe space for the community to gather to have dialogue while searching for solutions to its deep-seated historical problems.

Part V

ENGAGING USER AUDIENCES IN THE DIGITAL LANDSCAPE

Brigitte Billeaudeaux and Jennifer Schnabel

Introduction

SMALL- AND MEDIUM-SIZED cultural organizations face growing expectations from users to expand access to information about collections, programs, exhibitions, and other visitor services via the Internet. Smaller groups may feel outresourced by larger institutions that have a more robust web presence. However, the rise of the social web and other open source applications has made digital preservation and promotion more accessible for groups that want to provide cultural heritage material online. For smaller organizations, this can be difficult to manage, and building community partnerships can help them achieve their outreach goals. This section introduces ways to engage communities through digital collections and social media platforms. Two tools will be outlined as digital preservation solutions for staff with various levels of technical expertise as well as several options for promoting collections and services online. Though we primarily discuss how to best leverage collections and promote programs in the digital landscape, several case studies at the end of this section will illustrate other aspects of building a stronger digital presence.

Curate Digitized Content Using Open Source Tools

Organizations engaging the digital landscape for the first time will face a learning curve in identifying goals, selecting appropriate tools and content, and estimating the time needed to complete a digital preservation project. First, it is important to know the difference between digitizing items for preservation and digital preservation. Digitizing items for preservation is a onetime act, and digital preservation is the ongoing stewardship of digital material. Paul Conway explains the distinction well: digitization creates a valuable digital product and digital preservation is a set of tools and actions that will ensure the longtime use and value of the digital product.[1] This long-term commitment is made possible through a variety of tools outlined later in this part that are both easy to use and optimal for community engagement.

Staff should then consider the following questions: "How will the digital preservation tool benefit the organization and the community?," "What criteria should we use when selecting a digital preservation tool?," and "What do our users most want to access?" Digital preservation can grow costly for smaller organizations with little to no budgets, and this obstacle can end a project before it begins. However, the increase in open source products has created a community dedicated to sharing resources and digital tools that are plentiful and freely available. The user communities for these products are often active and serve as assets to smaller organizations with limited resources looking to adopt a digital preservation plan.

Practice Community-Driven Digital Preservation

Focused community outreach can help a small organization identify specific audiences, collection interests, and potential partnerships. Through these efforts, cultural heritage institutions can encourage stakeholders—visitors, scholars, and donors—to help determine which materials to include in online digital collections while highlighting the organization's commitment to preservation and access. Interview stakeholders in the community such as teachers, librarians, historians, and other cultural heritage professionals about the items they would most like to see represented in the digital collections. Examine responses closely and allow this feedback to help answer the staff's reflective questions about digital preservation and community access. Once a digital preservation project is in motion, look for ways to reengage stakeholders; notify educators so they can incorporate digital assets into curricula, and link them to digital preservation projects through websites, social media, and community events.

There are several ways for staff members and volunteers to learn more about digital preservation. Working groups, such as those through the National Digital Stewardship Alliance (http://www.digitalpreservation.gov/ndsa/) and the Digital Public Library of America (http://dp.la/), have member organizations that work together to solve issues related to digital preservation. Many working groups have valuable informational websites where small organizations can learn more about planning and executing a digital preservation project. Subscribing to listservs, blogs—such as "The Signal" published by the Library of Congress (http://blogs.loc.gov/digitalpreservation/)—and newsletters as well as attending meetings and conferences can benefit small organizations without access to community and regional partners. Institutions can seek assistance from groups that have established digital preservation programs and learn from their peers. Participation in working groups can also help organizations cross-promote activities and connect digital content to existing exhibitions or online collections. This can be done through the above-mentioned blogs and listservs as well as social media outlets. (Social media is a common resource used by cultural heritage organizations and will be discussed later in this part.)

Connect Content to Existing Displays

Multimedia displays can be problematic for spaces such as museums and libraries that are traditionally known for their silence. Video and audio material, generally left out of physical exhibitions for this reason, can be incorporated into digital displays. Bonus material not included in original analog exhibitions or displays with limited space and flexibility can be highlighted through digital presentations. Linking content to existing displays creates an electronic permanent collection that organizations can reuse to engage the community during the period of time between new exhibition installations.

Explore Digital Preservation Solutions

Smaller cultural heritage organizations are no longer bound by restricted budgets and organization size when seeking to provide a satisfying user experience online. The open source movement—the sharing of software and electronic code—has created a culture of sharing and access. An organization, Social Square, explains open source with a video that is available through a creative commons license; the video is available through Wikipedia and YouTube.[2] Some tools require more expertise than others, and vendors are responding by offering digital preservation products that use the open source code but offer a level of support at a smaller than normal price. Omeka (omeka.org; omeka.net) and the Internet Archive (archive.org) offer engagement opportunities for a broad range of organizations looking for digital preservation solutions.

The Internet Archive is a basic, user-friendly tool that can be used for digital preservation. The Internet Archive works as an Internet library, allowing users to upload, use, download, and share the content housed on the site.[3] The Illinois-based collective POWRR (Preserving Digital Objects With Restricted Resources) noted that the Internet Archive is a good tool for organizations that have no copyright restrictions on digital content and/or use an all-volunteer staff for digital preservation projects.[4] Digital objects are uploaded and housed on the Internet Archive's servers, and account holders provide metadata, or additional explanatory information about the digital object, to make them searchable. Once items are published, they are made available to the global audience. Visitors to the Internet Archive can use, view, and download content for free.

Organizations that want more control over their content displays on the front end and wish to use a digital preservation tool to also build online exhibitions should consider Omeka. This open-sourced, web-based platform is available in two versions: Omeka.org and Omeka.net. The dot org version of Omeka requires access to a server, either web hosted or physical, and offers unlimited website themes and capabilities and plug-ins, offering organizations many options as they build a customized digital collection.[5] The dot org version of Omeka is free to download but will require some technical expertise to install and set up.

Organizations looking for similar options but do not have access to technical expertise should explore the dot net version of Omeka. This version of Omeka is also freely available with a user account. Free accounts come with 500 megabytes of storage space on Omeka's hosted servers, and users are allowed to create and manage multiple sites with one account. Additional hosted space can be purchased with a premium package. Yearly fees range in cost from $49 a year to $999 a year with options to contact the organization for additional space needs.[6] As an incentive, premium user accounts have access to additional themes and site plug-ins.[7]

Empower Community Members to Become Digital Ambassadors

In 2001, Rowena Cullen touched on the "digital divide" and the disparities that are created by a lack of access to Information and Communications Technologies (ICTs).[8] The digital divide refers to a dichotomy of technological haves and have-nots and the knowledge to use those technologies to personal advantages.[9] This divide can be as simple as not owning a home computer or having limited or no access to Internet services because of geographic location. Individuals (and organizations) that fall into this divide lack the knowledge or experience needed to use and access digital preservation tools. Cultural organizations that make content available online must acknowledge there will be segments of the population that will not be able to access these materials.

Making items and collections available to the global audience is great, but simply putting digital items online is only half of the work. Falk and Dierking note that one way for cultural institutions to achieve organizational success in the twenty-first century is not related to size or historic reputation; it is about thinking outside of the box to meet the public's needs that go beyond the organization's mission.[10] Therefore, the success of a digital collection or library is not in its size, but what it provides to the user and who can and does access the material. While some cultural heritage collections are free and available online to the public, even the most user-friendly digital preservation platforms can seem intimidating to someone unfamiliar with computers. The tools that will house digitized information from the collections should be simple enough for widespread use on a number of different electronic devices. To ensure success, it is necessary for the organization to help close the divide that a digital library may create by offering educational opportunities within the community.

Organizations interested in digital projects should prepare to provide demonstrations and training to community stakeholders and user groups as well as organizational staff and volunteers. Community education does not have to be a grand, expensive venture; it can be as simple as offering tours of web applications used to house and display digitized collections, or providing multimedia tools, such as videos or written tutorials, that can guide users through digital preservation applications. At times, community education means helping people learn basic computer skills that will allow them to better access online content. Remember to include volunteers, docents, and staff members in community education opportunities. This group can demonstrate digital applications inside of the organization, encouraging visitors to revisit exhibitions and special topics after they leave the facility.

It can be difficult to determine where to begin offering community outreach opportunities. As staff members consider the target audience, they should ask such questions as, "Is the group capable of accessing the site?" and "Does the group know how to navigate the site?" so the organization will know where to focus outreach efforts. The goal for this type of community education is not to provide advanced skill sets to all, but to promote the digital resources to optimize use among the organization's strongest stakeholders. As staff members begin planning for outreach programs, consider the importance of location, equipment, training materials, and learning outcomes.

Accessibility, both geographic and technological, is most important when offering opportunities to your community. Visitors to the institution's physical space may feel more comfortable exploring the digital collections at home if they are able to learn how to do so on a computer located on-site. Additionally, providing guests with the website's URL, either on a printed brochure or on a takeaway item like a bookmark, can remind visitors to use the digital collections when they are no longer at the facility. Sometimes institutions are difficult to visit due to limited parking or public transportation options. Others may not have the space for more than a few visitors at a time. When planning an educational event, consider the primary community audience. For instance, an accessible and familiar off-site location may work best for senior groups, such as the local public library or community center, provided it has the space and equipment needed to accommodate the technological needs. For example, if the lesson is about digitizing photographs, make sure the facility hosting the training is equipped with enough computers and scanners to demonstrate scanning to a group of people.

Computers and tablets that may not be available through your organization may be available at public libraries, creating opportunities to test-drive digital preservation applications on various platforms. Partnering with public libraries can also build community capacity and opens opportunities to let people know about the organization through cross-promoting programs and events. Librarians frequently educate the public on how to use library resources, including technology; they are natural allies in any collaborative training session. These examples are value-added measures that can help smaller organizations achieve greater impact in the digital environment.

Teaching groups how to perform simple preservation measures, such as scanning or using an online form, can instill a sense of collective confidence in the future of the organization and the well-being of the collections. Providing these skills to targeted communities, such as senior citizens or young adult groups, places the organization in a position to become the local experts in digital preservation. Crowdsourcing, or inviting participants to assist with simple tasks such as describing an image or reading and describing manuscript items, grows from learning opportunities sponsored by cultural heritage institutions. For example, the Washington State Historical Society has achieved success with crowdsourcing for the Civil War Pathways Project by hosting a statewide read-in of Civil War materials from different cultural heritage organizations. The result is an Omeka.net website that displays a variety of archival items relating to the Civil War and Reconstruction in the Pacific Northwest.[11] Omeka.net showcases select projects on its website.[12] One site in particular is the SAILS Digital History Collection. This Omeka.net site houses and displays digitized content from a variety of libraries in Massachusetts.[13]

One of the case studies included in this section, the A. Schwab Digital Archive, details how Omeka.net is used to house digital artifacts.[14]

When offering preservation skills as community education opportunities, it is efficient and economical to use training materials that are already available online. Several of the open source tools mentioned at the beginning of this part have active user communities. Many participants create educational materials, such as tutorials and videos, and make them freely available. Identifying these educational materials and periodically checking links and media to ensure currency will make community education much easier to plan and execute successfully.

In addition to providing community education opportunities to promote the organization as a trusted expert in digital preservation and provide access to online content, it is equally important to connect with internal users. Without these individuals, many organizations would fail to communicate information about the organization's services, exhibitions, and collections to visitors. Teaching volunteers, docents, and staff basic skills in tool navigation and functions helps create a team of individuals that can engage visitors with the digital preservation tools both on- and off-site. Staff members in other areas of the institution are also important ambassadors when promoting digital preservation. They are often the first people to know about a new project or initiative and often serve as the public face of the institution in the community.

Engage Communities with Social Media

We often hear about "social media" in the news and in everyday conversation, but how can small institutions leverage free or low-cost tools available to engage the community? Social media is a term used for "blogs, wikis, Internet communities and online discussions" in which "content is created, at least in part, by users."[15] Organizations interested in expanding their outreach beyond traditional media outlets like newspapers, radio, and television can choose one or several of the free tools available to the public such as Facebook, Twitter, Pinterest, Flickr, Instagram, YouTube, Foursquare, Tumblr, or WordPress. In addition, Google products such as BlogSpot, Google+, Google Map Builder, and Google Tour Builder are easy to learn on the back end and user friendly on the front end. Each product's website features clear instructions, and other sites such as YouTube house a selection of helpful how-to videos.

Promoting collections and programs via social media can be key to disseminating content to wider audiences and inviting participatory community engagement. However, as Padilla-Melendez and Del Aguila-Obra (2013) warn, "It may be fashionable to use social media, but without a proper strategy, it could have more negative than positive outcomes."[16] There are several factors to identify and consider when determining which social media tools will support the outreach goals of a small institution: audience, collections and services, and time.

First, determine the target audience for social media content. Which platforms, if any, can they access or use easily? It may be tempting to only think of aspirational audiences, but it is important to perform a realistic, if informal, assessment of the current constituencies. Next, does the institution's collection include images, documents, or decorative arts? How would each translate on social media? Are there items that can be easily scanned or photographed, or does the collection only include oversized objects like maps or artwork?

Pinterest, Instagram, and Flickr are all image-based social media tools and are simple ways to connect visual representations of collection items with members of the public, many of whom may already use these platforms for personal communication. Map-building tools like Google Map Builder and Google Tour Builder can highlight locations important to the institution and its community as well as places significant to the provenance or context of the collection. Historypin (https://www.historypin.org/en/) uses the Google Map Builder to allow participants to upload photographs attached to a place. The images are overlaid on Google Maps reflecting what the image's site looks like today. Finally, is the institution primarily interested in sharing information about tours, hours, research appointments, and events? Twitter, with its 140-character message limit, allows organizations to communicate quickly and concisely. Facebook is useful for posting an image along with announcements and enables users to post comments. WordPress enables organizations to share lengthier posts about collections history, new acquisitions, and upcoming projects.

Organizations newer to social media or unsure of where to begin promoting their digital collections may want to consider choosing one project or theme and building two or three social media accounts, like Flickr and WordPress, around the content. Alternatively, an organization interested in promoting more general information about collections and services can start with a Facebook page and add a Twitter account, using text from the Facebook posts to feed the Twitter messages. Repeating information on more than one social media platform can be a helpful way to reach community members who may only check one tool or the other. Though it makes sense to investigate the social media efforts of comparable institutions, like other historical societies or historic house museums, small cultural organizations should also glean ideas from the social media activity of academic institutions and larger museums, libraries, and archives. One example is the Black Project at Bryn Mawr College (http://black atbrynmawr.blogs.brynmawr.edu/about/), which uses Google Tour Builder and a WordPress blog to engage an online audience. For digital mapping projects, consider exploring GRASS (https://grass.osgeo.org/), an open source geospatial information (GIS) tool. Also, it is crucial for the staff to identify the copyright ownership of materials selected for inclusion on social media and determine if the posted image represents a gift from a donor, a visitor's photograph, or a creative work in the public domain.

It is likely community members will only respond to social media efforts if they view the institution as an equally engaged participant. Social media is a useful outreach tool, but it can be detrimental to an organization's reputation to have several accounts with little or no fresh content. Sufficient time is needed to update social media; do staff members or volunteers have the available hours to update the accounts with original content on a regular basis (at least once a week)? Think about upcoming projects and events which may need extra attention, like an annual fundraiser or a new archive which needs processing. While such events may provide interesting content for social media accounts, the time involved in planning may prevent staff members from updating the institution's Facebook, Twitter, or Instagram accounts regularly. Before committing the institution to creating and maintaining a new social media account, reach out to colleagues from organizations with similar staff resources and a social media presence, and ask them about the time required to update their content.

Include and engage community members through crowdsourcing, mentioned earlier in this part, which invites social media users to help provide missing information about an image, document, or object. Small historical societies or even less formal associations can especially benefit from the knowledge and memory of their senior community members; see the West Tennessee Historical Society (https://www.facebook.com/West-Tennessee-Historical-Society-214160585283752/) and the Rendville (Ohio) Improvement Association (https://www.facebook.com/RendvilleIA/) Facebook pages for examples of such interactions. Guest blog posts can alleviate the staff workload and provide alternate perspectives on collections. Researchers who feel comfortable sharing their findings may want to post about an object or a related exhibition. Also, organizations may ask key community members to serve as social media advocates; if there is a community advisory group, encourage members to repost digital content on their personal and professional accounts.

In addition to original content (posted at least four times a month), staff members can repost relevant content from other local, regional, national, and even international institutions. The community will see how collections and services fit into the larger context and are integral to a collective cultural history. Institutions such as the Ohio History Center, a regional institution, explicitly encourage visitors to repost web content; others, such as the National Underground Railroad Museum, provide Twitter and Facebook buttons after each blog post, allowing readers to easily share with their own audiences.

Cross-promote with other historical and cultural institutions by creating a hashtag for common initiatives or community-wide celebrations. An example is the 2012 Memphis-area celebration of the birth of artist Carroll Cloar, for which the hashtag #summerof cloar was used by multiple organizations. Hashtags are user-created tags assigned to social media content. They use the symbol "#" coupled with tags generated by users that are linked to other content with the same tag and published to a social media platform. Hashtags are helpful because they allow users to discover content that has the same word or words attached. (A glossary of social media terms is available through the nonprofit consulting agency Socialbrite.)[17] Other ways to cross-promote include linking to websites and digital collections of relevant institutions and even co-producing digital exhibitions using materials from several partner museums or libraries. Look for ways to utilize your existing networks in order to help build this presence. This may mean talking to current users of the museum's collection, donors, board members, and researchers. Staff members can set up Google Alerts with keywords and names like "portrait miniatures" or "Ida B. Wells" as an efficient way to stay abreast of news items, exhibition reviews, upcoming programs, and recent research projects of interest to the institution and its community. Other methods include subscribing to news feeds, newsletters, listservs, and other resources sponsored by professional organizations such as the American Association for State and Local History (AASLH) and the Small Museum Association (SMA). Again, some of this content may be valuable to community members and worthy of reposting.

Make Lectures and Programs Accessible Online

Not all community members can visit an institution's physical space for exhibitions or lectures and performances. Recording programs, either as a video or an audio podcast, held in the venue or in other spaces and posting online is a way to engage community members who could not attend. Resources for novices can be found on the website for *Videomaker* magazine and online buying guides like CNET and B&H Photo Video Pro Audio. An organization can purchase an easy-to-use camera like a GoPro, a microphone (higher end is preferred for the optimal sound) and adaptor, and an inexpensive tripod. Adobe Premiere is a good choice for editing, and nonprofit institutions can obtain a special subscription rate by ordering through the Tech Soup website; one can contact the latter and ask questions over the telephone, as well. If the budget does not allow for such purchases, consider asking a local business or a board member to donate a camera and microphone or even funds for the equipment.

It's best to assign the task of recording programs to a staff member who could quickly learn how to operate the equipment. Is there a student filmmaker who would be willing to record a lecture as part of a journalism class? This option can work if the institution regularly hosts interns or employs graduate assistants; however, relying on student availability and individual skill sets could be a temporary solution and not always reliable for an ongoing plan to record events. Sometimes it is best to pay a professional the going hourly rate (approximately $100) to film an event as a way to ensure quality and consistency. Organizations with frequent need for professional videos or documentaries to promote collections and ongoing projects should consider hiring a professional either part-time or even full-time. In addition to documenting events, small institutions can film or record three-minute talks by curators or affiliated scholars about a specific object, display, or exhibition and post online to YouTube or add to an iTunes account. If the institution has a digital repository, include a link to the archived video or audio file on the homepage and promote via social media.

Conclusion

With the proliferation of open source digitization tools and social media platforms, all organizations have the opportunity to participate in the digital landscape. When cultural heritage institutions actively seek ways to reach visitor audiences online and provide access to important digital collections and online content, they instill confidence among the organization's user community. Opening a dialogue about audience interests helps the staff select content for online collections; involving community in the digital preservation process can also cultivate relationships with potential donors, volunteers, and partners (such as the local public library). Increased presence, both online and in the community, helps when it's time to promote collections, exhibitions, and events. Such engagement allows even the smallest organization in a position to strengthen their role in the communities they serve.

Acknowledgments

I would like to acknowledge Justin Thompson (Crosstown Arts, Memphis); Sarah Frierson (Folder and Box, Memphis); Ed Frank and Carol Perel (West Tennessee Historical Society); Wilford and Cyndi Preston (Columbus, Ohio).

Notes

1. Paul Conway, "Preservation in the Age of Google: Digitization, Digital Preservation, and Dilemmas," *The Library Quarterly: Information, Community, Policy* 80, no. 1 (2010): 61–79.
2. Social Square, "What Is Open Source Explained in LEGO," filmed March 2014, Wikimedia video, 4:40. Post October 2014 at https://commons.wikimedia.org/wiki/File:What_is_Open_Source_explained_in_LEGO.ogv.
3. Internet Archive, accessed December 27, 2015: https://archive.org/about/.
4. Jaime Schumacher et al., "From Theory to Action: 'Good Enough' Digital Preservation Solutions for Under-Resourced Cultural Heritage Institutions," Huskie Commons (2014), accessed December 27, 2015, at http://commons.lib.niu.edu/handle/10843/13610.
5. Information from Omeka website (see Omeka b 2015), accessed December 27, 2015.
6. Information from Omeka website (see Corporation for Digital Scholarship 2015), accessed December 27, 2015.
7. Information from Omeka website (see Omeka a 2015), accessed December 27, 2015.
8. Rowena Cullen, "Addressing the Digital Divide," *Online Information Review* 25, no. 5 (2001): 311–20.
9. Neil Selwyn, "Reconsidering Political and Popular Understandings of the Digital Divide," *New Media & Society* 6, no. 3 (2004): 341–62.
10. John H. Falk and Lynn D. Dierking, "Re-envisioning Success in the Cultural Sector," *Cultural Trends* 17, no. 4 (2008): 233–46.
11. American Association of State and Local History, "Civil War Pathways in the Pacific Northwest," accessed January 2, 2016, at http://awards.aaslh.org/award/civil-war-pathways-in-the-pacific-northwest/.
12. Omeka.net, "Showcase," accessed January 17, 2016, at http://info.omeka.net/showcase/.
13. SAILS Library Network, "SAILS Library Network: SAILS Digital History Collection," accessed January 17, 2016, at http://sailsinc.omeka.net/.
14. A. Schwab Digital Archive, "Welcome to the A. Schwab Digital Archive," accessed January 17, 2016: http://aschwab.omeka.net/.
15. Bob Franklin, *Key Concepts in Public Relations*, "Social Media," Los Angeles, CA: SAGE, 2009. Accessed December 29, 2015, http://www.credoreference.com/book/sageukpr.
16. A. Padilla-Melendez and A. R. Del Aguila-Obra, "Web and Social Media Usage by Museums: Online Value Creation," *International Journal of Information Management* 33, no. 5 (2013): 892–98.
17. Socialbrite, "Social Media Glossary: The Top 100 Words & Phrases in the Social Media Dictionary," accessed January 17, 2016, at http://www.socialbrite.org/sharing-center/glossary/.

Creating a Digital Library for Community Access

A. Schwab on Beale Street

Brigitte Billeaudeaux

D IGITAL LIBRARIES provide lots of opportunities to get information online and out to user communities. Items stored away in physical archives can now live online for all to see. While digital solutions have unearthed bits of cultural heritage once lost or forgotten, the online tools are vulnerable, take time and planning to create, and can be difficult to maintain. This case study reports on a digital library project of a family-owned store that has been present for over 130 years on Beale Street in Memphis, Tennessee. Beale Street is known worldwide for its connections to music, but it also has an older history as a hub for minority-owned businesses. The A. Schwab Trading Company was founded by French Jewish immigrant Abraham Joseph Schwab in 1876 and the Schwab family continued to operate the company for 135 years in its original location on Beale Street. In 2011 the Schwab family sold the trading company to the Saunders family. The Saunderses are no stranger to family businesses as their patriarch founded Piggly Wiggly, the first self-service grocery store chain in the nation. Along with the purchase of the Trading Company came the building and all of its contents, including a nineteenth-century basement with over a century's worth of Memphis memorabilia. Many of the items were in poor or compromised condition and the dank and dusty environment of the basement was less than ideal for storing artifacts with so much historic significance.

A. Schwab's has maintained a very small museum space for years on the mezzanine between the first and second floors of the store. The company was interested in highlighting items from its archives in an online presence but no one working in the company had the knowledge or time to accomplish this task. In an attempt to help the company highlight the history of the Schwab family's immigrant- and minority-owned business while providing some intervention to at-risk artifacts, Zachary Sandberg, Krista Oldham, and I partnered to create a digital library as a class project for the University of Tennessee Knoxville's Information Sciences program. We created guidelines for organizing, storing, and presenting archival items in a digital format along with simple workflows and guidelines to allow employees and volunteers to continue the work once our team was no longer involved.

Envisioning the Project

For this project, our team utilized the International Federation of Library Associations' (IFLA's) guidelines on collection development.[1] This internationally recognized group created the guidelines because of the lack of introductory information available on collection development policy.[2] The guidelines helped our team establish most aspects and criteria for the A. Schwab digital library. Team members wanted to provide an online product that could house and present digital items from A. Schwab's archives. Omeka's dot net platform is easy to use and very easy to setup (see the Resources Guide for further discussion of Omeka). Because of ease of setup and additional features offered through the site, Omeka.net was selected to be the web platform for the library. Omeka.net is the web-based counterpart to Omeka.org, an open source, or free and widely available, product developed by the Roy Rosenzweig Center for History and New Media at George Mason University.[3] The online platform was attractive because it did not require that team members or A. Schwab employees maintain a computer system in order to set up the site.

As a digital preservation tool Omeka.net is very user-friendly. The system is interoperable, meaning items put into Omeka.net can be transferred from one website to another. The system is initially free up to 500 megabytes of storage for anyone that creates a user account with Omeka. Five hundred megabytes can store several hundred low-resolution images, like those found on the Internet, but is not optimal for larger formats of media such as video or audio. Licensed packages with expanded premium features are available up to twenty-five gigabytes. For this project Zach and I suggested the silver package, a $99 yearly subscription, for A. Schwab because it would give the company ample room at two gigabytes to expand and grow the library in the future. The package also offered plug-ins like geolocation, a mapping tool that allows users to see a place associated with an item, and a feature that would allow for future user engagement opportunities.[4]

Zach and I facilitated meetings with the stakeholders, those that are invested in the company, to assess specific needs and wants that would grow out of this project. We conducted a community analysis of visitor information that had been collected from the time the Saunders family had taken ownership of the company until January 2013. These data, along with a collection evaluation, provided insights into the audiences that would benefit from an A. Schwab digital library. Three groups were identified: school groups, hobbyists and scholars, and history and heritage groups. The results of the community analysis provided insights on how to promote the digital library once it was in place. For school groups the library offered a product to return to once students and educators were back in the classroom. Hobbyists and scholars interested in the economic development and commerce of a large urban city in the south would benefit from many of the historic records that were found, digitized, and placed in the library. Because Schwab's is an immigrant- and minority-owned family business, history and other heritage groups would have an interest in learning more about the longevity of the store. Having materials accessible online to these communities could help further and foster new scholarship.

A myriad of materials was selected to seed the A. Schwab digital library. Vintage newsprint ads, manuals for health and beauty, metal stamping plates for advertising, letters from Memphis mayors to taxpayers, and images of Memphis and A. Schwab history are all examples of items that are part of the store's digital library. The physical items that can be found in the store's small museum were also included in the digital library. One example from the original museum is a congratulatory letter from a member of Memphis's chamber of commerce noting the store's 100th anniversary on Beale Street.

Implementing the Vision

Zach and I gathered and worked together to digitize the items and our third team member, Krista Oldham, took information that was being created and gathered and worked on the project remotely. Together we developed a comprehensive collections guideline for employees and volunteers. The guidelines included information on best practices for digitizing and storing artifacts and other information. Our group also worked collaboratively to create records for items in the digital library. Digital files were uploaded to the site and together we created metadata records, detailed information about the items housed in records, to accompany the materials.

A picture from 1916 of the Harahan Bridge that spans the Mississippi at Memphis, a poignant letter to one of the Schwab's from a man seeking a job in hard economic times, and a family portrait of the Schwab family were items that interested our team while we were building the library. These items were immediately identified as having importance to the collection. Over fifty items were selected to be included in the digital library. We could have selected many more objects, but for the initial creation of the library it was important that items fit within the initial scope developed in the collection guidelines. Some of the criteria for inclusion were that items had to be accessible and have a high historic value to the Memphis community or to the A. Schwab store.

The Project Results

Once the initial work of the digital library was completed and in place, A. Schwab stakeholders were informed and the final digital product (http://aschwab.omeka.net/) was turned over to the trading company. We set up meetings with stakeholders to tour the online site, review the collection guidelines, and open up a dialogue between members of the team and the company for further collaboration on the digital library. At the time that the project was handed over, A. Schwab was unable to manage the digital library site. Since taking ownership, the company was focused on adding a soda fountain to the store and developing the store's event space. These commercial ventures took precedence over maintaining and developing a digital library. No additions were made to the digital library and once renewal time for the digital library came due with Omeka.net, A. Schwab's did not do so and neglected to notify members of our team. This created a problem because the digital library site was removed and presumed to have been deleted by systems managers at Omeka.

Generally, Omeka provides a small window of time after a site's license lapses to transfer all of the data to another platform or server. (For users with free accounts this is not an issue; the site remains unless the user account is disabled.) Once this grace period passes, the site is deleted and is no longer accessible. Because stakeholders at A. Schwab lacked the expertise to work with these types of data and their failure to communicate the site's license lapse, all of that data was seemingly lost. Our team that worked on this project was devastated.

Lessons in Recovering a Lost Library

Over a year passed before anything additional happened with the digital library. Zach Sandberg and I were motivated to resurrect the digital library even if it meant rebuilding the site from scratch. Far too many weekends were dedicated to bringing the library to life and we were moved by the mementos and the artifacts that the Schwab family chose to keep to tell the story of their family and business. Zach discovered that the Internet Archive's Wayback Machine had successfully crawled or recorded and captured a snapshot of the website from January 22, 2014[5] (A. Schwab Digital Archive, 2014). This discovery gave us hope that there would be information to help us start rebuilding the digital library. The Internet Archive's Wayback Machine allows copies of websites to be made and stored on the Internet Archive's servers. The machine itself is actually a computer program that scans websites reading information that is publicly viewable. It takes all of the scanned information and then allows a search engine to recall the information when keywords or the website URL is searched. This is a cost-effective and very low-tech way for small organizations to archive websites. Because the A. Schwab site was crawled once, there was baseline information available about content on the website's pages to begin re-creating the digital library. Images and external links were rendered as broken but textual content from the site was available.

Before work began on the reconstruction of the site, Omeka was contacted to see if there was any salvageable material left on Omeka's servers of the defunct site. After being inactive for over a year, Omeka still had a complete copy of the A. Schwab digital library—a miracle only achievable in cyberspace! Omeka having a copy of the library meant that it could be recalled from Omeka's servers and the site could be restored to its original working order with all of the original content.

To fully resurrect the library Zach and I purchased a premium package of Omeka with the option to transfer information off at a future date. Also, decisions had to be made about the future of the site. How would the site grow? Where would new materials for the digital library come from? Because we made the financial commitment to bring the digital library back to life, we decided the site would be best maintained privately among members of the original project team. The site now has a section where visitors can contribute items to be included in the library just like the original site. This ability encourages visitors from the web community to contribute items to the digital library. Additionally, items from local organizations' archives will be digitized and included after obtaining the appropriate permissions.

Next Steps

The A. Schwab digital library has a future beyond the initial project because the team that created the library will continue to oversee its growth. The digital library tells a less widely known part of Memphis's history about a family-owned business that was present for all of the city's highs and lows. We plan to reach out to the Jewish community of Memphis, the Memphis Public Library, and the Preservation and Special Collections Department at the University of Memphis Libraries to continue to grow the A. Schwab digital library. Collaborating with the A. Schwab Trading Company for future artifact contributions is not out of the question, but for the interim the library is best maintained by community members that can oversee its consistent growth.

Material Expenses

Materials used in this project: Double bed scanner: Epson Perfection V750 Pro—this model is discontinued; comparable replacement is the Epson Perfection V850 Pro—retail $600–$995. Omeka.net plan for this project: $49–$99/year; plan prices range from free up to $999.

Acknowledgments

Thanks to Zachary Sandberg (Memphis University School, Memphis, Tennessee) and Krista Oldham (Haverford College, Haverford, Pennsylvania) for their work on this project.

Notes

1. International Federation of Library Associations. "Guidelines for a Collection Development Policy Using the Conspectus Model." Last modified September 22, 2015, http://www.ifla.org/publications/guidelines-for-a-collection-development-policy-using-the-conspectus-model.
2. Ibid.
3. Corporation for Digital Scholarship. "About: What Is Omeka.net?" Accessed December 2015, http://info.omeka.net/about/.
4. Corporation for Digital Scholarship. "Sign Up for a New Account!" Accessed December 4, 2015, https://www.omeka.net/signup.
5. A. Schwab Digital Archive. "Welcome to the A. Schwab Digital Archive." *A. Schwab Digital Archive.* January 22, 2014. Internet Archive, https://web.archive.org/web/20140401000000*/http://aschwab.omeka.net.

Separating the Glitz from the Practical in Social Media at the National Underground Railroad Freedom Center

Jamie Glavic and Assia Johnson

FROM FACEBOOK to YouTube, Pinterest to Snapchat—social media has changed the way we communicate. Thoughtfully crafted content is distributed in 140 characters, seven-second videos, or filter-edited images to dozens, hundreds, and thousands of people in order to share experiences, ideas, and information. According to an October 2015 report by Pew Research Center, nearly 65 percent of American adults use social networking sites—up from 7 percent when they began systematically tracking social media usage in 2005.[1]

What seemingly began as a trendy, booming tech start-up phenomenon has become a part of our day-to-day lives. However, ten years after Pew Research Center's initial social media use findings, there are still a few misconceptions:

"Our visitors aren't on social media."

Chances are you have more visitors on social media than not. While 90 percent of young adults are the most active on social media, 35 percent of Americans sixty-five and older report using social media, compared with just 2 percent in 2005. Additionally, 58 percent of rural residents, 68 percent of suburban residents, and 64 percent of urban residents report using social media.[2]

"Social media is free."

While there may not be an up-front monetary fee to access or use a number of social media platforms, it is not "free." The "cost" of social media lies in time, resources—not only delivering unique, rich content online, but also interacting with your audience in real time when they ask questions, share experiences, or post pictures. These multifaceted digital communication tools are accessible to organizations of any size or budget but will not be successful without consistency and a commitment to content development.

Social Media at the National Underground Railroad Freedom Center

The National Underground Railroad Freedom Center was not immune to the above misconceptions. The Freedom Center, located on the banks of the Ohio River in Cincinnati, Ohio, reveals stories about freedom's heroes, from the era of the Underground Railroad to contemporary times, challenging and inspiring everyone to take courageous steps for freedom today. As a museum of conscience with a limited marketing and communications department budget, we rely heavily on public relations and pitching stories for media coverage and utilize social media as communication, engagement, and information-sharing tools. Social media is an integral part of the institution's overall communications strategy.

In 2008, Jamie Glavic worked in the marketing and communications department as an assistant and offered to manage an abandoned Facebook page created by a volunteer. From 2008 to 2012 as Glavic's online responsibilities grew, the Freedom Center expanded its social media reach from Facebook to include a WordPress blog, Twitter account, Foursquare check-in, YouTube channel, Tumblr blog, and Instagram account. Not everything worked. Foursquare peaked in use over a period of two years but slowly faded. Tumblr, a platform that continues to grow in popularity, never gained steam with the Freedom Center's online audiences. This was both a period of online expansion and experimentation for the Freedom Center.

In spring 2015, Glavic returned to the National Underground Railroad Freedom Center as the director of marketing and communications and found the department struggling to manage several social media accounts without a centralized content strategy or reporting process. Prior to Glavic's hiring, the marketing and communications department consisted of one full-time employee for more than two years. While content was posted on a semiconsistent basis across platforms, the number of platforms being utilized proved to be difficult to manage; moreover, the day-to-day functions of the department took precedence over social media activity.

The Freedom Center had created more social media accounts than it could successfully manage, a common problem for small organizations. New platforms seem to pop up every month. Social media is a medium where organizations can easily get caught up in what's new, what's sexy, and what's in the news. We needed to separate the glitz from the practical and make our social media work for us and not the other way around.

Assessing the Freedom Center's Social Media Status

Glavic and Assia Johnson, public relations and social media coordinator, began separating the glitz from the practical in social media by taking a digital audit of the Freedom Center's current platforms: Facebook, Twitter, Instagram, Pinterest, Vine, Voices blog, and YouTube. We discovered the following:

- Our Facebook page had 25,438 followers, but they weren't engaging with our content. On average, we posted five to seven days a week, reaching between 300 and 1,200 followers with each post.
- Our Instagram account featured pictures from events and programming happening within the museum. Yet the 533 followers' participation on the platform was minimal, experimental, and haphazard.
- Our Pinterest page garnered 113 followers and 455 likes, but inconsistent postings simply didn't bode well for a platform that, by design, required constant activity.
- Our Twitter account was an invaluable tool for our institution. On average, we tweeted forty-two tweets a month to our 5,645 followers, making 6,000–30,000 impressions—or the number of times your content was displayed in a user's news feed, ticker, or page—depending on the content.
- Our Vine channel was a trendy new platform that reached the teenage to young adult audience we try to court with our mission.[3] On average, our vines, varying between two and ten posts a month, produced 828 loops (views per post) with 111 total followers. Participation in the platform was experimental—our posting schedule was inconsistent and unstructured.
- Our YouTube channel did not have a consistent schedule of engaging and diverse content and only had 182 subscribers.
- The blog on the Freedom Center website began in 2006 and was relaunched as The Freedom Blog in 2008. Bloggers consisted of two staff members, posting on an inconsistent basis with no editorial content outline. The website saw several redesigns in the last decade, making tracking of subscribers and followers nearly impossible. We added staff bloggers in 2010, but posts were only encouraged and not required, resulting in discontinuity of format, voice, and posts. Lack of consistent site management systems led to additional issues with time management, requiring staff and site managers to allot invaluable time, resources, and funds on multiple trainings.

Our next steps consisted of researching and using the following free resources to define and develop the value and goals of our social media use. Links to the reports below are listed in Part VI, the Resource Guide of this book:

- The Pew Research Center, a nonpartisan, nonprofit "fact tank," provides information on the issues, attitudes, and trends shaping America and the world. We subscribed to and evaluated reports from Pew's Internet & American Life Project with a focus on social media demographics and use practices.

- The Digital Engagement Framework, created by Jasper Visser and Jim Richardson, provides nonprofit professionals and volunteers with an easy-to-understand guidebook on how to develop and design a successful, consistent digital strategy. This is a great resource for beginners and longtime users.
- Hootsuite's Fundamentals of Social Media Marketing online courses provided a valuable introduction of different social media platforms through the fundamentals of social advertising and engagement.
- The 2015 Museum Horizon Report, a collaboration between the New Media Consortium and Balboa Park Online Collaborative, analyzes six key trends, six significant challenges, and six important developments in technology—identified across three adoption horizons over the next five years—that provide museum leaders and staff with a guide for strategic technology planning.

The information we gathered by walking through each of the resources and course work above helped us pinpoint our audience, create a consistent identity and voice online across multiple platforms, and learn how to build upon our successes by eliminating content and platforms that did not fit that identity or online goals.

Putting Our Assessment into Action

Following the audit, we decided which platforms were going to stay and which ones we would walk away from.

- Due to the number of followers and the ease of cross promotion with like-minded institutions and community partners, Facebook continues to be a priority.
- Instagram had great potential for our brand and target audience as its popularity and use increases. A content schedule would be created for audience building and consistency.
- Pinterest seemed like a natural fit for our core audience—thirty- to fifty-four-year-old women who love education and history, with at least a bachelor's degree, and have young children[4]—however, we did not have time or resources required to develop and create content to share boards on a regular basis. Due to capacity, we left Pinterest and archived our previously shared content for potential repurposing on other social media platforms.
- The genre most popular on Vine, comedy, did not fit our brand and voice. We were not alone—other museums of conscience were using the platform, but the time and resources needed to create such relevant and "viral" content befitting our brand greatly outweighed our return on investment. We deleted our Vine account and archived our previously shared content.
- YouTube continues to fit our brand and voice as an educational resource—one that can be used in classrooms and board rooms across the globe. Creating video content has become a marketing and communications priority.

After downsizing the number of platforms in use, we immediately noticed an increase in engagement on the platforms we kept with the development of our digital communication content calendar and revisiting already existing content—historical posts, inspiring images, quotes, and videos used on Vine, Pinterest, blog, and website. We continue to track, challenge, and expand our reach and engagement by using metrics, analytics, and insights either available through built-in platform metric trackers or with tools like Hootesuite (www.hootesuite.com), Buffer (www.buffer.com), and Sprout Social (www.sproutsocial.com). Analytic tools have helped us increase our monthly engagement and reach by providing our team with hard numbers on what types of content are most successful, by platform, time, audience, and interest. This snapshot led to the creation of engaging content that would garner over 8,842 interactions with our posts by 7,646 unique users with the potential reach of 1,919,211 people on Facebook and Twitter alone. As of December 2015, our Facebook page has grown to 29,000-plus followers, more than 600 followers on Instagram, and more than 6,000 followers on Twitter. We have had more than 100,000 views on our YouTube channel. These "free" platforms help us reach our audience with our content and mission to educate the public on how to use lessons from our past in order to take action on contemporary issues and struggles for freedom and equality in their online and IRL (in-real-life) communities. Additionally, we can reach new audiences and potential advocates for our mission by generating interest in our brand and involving them in the conversation by activating their communities to discuss topics we care about at length and to visit our museum for educational, community, and cultural enrichment.

Assessing our Assessment

There is no "one size fits all" when it comes to social media implementation. We discovered that by eliminating accounts that exhausted our resources and with little return, we were able to focus our efforts on platforms that capitalized on our institutional strengths. Understanding that it takes a lot of time to create, develop, and master a social media content strategy was critical. Equally important was our ability to find free or low-cost tools capable of distributing content across multiple platforms because these made our social media content development work more efficiently and saved time.

Through multiple conversations with volunteers and other professionals we learned those tasked with social media responsibilities often feel like they are on an island. We recommend creating fun, informational materials that not only educate colleagues and volunteers on how to share via selected social media platforms—helping spread your message in an approachable way that feels organic—but also invite them to participate in content development and brainstorming. Internal buy-in and excitement can greatly enhance engagement.

Focus your efforts on core audiences and utilize platforms that will reach a large segment of that audience, but remember that the way we communicate continues to transform. Experimentation in social media, when time allows, can expand your reach and expose your institution to new audiences online. However, it is important to note that experimentation on social media is not a life sentence. If something isn't working for your organization, it is perfectly acceptable to walk away from that platform. Decide how much time you are willing to spend trying out a new platform—we recommend no more than six months—and measure your results.

Social Media's Future in Museum Settings

In order to sustain our results, we must continue to monitor audience use and demographics on each of our social media platforms and stay informed of updates for users and platform managers as it can affect the way we create and distribute content. Social media is constantly changing and adapting—what was once the new "it" platform, like the once giant My-Space and the scrappy Friendster, and the next "big thing" can go the way of the dinosaurs. Don't dive into trends too soon—social platforms, too, are vying for eyes and engagement by exploring what content maintains and attracts new users, sometimes at great expense to content developers.[5]

Consider the following questions: What does your organization "look like" in the proposed new platform you're considering adopting? What kind of content will populate it, and how often would you post without a scheduling tool? Is the platform so new that the tool does not offer an option for scheduling? Can you visualize your coworkers or volunteers using the platform at the office or in their free time? More importantly, would it cannibalize or compete with another platform that is already wildly successful for your brand? If the pros outweigh the cons, do not adopt it—continue to monitor and vet the platform until you see an opportunity that would greatly extend the reach of your institution's mission.

Notes

1. Perrin, Andrew. "Social Networking Usage: 2005–2015." Pew Research Center. October 2015, http://www.pewinternet.org/2015/10/08/2015/Social-Networking-Usage-2005-2015/.
2. Perrin, Andrew. "Social Networking Usage: 2005–2015." Pew Research Center. October 2015, http://www.pewinternet.org/2015/10/08/2015/Social-Networking-Usage-2005-2015/.
3. Lenhart, Amanda. "Teen, Social Media and Technology Overview 2015." Pew Research Center. April 2015, http://www.pewinternet.org/2015/04/09/teens-social-media-technology-2015/.
4. Duggan, Maeve. "Mobile Messaging and Social Media—2015." Pew Research Center. August 2015, http://www.pewinternet.org/2015/08/19/mobile-messaging-and-social-media-2015/.
5. Andreeva, Nellie. "Snapchat to Shut Down Snap Channel. Laying off Team, Changing Content Plans." October 2015, http://deadline.com/2015/10/snapchat-snap-channel-shut-down-layoffs-original-content-strategy-1201577855/.

How a Simple, Inexpensive Podcast Engaged an Entire Community

Chick History, Inc.

Rebecca L. Price

WE ARE FIFTEEN YEARS into the paradigm of the twenty-first-century museum that encourages dialogue, relevancy, and civic responsibility. We are also fifteen years into Web 2.0, which emphasizes user-generated content, transparency, and virtual communities. These two ideas are a match made in heaven. I began Chick History in 2010 as an online "space" to experiment with these ideas, explore the opportunities digital resources offer, and to find new and innovative ways to tell women's history. Chick History soon evolved, expanded its scope, and partnered with other nonprofits and museums on collaborative programming. In 2015, Chick History incorporated and is now a 501c(3) nonprofit. Through programming, community outreach, and professional development, Chick History is dedicated to rebuilding history one story at a time.

Letting the Audience Take Ownership

One challenge with online engagement is that it takes a different form than on-site engagement. It is personal. It must be authentic. Most importantly, online engagement works best when it is user defined. By embracing these ideas, museums and cultural heritage institutions can experience a different type of engagement that reaches past their physical space and exhibitions when they go online to engage. This type of engagement can be significant to museums wanting to connect with and involve more diverse and underrepresented audiences, and are ready and willing for their targeted audience to become part of the process.

Chick History's first large-scale project was the #Herstory Podcast, a fifty-episode podcast in which I invited contemporary women to share the story of the historical woman who inspired her. The idea began with one simple question put to me from a fellow museum colleague: "How can I get involved?" She and I were discussing the state of women's history at a conference. I told her about Chick History and she told me she would love to do something for it. That was that, but the idea stuck in my head for several months.

What could she do? What would it look like? I pondered what a project would look like that gave full ownership to the audience, not the curator. This would go beyond surveying the audience and asking what they would like to learn; it would allow the audience to also tell the history. This became the basic idea for the #Herstory Podcast: What if you could choose someone in history you adored and talk about them on your own terms? As museum professionals, we get to do it every day. I was excited about the possibility of giving that to my audience. So, the #Herstory Podcast became the chance for women to share that story. The title references the herstory/history play on words, but it's also possessive. This would be "her story" that she was able to tell about a woman in history.

A User-Friendly Project

My first goal was reassuring all the participants that this was not a history lesson. Their enthusiasm and commitment to the project was secured once they understood they were in full control of who and what they wanted to share. This process was key to the project's success. This was also what some would argue was the biggest gamble: putting complete trust in your audience that they *already* know enough to speak intellectually and comfortably about a historical topic.

All participants were given the same three directives: (1) Tell us a little bit about the woman you have selected, (2) What do you find inspirational about her story?, and (3) What is one book you recommend to learn more about her? The questions were given to participants beforehand so they could prepare.

Each episode was intended to be approximately ten minutes in length and the historical woman had to have been deceased for at least twenty years. Once interviews began, it became immediately apparent that both of these guidelines needed to be amended. This was the first test of the "community curation" aspect of the project.

When I originally envisioned the concept, I set the requirement that the historical woman chosen must have been deceased for at least twenty years. The idea being that a minimum of two decades would be enough time to put her into historical context. For the most part, participants were able to do this. However, several women that I really wanted to participate would not have been able to do so, as they chose people who were recently deceased. Because their participation was important to the project, I made the decision to relax this requirement. In the end, it was the right decision as the quality of the project was enhanced with the diversity of women chosen.

As for the time frame of ten minutes, this also became a moving target, and participants were allowed to take as much or as little time as they needed. One participant completed her story in eight minutes, while the longest was approximately twenty-four minutes. This flexibility also added to the quality of the project and demonstrated the diversity of the contemporary women being interviewed.

Figuring Out the Technical Side and Promotion

The technical aspect of the project was implemented on a shoestring budget. Fortunately, there are many online resources that are free and inexpensive to get a podcast up and running, as well as basic software and recording tools. I used Skype to conduct all interviews and GarageBand for MAC to record and edit interviews. Once I had the final mp3 audio files, I hosted the files for free on Archive.org and used Blogger.com and then Feed-Burner.com to create the RSS feed needed to submit to iTunes and other online podcast directories. (See "Technical Guide" for step-by-step instruction.)

The only out-of-pocket expenses were a desktop microphone and purchasing Skype credit to use their telephone service. Skype is free from account to account, but if a participant did not have a Skype account, which was the case for about twenty participants, I used their telephone service.

The next step was promotion and marketing once the podcast was ready to disseminate. Fifty episodes would be aired over one year, with one episode a week. With a limited budget, only social media was used to promote, with a heavy emphasis on Twitter. Knowing that very few podcasts gain popularity without heavy social media marketing, I knew this would be very important in promoting the project. For each episode, a series of Twitter and Facebook posts were scheduled for the week. A built-in marketing bonus for the project was that many of the participants also had Twitter and Facebook accounts and could be tagged in all posts, and they in turn would help promote and share the project.

Unexpected and Rewarding Results

Two types of engagements were experienced with the #Herstory Podcast: one from the listeners of the podcast and one from the participants. As for the listeners, the success was measured in statistics and anecdotal data. In terms of reach, the podcast has been downloaded over 30,000 times since its release in 2012. Comments left on the blog and through social media also demonstrate the success of the project. Many listeners experienced the same type of "kinship" with the historical women that the participants did, expressing their agreement with how a story was told. In turn, they share something about the historical woman and why she inspires them, continuing the community dialogue aspect of the project.

The response and effect the project had on the participants has been extremely rewarding. Participants became ambassadors for the project. They helped to market and create additional content outside of their episodes, all for free. One participant who is a singer/songwriter wrote an original song for the project that was used as the musical

The #Herstory Podcast.

50 women...from the headliners to the lesser-known gems. A project by Chick History.

HOME   ABOUT   CONTACT   SUBSCRIBE

Chick History Podcast home page. Source: Created by author.

accompaniment. A second participant, SheHeroes, syndicated the podcast to their international audience in 2016.

Professional connections and relationships were also made between Chick History and participants that have proven beneficial to both parties. Many participants work for national organizations with similar interests and/or cause-driven work in the field of women's equality. This strong network of like-minded professionals has allowed Chick History to call on participants for support with other initiatives and collaborations. One spin-off project was a collaboration between Chick History and Girl Museum for an online exhibition. These lifelong connections will prove to be the most beneficial and rewarding outcome of the project.

Lessons Learned and Advice

The technical aspect of this project required the most research, and producing a podcast was more complicated than originally anticipated. Through trial and error, I did discover a free way to get a podcast published. For those interested in seeing how you publish a podcast for free, a step-by-step technical guide is at the end of this case study. Girl Museum has since followed this model for their podcast programming.

The demands of production were also very rigorous, and for anyone wanting to do a series of podcasts, I recommend having the run at least 50 percent complete before you start airing them, or at least recorded and ready for editing later. Scheduling fifty people for interviews, working with their schedules, and trying to meet a production deadline were challenging. There were some periods when a podcast was not published on a weekly basis.

It's important to note there are no hard-and-fast rules on podcasting frequency. Schedules vary from daily episodes that run like a radio program to podcasts that are released on a monthly basis to just a couple times a year. There are also serial podcasts, like the #Herstory Podcast, that have a set amount per series. *This American Life's Serial* podcast is the most famous of this type of podcasting. When deciding the frequency with which to publish, consider the workload and how much time you'll need to produce your podcasts. If monthly works for you, then go with monthly, etc.

The biggest lesson learned from producing a community project was to be flexible to the needs of the participants and truly incorporate them into the development process. Additionally, first-time users should adopt the attitude that using social media and online technologies is experimental. One size does not fit all. Trial and error is an important part of creating a successful online digital campaign and/or program. The same goes for negative feedback—anyone who ventures into the world of online programming and social media must accept that a certain amount of negative feedback will happen. The anonymity of the Internet has given strength to harsh critics, but it is all part of the process and should not deter the project.

What's Next and Keeping the Momentum

A plan to create a second season of episodes is intended and will be produced when the time and resources are available. Until then, other outlets of promotion are employed to continue to disseminate the first fifty podcasts to new audiences—and there are always new audiences on social media. Podcasts and other forms of digital content are different than exhibits and programs with a onetime use. This content lives in perpetuity on the web and iTunes and can be used over and over again. It remains searchable and usable as new people come across the project and then share it to their networks. Routine marketing helps promote the project, such as marking birthdays or anniversaries, to keep the content in circulation.

As mentioned earlier, SheHeroes is rebroadcasting the project to their audience. Other organizations have approached Chick History with similar ideas to reformat and broadcast that are currently in the works. The content of the episodes has also led to other uses outside podcasting. In September of 2015, I spoke about the project to a conference of young girls on self-esteem and leadership training.

Limited budgets, small staff, and physical restrictions (both the facility and the collection) can be obstacles that *unwillingly* prevent small museums from creating more engaging, community-centered programming offered on-site. Museums can work around financial and physical challenges by employing digital and online resources to engage audiences. Furthermore, by using a process that includes the audience and allows them to share with the museum, institutions can build trust with communities that are underserved or underrepresented in the museum's exhibitions and collection. This trust will lead to lifelong supporters of the museum that are thoughtfully and authentically engaged.

P.S. The woman from the conference who started it all? #Herstory 16: Mary Pickford by Eloise Batic.

Technical Guide: How to Podcast for Free

Professional podcasters make it look so easy. But anyone who has thought about and looked into podcasting knows it's more laborious than it looks and can cost money. There are services that will do the technical process of creating a podcast—storing your files, publishing, creating feeds, some even editing your audio files—but they will cost money.

There are ways to set up a podcast for free, and various free options are available online. This guide will focus on what was done for the #Herstory Podcast and the three free services used: Blogger.com, Archive.org, and FeedBurner.com.

Step 1: Set Up the Blog on Blogger.com

The blog serves as the main website and public interface where listeners go to learn more about the podcast and episodes. Each episode of your podcast will be a blog post. There are tutorials available for how to set up a blog on Blogger.com for those unfamiliar with the process.

Step 2: Host the Audio Files on Archive.org

Once you have your final audio file edited and just the way you want, it needs to be hosted (stored) online. Audio files are large. Blogger.com, and most blogs, will not store these large files that take up lots of space. So they need to go somewhere else and then be inserted into your blog. Create your Archive.org account and upload and host your files for free. Again, Archive.org will have tutorials on how to get started.

Step 3: Get Your mp3 File

Once you've uploaded the file to Archive.org, you'll need to get the URL for your mp3 file that is now online. It's just like any URL, but ends with ".mp3." Each file you upload to Archive.org will have its own page with several file types, including the mp3 version. Open the mp3 file in a new window and leave it open; we'll come back for it later.

Step 4: Create and Publish the Blog Post

Back in Blogger.com, create a new post with all the information you need for that episode. Don't forget to include the title and description! On the right are the "Post Settings." Look for the "Links" and open that up. You'll see a couple of entry fields, and the one you are looking for is "Enclosure Links." Go back to the Archive.org open browser with your mp3 file (from Step

3), copy the entire URL, and paste that into the field that says "Add Link" and press "Done." You've now enclosed your mp3 file into your blog. Your podcast won't work if you haven't done this. Now hit "Publish!" Tip: Keep the post as simple as possible to keep the code clean. Avoid images and hyperlinks.

Step 5: Set Up an RSS Feed

FeedBurner.com will turn a blog feed into the necessary RSS 2.0 feed that most podcasters, including iTunes, prefer. Log onto FeedBurner.com (since it's also a Google product, you can use the same email for your Blogger account). Here, you will paste your blog URL into a blank field that says "Burn a feed right this instant." Make sure you check the "I'm a podcaster!" button before hitting "next." You'll go through a couple of next steps with instructions on how to set it all up, and FeedBurner.com offers tutorials. Take note: it's in these steps that you will also enter the iTunes information for the name and description and image of your podcast for how it will appear in iTunes. A quick tip: your podcast image must be stored too, but you can do that on your blog!

Step 6: Hack Your RSS Feed

There is one hack you will need to do to your feed before you submit it to iTunes or other online directories. By default, Blogger.com feeds only pull the most recent twenty-five posts. Go to "Edit Feed Details" and look for the entry field called "Original Feed." Replace the last section with "default?max-results=500" and save. It should look like this:

http://theherstorypodcast.blogspot.com/feeds/posts/default?max-results=500

Step 7: Submit Your Podcast to iTunes

In FeedBurner.com, on your feed page is the orange RSS icon button. Click on that to take you to a new window that will have your feed in the URL. Copy that and submit it to iTunes, following their available tutorials for help. Your successful podcast feed will look something like this:

http://feeds.feedburner.com/theherstorypodcastfeed

Now all you need to do is repeat Steps 2–4 every time you have a new episode. Your feed from FeedBurner.com will automatically pick it up every time you publish and submit a podcast to iTunes.

Congratulations! You are now podcasting for free!

Recording the Neglected Sports Stories from the Backside

Holly Solis

ORAL HISTORY PROVED to be a critical component in documenting the contributions of the often neglected "backside" stories of the racetrack community. When added to the existing representations of the sport of horse racing, the Backside Stories oral history project provides a more holistic understanding of the total industry. Oral history projects can seem daunting and time-consuming. Planning, interviews, and transcription can be difficult and there is the added challenge of making interviews easily available to the public. But oral history does not need to be difficult. A museum without the resources to create, implement, or manage an oral history project can recruit volunteers or a student from a local educational institution whose research focus aligns with the project's topic. That is how the Backside Stories developed.

What follows is a how-to guide for working on a small oral history project through the eyes of a graduate student. My thesis project, Backside Stories, is an ideal type of partnership for a small museum. The work can be done by one or more people and has a flexible timeline. With good planning and partnerships, oral history projects can be a rewarding experience for all involved and help forge relationships with communities who have not gotten a chance to tell their stories.

Why Backside Stories?

I created Backside Stories through a combination of research and personal experience as a digital oral history project that focuses on Latino and Chicano labor on the backside of thoroughbred racetracks. The "backside" is the colloquial term for the stable area of the racetrack, and backside work involves the grooming, walking, and training of horses. My family is a part of the community that works quietly in the background of horse racing, a sport that is anything but quiet. Work in the horse-racing industry is not considered agricultural, but draws immigrants from rural areas of many Latin countries, including Mexico, Argentina, and Panama. These laborers are proud of the work they do, citing it as difficult and beautiful. However, they rarely are recognized for that work. This is one reason I created Backside Stories—to celebrate the work these laborers do every day and to help them step out of the shadow cast by jockeys, owners, and trainers.

Backside Stories brings these experiences to the forefront to offer a different horse-racing narrative. The project also exists to fill in a perceived gap in Southern California's labor history. Though sociological research about the backside of thoroughbred racetracks is plentiful, historical perspectives on backside labor in relation to Hispanic workers are rare. Many of the skills needed for this line of work are learned through word of mouth and on the job. This type of skill development makes oral history an important tool to engage the backside community, as the work itself is created through experience and personal contact.

The Plan

Backside Stories began with a project scope outline. This outline was a one-page document that included the reasons for the project (to document labor in the community's own words and place it within the context of other Latino and Chicano labor in California), possible interview subjects (anyone eighteen years or older who works or has worked in the backside of a Southern California racetrack and identifies as Latino or Chicano), and the expected use of the interviews (on a website, digital archive and exhibit, and the future inclusion in a museum exhibit). A project scope outline was useful for understanding and communicating the need for a project and how work can be allocated within an institution. Understanding future goals makes creating and conducting interviews easier.

Creating interview questions was the next and possibly one of the most difficult steps of the project planning process. Oral history is very different from other interview forms. Questions should not be too direct or elicit only "yes or no" responses. Open-ended questions that ask participants to describe something or relate experiences work well for oral history.[1] For Backside Stories, participants were asked to describe their daily work routine, the area where they grew up, and their first experience working with horses. Although a goal for oral history is to gather information on a set of specific topics or events, the process relies on slight prompting and very active listening. In one interview, a participant mentioned immigration raids. I had unintentionally prompted this answer by asking him to describe his experience working at Del Mar Racetrack near San Diego. Oral history is about letting the interviewee choose what they do and do not want to share. The process essentially gives the interviewee control over the extent of the history or narrative they share with the interviewer.

The project scope outline was also useful for completing Institutional Review Board (IRB) documents. An IRB is a committee established to review and approve research involving human subjects. Universities created IRBs to protect human research subjects from exploitation or unethical research practices, but other major institutions have adopted their standards. For oral history, IRBs are focused on protecting vulnerable populations including children, the mentally ill, and undocumented individuals. Ethical reviews of projects are critical and can create a more trusting connection between the community and your institution. The process consists of submitting an application, which, among other questions, requires a guarantee that the interviewee consents to the interview, a list of the proposed interview questions, and documents how the interview responses will be used and stored. The IRB process is important whenever personal information is being collected in the interview. It may be useful to contact a local university's history or public history department for help in reviewing a project, as they will be familiar with the process of IRB review.

As a part of Arizona State University's history department, the Backside Stories project required a formal review by the university's IRB office. The office had templates for consent and translation forms, recruitment flyers, and other documents. I created my own flyers and consent forms and revised them according to the IRB's recommendations. The entire process, from initial review to project approval, took about forty-five days. This timeline will depend on the IRB's revision requests and if a full project review is required. Backside Stories was exempt from a full project review, as are most projects that are not collecting highly personal and sensitive information.

The Recording Process

Once the project was approved, I began the interviews. I used a Zoom H5 Handy Recorder and a standard 8GB memory card, which cost about $240 and $20, respectively. I saved all interviews on the memory card as a .wav file. I was certain all file names were similar and stored together on a computer system. I made two copies of each interview and housed them separately in the event that one of the storage devices became corrupted.

I relied heavily on word of mouth for recruitment, though I also posted flyers in gathering spaces within the backside of Santa Anita Park. Getting in touch with organizations already embedded within the community was especially helpful. One of my contacts works in a clinic that serves backside workers at Santa Anita. This contact passed along information about the project to her friends who currently work in the backside. From there, interviews were set up in person or over the phone. The interviewee had control over the time and place of the interview, though a quiet, secluded area was the best setting to ensure good audio quality. Most interviews took place at the interviewee's home or a conference room at Santa Anita. Full transcription and editing took about three times as long as the interview's length, but longer if the interview was in Spanish. Edited audio interviews and their digital transcriptions were then copied onto CDs and given to their respective interviewees along with a letter of thanks for their participation. These CDs can be copied or shared with family members and friends, if the interviewee so chooses. This means that interviews can reach those without Internet access, or future generations that may not be able to access the website. Providing copies to interviewees also built trust and transparency in the project.

Results

Backside Stories, though focused on California history, has reached online visitors from all over the United States. Making oral histories accessible to those inside and outside the community

Backside Stories homepage on Omeka. Source: Created by author.

is key. My project used Omeka, a free digital archiving software created by the Roy Rosenzweig Center for History and Media Studies. This software allows almost any type of archive material to be easily available and citable for the public. Omeka allows creation of digital exhibits with just a push of a button and customization possibilities are almost limitless. (See articles by Bollwerk and Billeaudeaux, this volume.)

Backside Stories uses a free version of Omeka (see figure above) to host full interview audio (.wav files), transcriptions (.pdf files), photographs (.jpeg files), and related metadata.

Dublin Core

Title

Reinaldo Solis Sr.

Description

An oral history with Reinaldo Solis Sr., an immigrant from Panama. He has worked as a groom, foreman, and an assistant trainer. He speaks about his experiences with horses, his travels, and his day to day life on the backside. The smaller clip highlights his typical day of work.

Click the screenshot of the transcription to open the full PDF file.

Date

March 11, 2015

Creator

Holly Solis

Dublin Core metadata fields on Omeka. Source: Created by author.

Omeka is also useful because it makes the metadata entry process more efficient. Metadata, or data about data, provides additional information about resources stored in an archive. For example, for each of my audio interviews the metadata associated with the interview includes information about the date of creation, the creator, the interviewee, interview length, and topics covered within the interview. Metadata makes finding specific information related to records housed in an archive easier. The software comes preinstalled with Dublin Core (see figure at bottom of page 198), a group of metadata fields (or controlled vocabularies) that were created for broad use among a large group of items. For instance, Dublin Core provides standardized metadata fields for audio interviews, photographs, and transcription files. Fields include author, date, and subject. Instead of creating their own fields for each file again and again, the project team just plugs the information they have into the automatically generated Dublin Core fields. After plugging in the information, the team would just need to save and make the file public. Dublin Core fields reduce the time and resources spent on data entry; help to ensure different libraries, archives, and museums are using the same metadata terminology to describe objects; and have already been used by many institutions.

Backside Stories also uses Omeka for digital exhibits. Omeka's digital exhibit plugin allows the creator to pull items from other places in the archive. For example, I can upload a picture of the stable area at Santa Anita Park. In the digital exhibit area, all I would need to do is select that photograph from the archive and add a caption or explanatory text. From there, a visitor can click on the photograph and Omeka will automatically take them to the photograph's file and metadata.

Backside Stories uses WordPress as a project website (previous page). While Omeka is the project's online archive, WordPress allows for more in-depth summaries of interviews, definitions of the different types of backside labor, and project sources. The WordPress site is intended to serve as an introduction to the project, one that links back to the Omeka archive so that visitors can learn more about specific topics through oral histories or other archive material. For example, the WordPress site contains names and descriptions of many backside jobs. Visitors can click on a job title and be redirected to the Omeka collection of interviews that corresponds to that particular job. WordPress is easy to use, free, and fully customizable. Of course, WordPress can also be replaced by a museum's existing website by simply setting up a hyperlink to the Omeka archive item.

Lessons Learned

The most important lesson I learned from this project is to begin early. Planning, funding, and possible IRB processes took up a substantial part of my project timeline. Speak to community organizations and possible interview subjects early and let them be a part of the planning process. Their contributions and feedback are important for understanding how the community you are working with will view your project and can have an impact on the quality and quantity of interviews collected. Keep in mind the importance of having the community's voice in the forefront of the project.

Language barriers can be difficult to overcome. I encountered both English and Spanish speakers, bringing translation to the forefront as an issue to address. As a semifluent Spanish speaker, I could competently conduct interviews but would also complete interviews in two parts if necessary. I would contact the participant for a second interview in case I had additional questions or needed clarification about a topic discussed in the first part of their interview. This two-step interview process gave me more time with the translation in case I misinterpreted something during the original interview. The project also had an individual who sat in on an interview and helped with the translation of my questions for the interviewee. I edited their Spanish translations out of the interview, so as not to confuse listeners with two sets of questions and speakers.

Carrying Backside Stories Forward

Backside Stories is currently collecting more interviews to populate the Omeka archive. My next step is to expand the digital exhibit on Southern California Latino labor history and its connection to backside work. The project will create its own domain through a WordPress site and focus the content of the digital exhibit to include Southern California Latino labor history and its connection to backside work. After the digital exhibit is complete, the project plans to create a physical exhibit based on the oral histories for display at the racetracks where participants work or local museums in close proximity to the racetracks.

Oral history projects are a partnership with the community. Keeping in touch with participants after their interviews to inform them that their interviews have been uploaded, or if their interviews are being used in an exhibit, and being open to ideas from the community itself is key to being a good community partner. Backside Stories has already begun to shine a light on the experiences of backside workers. The finished interviews have given current audiences a broader understanding of backside labor and the sport of horse racing. Interview subjects, colleagues, friends, and family have been excitedly spreading the word about the project. From these word-of-mouth exchanges, the project can reach broader audiences that may have originally been unaware of this type of labor at a thoroughbred racetrack.

Note

1. For more information, see Shopes, Linda. "Human Subjects and IRB Review," in *Oral History in the Digital Age*, edited by Doug Boyd, Steve Cohen, Brad Rakerd, and Dean Rehberger. Washington, DC: Institute of Museum and Library Services, 2012, http://ohda.matrix.msu .edu/2012/08/making-sense-of-oral-history/.

Small Museum Website Creation with a Limited Staff and Budget

The Arden Craft Shop Museum

Kelsey Ransick

Tucked away in the 1950s-style suburbs of northern Delaware sit the Ardens, a community of three villages founded on the economic ideals of Henry George and the aesthetic tastes of William Morris. Sculptor Frank Stephens and architect Will Price admired Georgist economic principles, often simplified as "tax land, not labor," and wanted to prove that Single Tax theory was feasible in practice. Stephens and Price purchased an old farm and founded Arden in 1900 as a summer retreat for those seeking refuge from the hustle and bustle of nearby Wilmington and Philadelphia. Creative and cultural "gilds," such as the Shakespeare Gild and Weaver's Gild, sprang up with the founding of the community organization the Arden Club in 1908. By 1922, when the neighboring village of Ardentown was founded, Arden had a growing population of summer residents and some year-round residents. The villages grew, expanded gild offerings, welcomed new residents, and made improvements to the leaseholds—parcels of publicly held land available to residents under a ninety-nine-year lease. In 1950, Ardencroft was added to the community, and the three villages of the Ardens flourished. Artists, writers, freethinkers, reformers, anarchists, socialists, and scores of other creative types have long been drawn to the villages, and the community boasts an interesting history as part of the Arts and Crafts movement.[1] Today, the villages retain their commitment to Georgist economic principles and creative endeavors.

In the 1990s, a group of residents began pushing for the creation of a museum to showcase the villages' artists and house almost 100 years of amassed archival material. In 2001, Arden Craft Shop Museum, Inc. was founded to help create and oversee a new museum focused on local history and artistry. Villagers raised funds to purchase and renovate the old Craft Shop, and in 2004, the Arden Craft Shop Museum (ACSM) opened its doors. Acting as a repository for local crafts, artwork, literature, and historical artifacts, the ACSM has since put on over twenty exhibitions, organized and made accessible ten linear feet of archival material, and celebrated its ten-year anniversary—all without a single full-time staff member. Today, the museum is open two days a week, thanks to one staff member who works eight hours per week and the dedicated Museum & Archives Committee of ten volunteers.

Planning for an Online Presence

The museum enjoyed success with local visitors—many residents of all three villages visited the museum in its opening year, and continued to do so over the next decade. However, the volunteer-run museum needed to reach a larger audience. Museum volunteers wanted to make the collections more accessible and spread general awareness of the museum. The ACSM hired its first museum professional, Keith Minsinger, as a curator in 2010. Minsinger set up an online presence for the museum, a Facebook page with hours and location information. The museum's first website went live in 2012, thanks to the next curator (and again sole staff member), Robin Valencia MacDonald. Built on WordPress, ardencraftshopmuseum. com was an attractive and straightforward blog. MacDonald did most of the maintenance, taking about an hour each month to post an Object of the Month blog, perform updates, and respond to blog comments. Considering her limited hours and numerous other duties at the museum, an hour was about all the time that could be spared for the website.

Shortly after I took over as curator for MacDonald in 2013, WordPress announced that it would begin placing third-party advertisements on websites held by free accounts. In true Freemium[2] style, users could purchase an ad-free upgrade for about $30 per year. Since we were already paying $18 for the domain and $5 to connect it to WordPress, this would bring our website expenses to about $55 per year. I brought this to the attention of the committee, who agreed that we did not want advertisements we could not control on our site. I suggested that if we were going to pay more for the website, we should consider options that might give us more flexibility with the look and setup of our site.

The website needed to be something that volunteers and future staff members could easily learn to update. That way, our blog could be populated by a variety of voices but our website could look professional and clean. I began by investigating a number of What You See Is What You Get (WYSIWYG) editors, including Wix and Squarespace. I compared each editor's fees to host a website, built-in designs and templates, data storage limits, and extra features. The three finalists were Weebly, WordPress, and GoDaddy, leaving us with three options: moving the domain to GoDaddy and hosting to Weebly, upgrading the WordPress account, or moving both the domain and hosting to GoDaddy.

The three most important factors were price, extra features, and aesthetics. After speaking with a few committee members, we narrowed it down to Weebly and WordPress, and at the next monthly meeting we discussed what would work best for our institution. We knew we wanted to put parts of the collection online, including numerous images. We also wanted to be able to take donations and sell a limited selection of gift shop items through the website. Since we were changing the website up anyway, we decided we wanted a website that looked more like a website and less like a blog. However, keeping the blog component (with comments) was important, especially as we had upcoming exhibitions that would benefit from community input or information crowdsourcing. The committee reviewed the information and our site goals and approved a switch to GoDaddy domain registration and Weebly website hosting as soon as the new website could be set up.

Creating an Expanded Web Presence

Creating the new website (http://www.ardencraftshopmuseum.com/) took about two months. The content from the old website was copied into new Microsoft Word documents. Because of the structure of WordPress blogs, there were only two pages to be moved, an About page and a blog, though the content of the latter would not transfer easily. We began by reviewing the About page for accuracy and augmenting it with additional information. We created documents for more "traditional" website pages (e.g., Visit, Collection & Archives, Support Us) and drafted content for these pages. Then we revised, revised, and revised.

While the editing process continued, we began the domain registrar transfer from WordPress to GoDaddy. This involved unlocking the domain with the current registrar (WordPress), purchasing a domain transfer from GoDaddy, authorizing the domain transfer, and then waiting for GoDaddy to complete the transfer, during which time the site would stay at WordPress until the domain could be mapped to the new Weebly site.[3]

To get the Weebly site started, we looked over the built-in themes from Weebly and selected one that looked functional, flexible, and appropriate for the tone of the museum. With approval from the committee, we began migrating content from the Word documents into the Weebly editor. When the new site looked satisfactory, the switch began. There was some concern among the committee that the site would be down while the domain and hosting were transferred. Though one version of the website (either WordPress or the new Weebly one) would always be available, we chose a Wednesday evening in case anything did go wrong during the switch, hoping that fewer people would chance by the website during that time. Weebly provided step-by-step instructions for upgrading a site and connecting it to a GoDaddy domain.[4] The transfer was initiated with a few clicks of the mouse and the switch completed about four hours later, during which time some visitors saw the old website and some the new, depending on their browsers and cookie history.

Benefits of the Expanded Website

New features on the website included an RSS feed reader on the homepage to keep the front page content fresh, an online donation portal and gift shop, and a calendar for upcoming exhibitions. The donation portal and gift shop were especially valuable a year later when we sold tickets online for a fundraising event. Thanks to PayPal's nonprofit rate and easy integration with Weebly, we collected numerous donations in addition to selling almost thirty advance tickets. The calendar, linked to our Gmail account, included our somewhat unusual hours (Wednesdays 7:30–9:00 pm and Sundays 1:00–3:00 p.m.), upcoming exhibitions, programs, and other museum-sponsored events.

About a year after we launched the new site, we began planning a new exhibition about authors from the three villages. In an effort to capture information about these authors, we turned to the community for names, published works, and biographical information. Our new website accommodated both a document with a running list of the authors for whom we had information and also a submission form via which Ardenites could share information with us.[5]

We announced the new website on Facebook, in the village newsletter, and in person to our visitors, encouraging everyone to look at the new site and engage with it. Links to new blog entries and major updates were posted to Facebook and the website featured social media buttons on every page. Some community members liked our website so much that they approached us about making their own websites. One Ardenite sought help to set up his website on Weebly, www.henrygeorgeacademy.org. He has since learned how to edit on Weebly and has taken over management of his site.

Lessons Learned

During the process, we learned a great deal about website development and design. Firstly, content management is no cakewalk, but it can be made manageable. Even the simplest two-page site requires dedicated upkeep. Moving to a fifteen-page website meant a lot of content creation, even if most pages only had a paragraph or two of text. Secondly, website platforms often change up their offerings and plan costs. It is worthwhile to shop around for other platforms and plans, especially if it seems likely that a platform will keep increasing prices.

One downside to switching websites is that our old blog posts either had to be individually migrated or left behind. Since WordPress could continue to host our old site as a free blog (with WordPress advertising and no customized URL), we decided to place a link to the old website on the new site. That way, interested parties could still visit past blog posts. Our Search Engine Optimization (SEO) was briefly thrown off because any hits on the old blog posts would not transfer to the new site. Once enough visitors made it to the new site, the SEO caught up and the website now appears on the first page of most search engines.

Moving Forward

Looking back with two years' hindsight, we now see two missed opportunities, both involving the domain. When the ACSM's first website launched, it had a dot-com extension. We were hesitant to change it to a dot-org during the update because all of our brochures and publicity had the dot-com address. While dot-orgs are traditionally associated with nonprofits and dot-coms with other companies, these extensions are not necessarily regulated and different domain registrars charge different prices for them. In some ways, extensions had begun to lose their strict meanings. However, at the end of 2015, Internet domain names underwent a major update, and dozens of new domain extensions (e.g., .tech, .news, .guru) were opened up, which may mean that visitors will start paying more attention to extensions. This could work against us when seeking donations if people mistake us for a for-profit company. In the future, we may dedicate additional funds to purchase both the dot-com and the dot-org versions of our domain and redirect everything to the dot-org.

We have not completely missed the second opportunity: Google is also a domain registrar, one that offers free emails and analytics with a domain purchase. We can switch registrars at any time to take advantage of this, though we are unlikely to do so because GoDaddy gave us a good deal on our domain purchase ($74 for nine years of domain registration). Perhaps when our renewal comes up, we will. In the meantime, Weebly runs some stats and visitor demographics for us and we have signed up for Google for Nonprofits, which also gives us free email under "@ardencraftshopmuseum.com."

Table 5.1.   WYSIWYG Editors Compared

	WEEBLY	WORDPRESS	GODADDY
Aesthetics	Very nice, professional built-in templates	Beautiful built-in templates but limited editing ability unless we purchase a CSS-editing upgrade ($30/year)	Nice built-in templates
Platform Flexibility	Templates don't require much updating, but do offer variety of color schemes; page content and layout can be quite varied	Limited—on a platform built for blogs (i.e., restricted page structure and organization)	Untested platform abilities (fairly new WYSIWYG editor); cannot switch themes without losing content
Ease of Use	Drag-and-drop functionality is easy to learn	Blog posting is easy, but other editing requires practice	Drag-and-drop functionality is easy to learn
Extra Features	Has e-commerce functionality and can integrate with PayPal; allows HTML coding	Allows limited HTML coding within posts; has numerous plug-ins, but these can be tough to integrate	No e-commerce (donations or gift shop purchases will have to go through third-party website)
Data Storage	Unlimited	3 GB	1 GB
Cost	$7.99/year GoDaddy domain + $3.33/month Weebly hosting = approximately **$48/year**	$18/year WP domain + $5/year domain connect + $30/year ad-free upgrade = **$53/year**	$7.99/year GoDaddy domain + $3.50/month hosting = **$49.99/year**

Moving forward, we are determined to keep our online presence active. While we already update the calendar and post to the blog once or twice per month, additional blog posts would keep visitors coming back on a regular basis. One of our committee volunteers has become more active on Facebook, routinely linking back to our website. Hopefully, we can persuade a few more volunteers into actively posting and drawing attention to our website and the museum's activities. Additionally, as we move to offer more community-based exhibitions, we would like to take advantage of the many voices in such an active community. We can do this by asking Ardenites to submit comments and photos on Facebook and through the website. Ideally, the website will become a resource for researchers as well. We have already posted one finding aid for a major collection, but additional finding aids will expand information available to long-distance researchers. Maintaining and expanding our online presence will help us be more efficient with our limited hours. A few minutes here and there checking our Facebook page or looking at form submissions for co-created exhibitions will help us maximize our reach and deepen community engagement.

Notes

1. The Arts and Crafts movement, a reaction to the Industrial Revolution, valued individualistic design and hand-crafted goods rather than uniform and manufactured products that fed into the progression of capitalism.
2. A pricing system in which the main or basic product is available for free, but premium versions or upgrades are sold to a smaller part of the user base. Learn more at www.freemium .org/what-is-freemium-2.
3. Most domain registrars provide step-by-step instructions for these switches. GoDaddy's can be found at www.godaddy.com/help/transfer-domain-to-godaddy-1592.
4. Found at http://hc.weebly.com/hc/en-us/articles/201103158-Use-a-GoDaddy-Domain-with-Your-Site.
5. We received three submissions, which were quite helpful, though we had hoped for more.

Part VI

RESOURCE GUIDE

www.museumcommunities.com

T O COMPLETE THIS how-to-guide we include a link to our digital Resource Guide to support the application of the projects reported by our contributors in this volume. As well, we asked our contributors to draw on their collective experience to provide a list of their go-to resources on all of the volume topics. The content of the guide is not intended as a definitive or even comprehensive set of links to the many resources available for museums to manage work in their communities. However, we are confident that many readers will find that the guide links provide them with all of the information they need to launch projects like those reported by our contributors. Others will find the guide an excellent starting point to direct the further investigation for project resources.

The Resource Guide links are organized by the same topics as the six parts of this book: Introduction, Education, Participatory Experiences, Advocacy, As a Community Resource, and Digital Technology.

To make this Resource Guide as user friendly as possible, the content is presented in a digital format at www.museumcommunities.com. We chose to use a digital presentation for several reasons:

- First, the sheer length and tedious need to copy long URLs by hand from the printed page into the browser window seemed an overly cumbersome process. Further, as the resource guide content required an Internet connection for accessing, it seems wholly logical to simply place the links online as well. The Works Cited section of this volume, along with chapter end notes, contain the hard-copy references authors used in the volume.
- Second, the Resource Guide also curates pdf and other files referenced by the authors. Again, as digital access is necessary to download the files, it seems wholly logical that the guide itself be online.
- Finally, we will continue to update the user guide. As you read these words, the Resource Guide has been updated and expanded from the original version. As we are all aware, the Internet is not a static place—things change. For example, with the 2012

name change of the American Association of Museums to the American Alliance of Museums, all of the URL addresses for the organization's webpages also changed. The Society for American Archaeology's over 400 *For the Public* linked webpages are currently being updated and those links will likely change too. We were quite concerned that within one year, many of the links in a hard-copy Resource Guide would also have changed. Although we can readily update the Resource Guide website, obviously, reprinting regular updates to the printed volume is not practical.

We intend for the Resource Guide website to be an active hub for sharing information between museums and the communities that they serve. If you know of a great resource not included in the Resource Guide, we encourage you to submit the content. So be certain to visit the Resource Guide website (www.museumcommunities.com) now and often!

Project Financing

We did want to include one section of resources in print—Project Financing—a topic that causes many cultural heritage institutions, particularly smaller ones with limited or no staff, to not consider implementing the types of projects our contributors report. We wanted to address this concern from the very outset. That is why we required our contributors to report on projects that could be completed for under $1,500 plus labor and assuming access to normal business equipment and supplies. In addition, we asked all of our contributors to tell us about their "go-to" resource to obtain $1,500 to fund a special project. We posted the same query to the museum professionals who subscribe to the Museum-L listserv. The responses we received were less about specific links and more about strategic approaches. We received a considerable diversity of feedback that can be divided in several categories:

- In our contributors' case studies, labor was intentionally excluded from the cost estimates. However, funding for those projects could be a substantial expense if the skills are not already available from the museum staff. A substantial number of our case studies either directly or indirectly relied on skills of students to carry out the projects. As Robert Connolly, Holly Solis, Brian Failing, and Suzanne Francis-Brown note, engaging university students in the form of internships, volunteers, and for class projects can prove a critical resource for completing projects of all types.
- Nonprofit Tech for Good (http://www.nptechforgood.com/) is representative of the growing number of websites that consult on digital fundraising. Several of the contributors find this particular site useful because of its weekly e-newsletter that contains ten to fifteen links to relevant reports or infographics, links to free introductory webinars, and an extensive archive of curated material. The site is administered by Heather Mansfield, the author of two volumes on social media and fundraising for nonprofits. Of particular value Mansfield integrates multiple social media tools, each with its own function, into a nonprofits total social media and fundraising program.
- Perhaps the most common and diverse set of responses we received from both our Museum-L query and the volume contributors focused on local organizations and

special-interest groups. For example, a Visiting Nurses Association in South Carolina helped to fund educational outreach trunks. Rotary Clubs and other civic organizations were also favored funders for small projects. The Manassas Museum reported a longstanding relationship with the local women's club for funding projects in the $2,000 range.

- Melissa Prycer notes in her case study for this volume, as did several of our Museum-L responders, the ability to tap into existing government small grants programs. For example, in an email response Kathie Gow from the Hatfield Historical Museum in Massachusetts wrote that "each city and town has its own cultural council, a subsidiary of the state cultural council. We're a small town, and our cultural council usually has about $4,000 annually to spend, divided up among 8–15 applicants. . . . There's also the nonprofit fundraising organization connected with our small school system. They have about $10K they raise each year and offer grants between a few hundred dollars and a few thousand." As well, local and regional arts, libraries, and humanities endowment organizations were considered by our volume contributors as favored resources.

- Special focus organizations serve as information clearinghouses around specific issues. For example, the Tennessee Environmental Education Association publishes a monthly e-newsletter (http://eeintennessee.org/) that contains a list of relevant grants and resources.

- Corporate sponsorships were another prime means our contributors reported for funding opportunities. Local businesses can be approached to provide in-kind services such as printing, construction materials, or supplies. Major corporations routinely offer small (and large) grant awards for community-based projects (e.g., http://www.homedepotfoundation.org/; http://giving.walmart.com/foundation).

- Crowdfunding for nonprofits that are both 501(c)3 and nonprofits in name only is a fast growing means to achieve small to moderate amounts of money in a matter of weeks. Organizations such as Kickstarter (https://www.kickstarter.com/) and GoFundMe (https://www.gofundme.com/) are examples of crowdfunding organizations. Typically, the crowdfunding organization receives about 8 percent of the funds raised as fees. The actual crowdfunding organizations only make money if campaigns are successful so they provide excellent advice on how to organize the effort. Our volume contributors Gustavo Valencia Tello and Elizabeth Cruzado Carranza successfully raised over $2,000 in less than two weeks as partial support for their ongoing project. Of importance, simply being listed on the crowdfunding platform will not be the basis for a campaign's success. Rather the platform simply serves as a host for the fundraiser to tell their story and accept donations. The fundraiser must promote the campaign through their social media outlets and other sources.

- Our contributors provided several general caveats and recommendations for fundraising of all types. First and foremost was accountability and communication. Even if the ask is only for $500, presenting a budget along with the request assures the potential donor that the program is well conceived with a greater probability to succeed. Further, success begets success. Having successful past programs to show funders provides more assurance of future success. Our volume contributors report the importance in following up initial donations with an acknowledgment of the gift and follow-up reporting on the progress of the project so that the donor knows their money is well spent.

Be certain to check the Resource Guide website (www.museumcommunities.com) for more financial resources.

Works Cited

Adair, Bill, Benjamin Filene, and Laura Koloski (eds.). *Letting Go? Sharing Historical Authority in a User-Generated World*. Philadelphia: Pew Center for Arts & Heritage, 2012.

American Association of State and Local History. "Civil War Pathways in the Pacific Northwest." Accessed January 2, 2016, http://awards.aaslh.org/award/civil-war-pathways-in-the-pacific-northwest/.

Ames, Michael M. *Cannibal Tours and Glass Boxes: The Anthropology of Museums*. Vancouver: University of British Columbia Press, 1995.

Andreeva, Nellie, "Snapchat To Shut Down Snap Channel. Laying off Team, Changing

Content Plans." October 2015. http://deadline.com/2015/10/snapchat-snap-channel-shut-down-layoffs-original-content-strategy-1201577855/.

Boast, Robin, and Peter Biehl. "Archaeological Knowledge Production and Dissemination in the Digital Age." In *Archaeology 2.0: New Tools for Communication and Collaboration*, edited by Eric C. Kansa, Sarah Whitcher Kansa, and Ethan Watrall, 119–56. Los Angeles: Cotsen Institute of Archaeology Press, 2011.

Bohaker, Heidi, Alan Ojiig Corbiere, and Ruth B. Phillips. "Wampum Unites Us: Digital Access, Interdisciplinarity and Indigenous Knowledge Situating the GRASAC Knowledge Sharing Database." In *Museum as Process*, edited by Raymond Silverman, 45–66. New York: Routledge, 2015. Website: https://grasac.org/.

Bonney, Rick, Heidi Ballard, Rebecca Jordan, Ellen McCallie, Tina Phillips, Jennifer Shirk, and Candie Wilderman. "Public Participation in Scientific Research: Defining the Field and Assessing Its Potential for Informal Science Education. A CAISE Inquiry Group Report (2009)," accessed February 10, 2015, http://informalscience.org/images/research/PublicParticipationinScientificResearch.

Bria, Rebecca, and Elizabeth Cruzado, "Making the Past Relevant: Co-Creative Approaches to Heritage Preservation and Community Development at Hualcayán, Ancash, Perú," *Advances in Archaeological Practice*, 3 (2015):208–222.

Bria, Rebecca, and Elizabeth Cruzado. "Making the Past Relevant: Co-creative Approaches to Heritage Preservation and Community Development at Hualcayán, Rural Ancash Peru." *Advances in Archaeological Practice* 3(2015):208–22.

Brown, Aleia. "On Race and Museums: Starting Conversations, Embracing Action." *Museums & Social Issues* 10(2015):109–12.

Brown, Aleia, and Adrianne Russell. "Museums & #Black Lives Matter." In *Code | Words: Technology and Theory in the Museum*, edited by Ed Rodley, Robert Stein, and Susan Cairns. London: MuseumsEtc, 2015.

Butler, Shelley R. "The Politics of Exhibiting Culture: Legacies and Possibilities." *Museum Anthropology* 23(2000):74–92. doi:10.1525/mua.2000.23.3.74.

Cairns, Susan. "Mutualizing Museum Knowledge: Folksonomies and the Changing Shape of Expertise." *Curator: The Museum Journal* 56(2013):107–19. doi:10.1111/cura.12011.

Cameron, F. R. "Beyond the Cult of the Replicant Museums and Historical Digital Objects: Traditional Concerns, New Discourses." In *Theorizing Digital Cultural Heritage: A Critical Discourse*, edited by F. R. Cameron and S. Kenderine, 49–76. Cambridge, MA: MIT Press, 2007.

Cameron, F. R. "Object-Oriented Democracies: Conceptualizing Museum Collections in Networks." *Museum Management and Curatorship* 23(2008):229–43.

Cameron, F. R., B. Hodge, and J. F. Salazar. "Representing Climate Change in Museum Space and Places." *WIREs Climate Change* 4(2013):9–21. doi:10.1002/wcc.200.

Christen, Kimberly. "Archival Challenges and Digital Solutions in Aboriginal Australia." *SAA Archaeological Record* 8(2008):21–24.

———. "Opening Archives: Respectful Repatriation." *The American Archivist* 74(2011):185–2010.

———. "Does Information Really Want to Be Free? Indigenous Knowledge Systems and the Question of Openness." *International Journal of Communication* 6(2012):2870–93.

———. "Tribal Archives, Traditional Knowledge, and Local Contexts: Why the 'S' Matters." *Journal of Western Archives* 6(2015):1–19.

Connolly, Robert P., Samantha Gibbs, and Mallory Bador. "The C.H. Nash Museum at Chucaliss: Community Engagement at an Archaeological Site." *Museums & Social Issues* 7(2013):227–43.

Connolly, Robert P., and Natalye B. Tate. "Volunteers as Mission." *Collections* 7(2011):325.

Connolly, Robert P. "Co-Creation as a Twenty-First Century Archaeology Museum Practice." *Advances in Archaeological Practice* 3(2015):188–97. doi:10.7183/2326-3768.3.3.188

Connolly, Robert, Rebecca Bria, and Elizabeth Cruzado, "Co-Creation and Sustainable Community Engagement." In *Collections Care and Stewardship: Innovative Approaches for Museums.* Lanham, MD: Rowman & Littlefield, 2015.

Conway, Paul. "Preservation in the Age of Google: Digitization, Digital Preservation, and Dilemmas." *The Library Quarterly: Information, Community, Policy* 80, no. 1 (2010): Press: 61–79.

Corporation for Digital Scholarship, "About: What is Omeka.net?" Accessed December 4, 2015, http://info.omeka.net/about/.

Corporation for Digital Scholarship. "Sign Up for a New Account." Accessed December 2015, https://www.omeka.net/signup.

Crooke, Elizabeth M. *Museums and Community: Ideas, Issues, Challenges.* London: Routledge, 2007.

Cullen, Rowena. "Addressing the Digital Divide." *Online Information Review* 25, no. 5 (2001): 311–20.

Duggan, Maeve, "Mobile Messaging and Social Media—2015." Pew Research Center. August 2015. http://www.pewinternet.org/2015/08/19/mobile-messaging-and-social-media-2015/

Evans, Mary A. *Effigies.* Scottsdale, AZ: Poisoned Pen Press, 2007.

Failing, Brian, "Using Postcards as Historical Evidence," *Eastern Illinois University*, Fall 2014, Accessed November 30, 2015, http://www.eiu.edu/localite/postcardshisthome.php.

Falk, John H., and Lynn D. Dierking. "Re-envisioning Success in the Cultural Sector." *Cultural Trends* 17, no. 4 (2008):233–46.

Finnis, Jane, Sebastian Chan, and Rachel Clements. "Let's Get Real: How to Evaluate Online Success." *Action Research Project.* Brighton, UK: Culture 24, 2011.

Frankle, Elissa. "More Crowdsourced Scholarship: Citizen History." 2011. Accessed January 2, 2016, http://futureofmuseums.blogspot.com/2011/07/more-crowdsourced-scholarship-citizen.html.

Franklin, Bob. *Key Concepts in Public Relations*. "Social Media." Los Angeles, CA: SAGE, 2009, Accessed December 29, 2015, http://www.credoreference.com/book/sageukpr.

Garcia, Ben. "What We Do Best: Making the Case for the Museum Learning in Its Own Right." *Journal of Museum Education* 37(2012):47–56. http://museumeducation.info/wp-content/up loads/2012/06/jme.v37.n2.FREE.pdf.

Golding, Viv, and Wayne Modest (eds.). *Museums and Communities: Curators, Collections, and Collaboration*. London: A&C Black, 2013.

Gorgels Peter. "Rijksstudio: Make Your Own Masterpiece!" In *Museums and the Web 2013*, edited by Nancy Proctor and Rich Cherry. Silver Spring, MD: Museums and the Web 2013. Accessed February 15, 2016, http://mw2013.museumsandtheweb.com/paper/rijksstudio-make-your-own-masterpiece/.

Ham, Sam H. *Environmental Interpretation: A Practical Guide for People with Big Ideas and Small Budgets*. Golden, CO: North American Press, 1992.

Harden Susan B., Paul N. McDaniel, Heather A. Smith, Emily Zimmern, and Katie E. Brown. "Speaking of Change in Charlotte, North Carolina: How Museums Can Shape Immigrant Receptivity in a Community Navigating Rapid Cultural Change." *Museums & Social Issues* 10 (2015):117–33. doi:10.1179/1559689315Z.00000000039.

Hirzy, Ellen, "Mastering Civil Engagement: A Report from the American Association of Museums," *Mastering Civil Engagement* (2002):9–22.

Internet Archive. "About the Internet Archive." Accessed December 29, 2015, https://archive.org/about/.

Jennings, Gretchen. "The #museumsrespondtoFerguson Initiative, a Necessary Conversation." *Museums & Social Issues* 10(2015):97–105. doi:10.1179/1559689315Z.00000000036.

Johnson, Ken. "No Detail Goes Unnoticed When Art Is a Click Away: Art Museums Are Increasingly Adding Their Collections Online." *New York Times*, January 29, 2015, http://www.nytimes.com/2015/01/30/arts/design/art-museums-are-increasingly-adding-their-collections-online.html?_r=0.

Karp, Ivan, and Steven D. Lavine (eds.). *Exhibiting Cultures: The Poetics and Politics of Museum Display*. Washington, DC: Smithsonian Institution Press, 1991.

Karp, Ivan, Christine Mullen Kreamer, and Steven D. Levine (eds.). *Museums and Communities: The Politics of Public Culture*. Washington, DC: Smithsonian Institution Press, 1992.

Karp, Ivan, Corinne A. Kratz, Lynn Szwaja, and Tomás Ybarra-Frausto with G. Buntinx, B. Kirshenblatt-Gimblett, and C. Rassool (eds.). *Museum Frictions: Public Cultures/Global Transformations*. Durham, NC: Duke University Press, 2006.

Kedmey, Karen. "These New York Museums Let Visitors Go behind the Scenes to Explore Their Brimming Storage Facilities." *Artsy Editorial*. February 12, 2016, https://www.artsy.net/article/artsy-editorial-new-york-museums-open-their-storage-to-the-public-putting-their-vast-col lections-on-display.

Kehl, Winifred. "Turning the Museum Inside Out: Opening Collections, Engaging Audiences." *Museum*. September/October 2015, http://www.aam-us.org/docs/default-source/museum/burkemuseum.pdf.

Kohn, Richard H. "History and the Culture Wars: The Case of the Smithsonian Institution's Enola Gay Exhibition." *The Journal of American History* 82, no. 3(1995). 1036–63. doi:10.2307/2945111.

Krouse, Susan A. "Anthropology and the New Museology." *Reviews in Anthropology* 35(2006): 169–82. doi:10.1080/00938150600698336.

Kuo Wei Tchen, John. "Creating a Dialogic Museum: The Chinatown History Museum Experiment." In *Museums and Communities: The Politics of Public Culture*, edited by Ivan, Karp, Christine Mullen Kreamer, and Steven D. Lavine, 285–326. Washington and London: Smithsonian Institution Press, 1992.

Lenhart, Amanda, "Teen, Social Media and Technology Overview 2015." Pew Research Center. April 2015. http://www.pewinternet.org/2015/04/09/teens-social-media-technology-2015/.

McKensie, Bridget. "Towards the Sociocratic Museum: How, and Why, Museums Could Radically Change, and How Digital Can Help." In *Code | Words: Technology and Theory in the Museum*, edited by Ed Rodley, Robert Stein, and Susan Cairns. London: MuseumsEtc, 2015.

Metcalf, Fay D., and Matthew T. Downey, *Using Local History in the Classroom*. Nashville, TN: The American Association for State and Local History, 1982.

Omeka a. "Features and Plugins." Omeka Features and Plugins Comments. Accessed December 27, 2015, http://omeka.org/about/imls-final-grant-report/features-and-plugins/.

Omeka b. "Project: Omeka Project Comments." Omeka Project Comments. Accessed December 27, 2015, http://omeka.org/about/.

Padilla-Melendez, A., and A. R. Del Aguila-Obra. "Web and Social Media Usage by Museums: Online Value Creation." *International Journal of Information Management* 33, no. 5 (2013):892–98.

Perrin, Andrew, "Social Networking Usage: 2005–2015." Pew Research Center. October 2015. http://www.pewinternet.org/2015/10/08/2015/Social-Networking-Usage-2005-2015/

Phillips, Lori Byrd. "The Role of Open Authority in a Collaborative Web." In *Crowdsourcing Our Cultural Heritage*, edited by Mia Ridge, 247–68. London: Ashgate Publishing, Ltd., 2014.

Phillips, Lori Byrd. "The Temple and the Bazaar: Wikipedia as a Platform for Open Authority in Museums." *Curator: The Museum Journal* 56(2013):219–35.

Proctor, Nancy. "Crowdsourcing—An Introduction: From Public Goods to Public Good." *Curator: The Museum Journal* 56(2013):105–106. doi:10.1111/cura.12010.

Proctor, Nancy. "Digital: Museum as Platform, Curator as Champion, in the Age of Social Media." *Curator: The Museum Journal* 53(2010):35–43. doi:10.1111/j.2151-6952.2009.00006.x.

Reed, Caroline. "Is Revisiting Collections Working? A Summary Report." Accessed February 20, 2016, http://ourmuseum.org.uk/wp-content/uploads/Is-Revisiting-Collections-working_summary.pdf.

Ridge, Mia (ed.). *Crowdsourcing Our Cultural Heritage*. London: Ashgate Publishing, Ltd., 2014.

Ridge, Mia. "From Tagging to Theorizing: Deepening Engagement with Cultural Heritage through Crowdsourcing." *Curator: The Museum Journal* 56(2013):435–50.

Rodley, Ed. "The Virtues of Promiscuity, or Why Giving It Away Is the New Future." In *Code | Words: Technology and Theory in the Museum*, edited by Ed Rodley, Robert Stein, and Susan Cairns. London: MuseumsEtc, 2015.

Rodley, Ed, Robert Stein, and Susan Cairns (eds.). *Code | Words: Technology and Theory in the Museum*, edited by Ed Rodley, Robert Stein, and Susan Cairns. London: MuseumsEtc, 2015.

Rowley, Susan. 2013. "The Reciprocal Research Network: The Development Process." *Museum Anthropology Review* 7(1–2):22–43. Website: https://www.rrncommunity.org/.

Rowley, Susan, Dave Schaepe, Leona Sparrow, Andrea Sanborn, Ulrike Tadermacher, Ryan Wallace, Nicholas Jakobsen, Hannah Turner, Sivia Sadofsky, and Tristan Goffman. "Building an On-Line Research Community: The Reciprocal Research Network." In *Museums and the Web 2010: Proceedings*, edited by J. Trant and D. Bearman. Toronto: Archives & Museum Informatics, 2010. Accessed December 30, 2014, http://www.museumsandtheweb.com/mw2010/papers/rowley/rowley.html.

Roy Rosenzweig Center for History and New Media. "Omeka." Accessed December 4, 2015, http://chnm.gmu.edu/omeka/.

Satwicz, T., and K. Morrissey. "Public Curation: From Trend to Research-Based Practice." In *Letting Go? Sharing Historical Authority in a User-Generated World*, edited by Bill Adair, B. Filene, and Lisa Koloski, 196–205. Philadelphia: Pew Center for Arts and Heritage, 2011.

Schultz, Lainie. "Collaborative Museology and the Visitor." *Museum Anthropology* 34(2011):1–12. doi:10.1111/j.1548-1379.2010.01103.x.

Schumacher, Jaime, et al. "From Theory to Action: 'Good Enough' Digital Preservation Solutions for Under-Resourced Cultural Heritage Institutions." 2014. Accessed from http://commons.lib.niu.edu/handle/10843/13610.

Selwyn, Neil. "Reconsidering Political and Popular Understandings of the Digital Divide." *New Media & Society* 6, no. 3 (2004):341–62.

Shannon, Jennifer. "Projectishare.com: Sharing Our Past, Collecting for the Future." In *Museum as Process*, by Raymond Silverman, 68–89. New York: Routledge, 2015. Website: http://en.projectishare.com/about.

Shirky, Clay. *Here Comes Everybody*. New York: Penguin Books, 2012.

Shopes, Linda, "Human Subjects and IRB Review," in *Oral History in the Digital Age*, edited by Doug Boyd, Steve Cohen, Brad Rakerd, and Dean Rehberger. Washington, DC: Institute of Museum and Library Services, 2012, http://ohda.matrix.msu.edu/2012/08/making-sense-of-oral-history/.

Simon, Nina. *The Participatory Museum*, 2014 Accessed December 1, 2014, http://www.participatorymuseum.org/read/.

Sleeper-Smith, Susan (ed.). *Contesting Knowledge: Museums and Indigenous Perspectives.* Lincoln: University of Nebraska Press, 2009.

Smith, Laurajane, Geoff Cubitt, Ross Wilson, and Kalliopi Fouseki (eds.). *Representing Enslavement and Abolition in Museums: Ambiguous Engagements.* New York: Routledge, 2011.

Society for American Archaeology. "Archaeological Practice on Reality Television." Special Issue. *The SAA Archaeological Record* 15, no. 2 (2015), http://www.saa.org/Portals/0/SAA/Publications/thesaaarchrec/March2015.pdf.

Srinivasan, Ramesh, Robin Boast, Jonathan Furner, and Katherine M. Becvar. "Digital Museums and Diverse Cultural Knowledges: Moving Past the Traditional Catalog." *The Information Society* 25, no. 4 (2009):265–78.

Stein, Jill, Cecilia Garibay, and Kathryn Wilson. "Engaging Immigrant Audiences in Museums." *Museums & Social Issues* 3(2008):179–96. doi:10.1179/msi.2008.3.2.179.

Stein, Robert. "Museums . . . So What?" In *Code | Words: Technology and Theory in the Museum*, edited by Ed Rodley, Robert Stein, and Susan Cairns. London: MuseumsEtc, 2014.

Stocking, George. *Objects and Others: Essays on Museums and Material Culture.* Madison: University of Wisconsin Press, 1988.

Tate, Natalye B. "Museums as Third Places or What? Accessing the Social without Reservations." *Museums and Social Issues* 7(2012):269–83. doi:10.1179/msi.2012.7.2.269.

Tayac, Gabrielle (ed.). *IndiVisible.* Washington, DC: Smithsonian Books, 2009.

Tello, Julio C. *Arqueología del Valle de Casma.* Lima: Editorial San Marcos, 1956.

Tilden, Freeman. *Interpreting Our Heritage*, 3rd ed. Chapel Hill: University of North Carolina Press, 1977.

Waibel, Gunter, and Ricky Erway. "Think Globally, Act Locally, Library, Archive, and Museum Collaboration." *Museum Management and Curatorship* 24(2009):323–35. doi:10.1080/09647770903314704.

Weil, Stephen. *Making Museums Matter*. Washington, DC: Smithsonian Institution Press, 2002.

Wong, Amelia. "The Complexity of 'Community': Considering the Effects of Discourse on Museums' Social Media Practices." *Museum & Society* 13(2015):302–21.

Wood, Elizabeth. "Museums and Civic Engagement: Children Making a Difference." In *Museums and Communities: Curators, Collections and Collaboration*, edited by Viv Golding and Wayne Modest, 217–31. London: A&C Black Press, 2013.

Zorich, Diane, Gunter Waibel, and Ricky Erway. *Beyond the Silos of the LAMs: Collaboration Among Libraries, Archives and Museums*. Report produced by OCLC Research, 2008. Published online at: http://www.oclc.org/research/publications/library/2008/200805.pdf.

Index

About the Contributors

Nur Abdalla received her BA in anthropology and Japanese MA in applied anthropology from the University of Memphis (Memphis, Tennessee). Her research interests include connecting museums with educational institutions as tools for empowerment.

Melanie A. Adams is the senior director, guest experiences and educational services, Minnesota Historical Society. She received her PhD in educational leadership and policy studies from the University of Missouri-St. Louis.

Brigitte Billeaudeaux is an assistant professor and archivist at the University of Memphis Libraries in the department of Preservation and Special Collections. She holds an MA in anthropology from the University of Memphis and an MS in information science from the University of Tennessee at Knoxville.

Elizabeth A. Bollwerk holds a PhD in anthropology from the University of Virginia and is an archaeological analyst for the Digital Archaeological Archive of Comparative Slavery (DAACS) at the Thomas Jefferson Foundation. She has published pieces on Open Authority and digital public archaeology in *Museums and Social Issues* and *Advances in Archaeological Practice.*

Robert P. Connolly currently teaches in the Museum Studies Graduate Certificate Program at the University of Memphis, where for the past decade he also served as the director of the C.H. Nash Museum at Chucalissa. He has published numerous articles on his co-creative research projects in both the United States and Perú. He blogs at *Archaeology, Museums and Outreach.*

Shana Crosson is a former teacher turned museum professional who has developed museum exhibits, curriculum products, and websites, all delivering historical content to teachers, students, and families. She leads the Minnesota Historical Society's efforts to move toward a digital delivery of historical content for the K–12 audience.

Elizabeth K. Cruzado Carranza has worked for over ten years as an archaeologist in her native Perú. She received her BA and license in archaeology from the Universidad Nacional Mayor de San Marcos in Lima, Perú and MA in archaeology from the University of Memphis and is currently enrolled in the PhD program in anthropology at Louisiana State University.

Ember Farber is currently the advocacy director of the American Alliance of Museums, where she has worked since 2003. She holds an MA degree in nonprofit lobbying and corporate public affairs from George Washington University.

Mary Anna Evans is an assistant professor at the University of Oklahoma, where she teaches fiction and nonfiction writing.

Brian Failing is the executive director of the Aurora Regional Fire Museum in Aurora, Illinois. He holds an MA degree in public history from Eastern Illinois University.

Assia Johnson is a public relations and media specialist who is passionate about the museum field and non-profit marketing. As the National Underground Railroad Freedom Center PR & Social Media Coordinator, she plays an integral role in managing and developing print and online content.

Suzanne Francis-Brown is the curator of the University of West Indies Museum. Her PhD in History from the University of the West Indies, Mona is built on an MA in heritage studies from the same institution, where she has worked on heritage-related projects.

Jamie Glavic is the director of marketing and communications at the National Underground Railroad Freedom Center in Cincinnati, Ohio. She serves on the board of the Ohio Museums Association, is a graduate of Developing History Leaders at the Seminar for Historical Administration, and blogs on current issues in museums at themuseumminute.com.

Allison Hennie holds an MA degree in applied anthropology from the University of Memphis and is a project manager for the Urban Art Commission in Memphis.

Colleen McCartney graduated with a BA in anthropology from Texas Tech University and an MA in applied anthropology and graduate certificate in museum studies from the University of Memphis. She was awarded the Tennessee Association of Museums' Emerging Museum Professional of the Year for 2016.

Sarah E. Miller is a historical archaeologist with experience in public archaeology, municipal archaeology, and cemetery care and preservation. She currently serves as the director of the Florida Public Archaeology Network's Northeast and East Central Regions hosted by Flagler College.

Porchia Moore is a PhD candidate dually enrolled in the University of South Carolina in the School of Library and Information Science and the McKissick Museum Management Program. Her research interests include using Critical Race Theory to examine the intersections between race, technology, community, identity, and social media in cultural heritage museums.

Lyndsey Pender received her BA in anthropology from Western Kentucky University. She is currently pursuing her MA in applied anthropology with a focus in medical studies at the University of Memphis.

Rebecca L. Price is the founder and president/CEO of Chick History, Inc., a nonprofit dedicated to rebuilding history one story at a time by focusing on women's history, original programming, and community outreach. She holds an MA in museum studies from George Washington University and has worked for the National Museum of Women in the Arts, the Institute of Museums and Library Services, and the American Association for State and Local History.

Melissa Prycer, after serving as educator for a decade, is now executive director of Dallas Heritage Village. She is passionate about community development, history education, and literature.

Kelsey Ransick received her MA from University of Delaware. She has done curatorial and archival work, web design, and sundry other small museum tasks.

Ashley Rogers is the director of Museum Operations at the Whitney Plantation in Wallace, Louisiana. She holds degrees in history from Colorado State University and Warren Wilson College. She lives in New Orleans.

Jennifer Schnabel is currently an assistant professor and English librarian at The Ohio State University and recently served as assistant to the dean for community engagement at the University of Memphis Libraries.

Susan Sekaquaptewa is a Hopi museum specialist and a trustee for the Museum of Northern Arizona. She is also a researcher and facilitator for various projects that include Hopi community involvement, such as Hopivewat: Resource and Learning Center, that emphasizes responsible stewardship and management of Hopi culture through traditional Hopi values.

Holly Solis is a public history graduate student at Arizona State University. Her research interests include Latino and Chicano history and museum studies.

Jody Stokes-Casey has an MA degree in art history and a graduate certificate in museum studies at the University of Memphis. She is currently an art instructor for Shelby County Schools and served as the interim director of interpretation, education, and collections at the National Civil Rights Museum, the interim associate director of education, and an educator in K–12 classrooms.

Gustavo Valencia Tello is a social sciences teacher in the village of Nivin on the rural coast of Ancash, Peru. He advocates for the preservation of the culture and environment in the region through sustainable community projects and student based projects.

Leodan Alejo Valerio is a history teacher in highland Ancash, Peru. His interests include Quechua language revitalization in the schools and linking contemporary events with prehistoric archaeological sites to strengthen the cultural awareness of his students.

Mary Wildermuth is the executive rirector of the Muscatine History and Industry Center and a retired librarian, special projects administrator, and grant writer from the Muscatine Community School District. She also currently serves as the secretary of the Muscatine Convention and Visitors Board.

Lisa C. Young, PhD, is a lecturer in anthropology at the University of Michigan and university associate at the University of Arizona's Arizona State Museum who is interested in the changing relationship between museums and source communities. Her archaeological research in the Homolovi area of northeastern Arizona includes collaborative exhibit projects and engaged student learning opportunities.